Library of
Davidson College

EVALUATION FOR DECISION-MAKING IN THE SCHOOLS

JOHN W. WICK
Northwestern University

DONALD L. BEGGS
Southern Illinois University

HOUGHTON MIFFLIN COMPANY

BOSTON · New York · Atlanta
Geneva, Illinois · Dallas · Palo Alto

HOUGHTON MIFFLIN COMPANY
EDITORIAL ADVISORY COMMITTEE IN EDUCATION

C. Gilbert Wrenn, *Macalester College*
Van Cleve Morris, *University of Illinois at Chicago Circle*
Samuel A. Kirk, *University of Illinois*
William Van Til, *Indiana State University*
Charles S. Benson, *University of California, Berkeley*
Robert H. Anderson, *Harvard University*

371.2
W636e

71-10822

Copyright © 1971 by John W. Wick and Donald L. Beggs

All rights reserved. No part of this work may be reproduced or transmitted in any form or by any means, electronic or mechanical, including photocopying and recording, or by any information storage or retrieval system, without permission in writing from the publisher.

Printed in the U.S.A.

Library of Congress Card Number 71-129846

ISBN: 0-395-05533-4

EDITOR'S INTRODUCTION

All over the world, decision-makers in education—teachers and their administrators—practice their trade in a conventional way. At higher levels of decision-making, administrators rely on bureaucratic hunches while responding to political pressures. In the classroom, actual practice reflects a blend of ancient collective wisdom and the private intuition of the individual teacher. It is a matter of wonder that so much of the new knowledge created during the last three decades can be imparted in what is essentially an unchanging, static environment of instructional processes. We would be astonishingly more effective in education if we could accurately assess the consequences of our actions; if we could predict consequences of those alternative actions we might take in the future; and (simply to recognize budget constraints) if we could obtain these kinds of useful information at less-than-prohibitive costs. The authors of this volume take us a long way toward finding the means to provide ourselves with quantitative analysis of our professional problems.

The range of questions amenable to analysis, it turns out, is quite substantial. One would expect to find in this volume quantitative manipulations of students' achievement scores, along with discussions of their uses (e.g., assignment of students to homogeneous groups). But we see that quantitative analysis is useful in many other types of planning activities—for example, in evaluation and redesign of in-service training programs, development of improved procedures to select faculty and to raise the rate at which experienced faculty can be retained in service of the given school district, determining the best time to launch a bond issue campaign, and analysis of progress toward the goal of school integration. The list is impressive. And it should be pointed out that the uses of analysis in social planning are far more widespread than can be indicated in this volume.

In view of the growing interest in new methods of analysis for problem-solving, it is important that educators become familiar with the techniques. This book will give the reader a lasting sense of understanding of most of the main ideas on which systematic treatment of problems is based. No special knowledge of mathematics is required to follow the text. Mathematically inclined readers may be so intrigued that they will continue with serious study of operations research techniques. The general reader will come to know how and when analytical techniques can be applied to the solution of particular problems, how to converse with analysts and judge their probity, and how to avoid pitfalls that always lurk ahead when we try to assess and predict human actions.

I hope the reader will find the style of this volume as delightful as I do. Be not misguided, however: the topics treated here are serious and important.

Charles S. Benson

PREFACE

We hope this book will function as a bridge between two important groups of educators. Practicing educators make up the first group. The group includes teachers, administrators, professional specialists in the schools, as well as students in training for these positions. The contents are focused on these people.

The second important group includes quantitative researchers, statisticians, and test experts in education. Their common denominator is a relatively high degree of mathematical sophistication. The reports and research of this second group do get published in educational books and journals. These reports have not always been widely read by members of the first group, however, for the texts include a considerable amount of mathematical shorthand and terminology unfamiliar to those not working full-time in the quantitative areas.

This book is written for the first group—the practitioners and students in training. No special mathematical background is assumed. But it is written about the reports and research from the second group. In attempting to build this bridge, the authors have selected topics based on important decision points for the practitioners in the schools. Thus the book can function quite satisfactorily as a nontechnical supplementary text in courses like the following:

A first or second undergraduate measurements course; or as part of an overview course at the junior college level.

Introductory graduate courses dealing with the psychological foundations of education.

Introductory graduate courses for educational administrators, guidance and personnel specialists, and other professional specialties in education.

In each of these areas, this book could function as an introduction to the contributions educational research and measurement can make at certain important decision points for the practitioner.

We have broken with tradition in the presentation of certain topics. We have advocated a general evaluation approach called continuous assessment (in lieu of the more traditional pre- and post-test approach); we have taken a strong stand on such diverse topics as homogeneous grouping and the evaluation of teacher effectiveness; and we have traced the history of desegregation efforts in the schools, showing the role of educational measurements in the struggle for educational equality. Other topics include the evaluation of in-service programs, the use of achievement tests, staff attitude and morale, and teacher recruitment and retention. The reader is directed to the last section of Chapter 1 for a complete overview of each chapter.

We are indebted to Professor Robert J. Coughlan of Northwestern University who outlined and drafted Chapter 7, and to Mr. James Fletcher of Northwestern University who reviewed the legal references and offered suggestions for Chapter 11. Many colleagues read and commented on chapters in the book. These include Professors James Hall, Gail Inlow, and Lindley Stiles at Northwestern University, Keith McNeil and John Mouw at Southern Illinois University, and Mrs. Grace Duff of the Cairo (Illinois) Public Schools. And the authors owe a deep debt to their wives, Janet Wick and Shirley Beggs, who supplied technical support as typists and readers, as well as much-needed moral support.

John W. Wick
Donald L. Beggs

CONTENTS

1 EVALUATION AND THE LEARNING CLIMATE / 2
Evaluation and the learning climate: Which way?
Program objectives or behavioral differences?
The costs and benefits of measurement
The time schedule in evaluation
Overview of the book

2 OUTCOME EVALUATION / 22
An example of outcome evaluation
Specifying behavioral outcomes
The control group
Measuring the four outcomes
Statistical significance and predictive association

3 CONTINUOUS ASSESSMENT / 52
Five basic concepts of continuous assessment
Individualized continuous assessment: The corridor approach
Other uses for continuous assessment

4 USING ACHIEVEMENT TESTS / 78
Primary uses of standardized achievement tests
Using norms for comparison
Conversion of raw scores
Using achievement tests to measure growth
Using achievement tests for fixed time interpretations
Reporting test results

5 HOMOGENEOUS GROUPING / 98
A brief review of research
Dimensions of ability grouping
Placement errors due to measurement errors
Placement errors due to infrequent testing
Placement errors due to cultural bias
Errors due to use of IQ as determinant
Effects of misplacement

6 EVALUATION AND IN-SERVICE PROGRAMS / 126
Reasons for in-service education
Example of a planned in-service program
Evaluation of the in-service program

7 STAFF ATTITUDE AND MORALE / 146
The concept of morale
Measuring staff morale
Research about morale in schools
The attitude survey
Continuous assessment of staff morale

8 RECRUITING AND RETAINING TEACHERS / 172
Research about teacher recruitment and retention
Models for decision-making
Problems of teacher retention
Gathering data to improve recruitment and retention

9 EVALUATING TEACHER EFFECTIVENESS / 192
Considerations in measuring teacher effectiveness
Personality measures
Evaluation by expert observation
Measurement by pupil performance
Measurement by pupil behavior in the community
Decision-making model

10 ASSESSING COMMUNITY ATTITUDE: THE SCHOOL BOND ISSUE / 210
Hiram Public School: An example
Expressed attitudes and actual behavior
Some sampling decisions
The questionnaire
Sample size and accuracy of prediction
Statistical procedure and decision-making
Measuring other community attitudes
Continuous assessment of community attitudes

11 EDUCATIONAL MEASUREMENT AND DESEGREGATION / 234
History of litigation: Why the delays?
Six statements of cause
Hobson v. Hansen: The track system
Summary

EVALUATION AND THE LEARNING CLIMATE

Evaluation and the Learning Climate: Which Way?
The learning program as experimental conditions
The learning climate as a function of evaluation

Program Objectives or Behavioral Differences?

The Costs and Benefits of Measurement

The Time Schedule in Evaluation

Overview of the Book

A multitude of decisions, simple to complex, are made each day by the members of a school's professional staff. This staff, which includes the superintendent, principals and assistant principals, curriculum directors, psychologists, guidance and counseling personnel, teachers, and others, frequently must choose from among many different alternatives in solving problems. The authors' primary purpose in this book is to identify important ways in which the educational staff can use research and measurement methods to make decisions, and to show how these methods are best implemented. Due to the multidimensional complexity of the human animal with which educators work, measurement in education is not as accurate as in the physical sciences, where thermometers and micrometers tell us temperature and thickness to almost any degree of precision. For this reason, we have coupled our discussion of measurement methods with discussions of the magnitude of errors which are inherent in such measures.

This book is an applied measurement and research aid for educators in the field. Obviously we could not include all types of decisions made by the school administrator. Some things cannot be quantified. When a man asks, "Should I wear a coat?" quantitative methods can be used—he need only look at a thermometer. But when he asks, "Which color will look best with these trousers?" the question is aesthetic, and not quantifiable.[1] Let us first say that this book is limited to the quantifiable questions. But let us quickly add that more and more questions in education are leaving the domain of the aesthetic and moving over to the domain of the quantifiable. Two excellent examples are contained in the chapters on assessment of community attitudes and the bond issue, and on the measurement of staff attitude and morale.

EVALUATION AND THE LEARNING CLIMATE: WHICH WAY?

A substantial number of teachers and administrators neither proclaim nor decry the techniques of educational measurement (tests, scales, etc.). Quantitative evaluation, to this group, is simply a concept outside the domain of important

---

[1] Except in the normative sense, where the color-coordination preferences of some group might be measured.

educational matters. After all, they will argue, who knows the students better than the teacher who is with them daily over the school year? It seems obvious to these teachers that the learning climate, under their direction, must come first; they do not even suspect that evaluation techniques might determine the classroom learning climate. The proposition that learning climate *follows* evaluation techniques may seem absurd; but suppose we nevertheless develop it further.

THE LEARNING PROGRAM AS EXPERIMENTAL CONDITIONS

Using research terminology, the learning program undertaken by the teacher might be termed, in a very real sense, the "imposition of experimental conditions." The teacher should be aware that the period of time during which most of these experiments are operating (i.e., when the class is in session or when this topic is high in the student's consciousness) is quite small when contrasted with the total consciousness of the participating subjects. Furthermore, the impact of the imposed experimental conditions is probably not consistently intense—distractions do occur in the classroom. For these and other reasons, it is usually unreasonable to expect profound alterations in the fundamental behavior pattern of the students.

For example, consider a sixth-grade social studies course. Assume the maximum: That the curriculum calls for a full fifty minutes of social studies each day. Assuming the average student's waking hours total fifteen, this amounts to about 5.5 percent of his consciousness—a substantial segment, taken over the course of nine months. But weekends and vacation periods must be excluded, so that the percentage is decreased to 3.6 percent. Is this still too high? Only those who have ever taught or attended school will answer in the affirmative. The student may be in class fifty minutes per day, five days per week, but physical presence does not allow us to conclude that social studies concepts were at all times on the surface of consciousness. The final 3.6 percent figure might be looked upon as a maximum, to be achieved only in the ideal situation. To be realistic we must be prepared to accept a figure somewhere between zero and 3.6 percent. If the social studies teacher can do a major reshaping job on the child, given perhaps two percent exposure for a nine-month period, he is to be commended (or damned, depending on the result).

This leads to the following fundamental proposition:

> The great majority of learning programs in education are not extensive enough to cause major alterations in the total psychological makeup of the subjects, so that the inclusion of broad generalities (such as "to develop good citizenship") in the list of objectives is not warranted.

The plain truth is that too often program planners, perhaps unwittingly, include such unwarranted generalities in their lists of objectives to avoid grappling with the more difficult problem of delineating the specific behavioral outcomes which should occur if the hypotheses which motivated the implementation of their program are correct. Undoubtedly many current experimental packages would suffer from inspection in this light if their wrappings of nebulous verbiage were removed.

A learning climate of some type exists in every room and that climate is not the total responsibility of the teacher. There are, after all, factors which exist in the school which cannot be manipulated by the teacher. The tone of different schools varies considerably along a continuum of contentedness—from open hostility to great mutual understanding. The tone of intellectualism in the community is also a variable, ranging from distrust of any new and innovative technique to its antithesis—change for the sake of change—and passing through many states of lethargy between. Perhaps it is time to take the teachers off the hook on this matter, and admit that there are some nonlearning situations which are not within the teacher's control, and he may not be to blame if learning does not occur.

But these uncontrollable situations are surely not the norm, or we could not have moved ahead as effectively as our history indicates. In many situations the teacher *can* control the learning climate. What should he aim for?

THE LEARNING CLIMATE AS A FUNCTION OF EVALUATION

The question of whether evaluation should determine the learning climate is still unanswered. But we must digress further, to review a scheme for the classification of learning skills. The classification system, assembled under the leadership of Bloom (1956), defines three domains of learning objectives. The first of these three, the *cognitive* domain, is concerned with the recall of knowledge once learned, and with using such knowledge in problem-solving situations. The second domain includes the *affective* objectives. The key word for this domain is *feeling,* for it includes interests, attitudes, and values. Quite obviously most of our courses of instruction in the schools have affective objectives. The final domain includes the *psychomotor* objectives. These objectives would require some sort of muscular or motor skill, or neuromuscular coordination. Such objectives might be found most often in physical education, trade, or technical courses, as well as in handwriting and speech classes.

Most educational objectives fall in the cognitive domain. The Bloom taxonomy lists six subgroups under this heading, arranged in order of ascending complexity. These are *knowledge, comprehension, application, analysis, synthesis,* and *evaluation.* Before a student can comprehend a concept, he must know certain facts (knowledge) about the concept. Before the student can apply a concept in some real instance, he must have comprehended the concept. This buildup could continue through the last three subgroups—analysis, synthesis, and evaluation. Each new heading builds on the subgroups which precede it.

The behavioral objectives listed by the typing teacher could include one in the cognitive and psychomotor domains such as: "The student should be able to take a letter from a dictating machine, and type the letter in a modified-block format." A junior high school history teacher might have as one of his affective behavioral objectives that: "The student should manifest his interest in current events by reading from at least five newspapers or periodicals each week." And a second-grade teacher most likely would agree that this behavioral objective in the motor skills domain is important: "The students should be able to complete all parts of a worksheet in the spaces provided, and in a legible manner." The concentration of objectives in any one domain is very much a function of the course of instruction in question. We would expect, for example, more motor-oriented objectives from the typing teacher than from the social studies teacher.

Suppose a social studies teacher sets this important objective up for his class: "The student should develop the ability to *distinguish* between fact and opinion, given articles from newspapers and news magazines." This objective would be included under the "analysis" category of the Bloom taxonomy. The teacher assembles illustrative materials from these sources to illustrate different degrees of impartiality in information presentation. Some would be crisp; others would be no more than the ravings of a demagogue. The teacher could help the students find the "weasel words" reporters often use to give the impression of factuality where they are really only giving an opinion. Examples of such words are "there is a possibility that" or "some seem to think that . . ."

At some point the teacher must begin making assessments regarding the relative performance of the students. This does not necessarily mean tests. It can include that quick smile of encouragement, that extra thirty seconds of attention, or the negation of these two. It can mean written assignments, and the kinds of responses the teacher makes to these. And it can include tests devised by the teacher. In all of these situations the teacher assesses and evaluates, and we submit that:

> *The student's subsequent responses are not independent of the earlier assessments by the teacher.*

A favorable assessment—be it only a nod or a word of encouragement—affects the student's perception of subsequent situations. Narrowing this line of thought to that important part of assessment which includes evaluation with tests, it necessarily follows that

> *The student will learn material according to his perception of the evaluation techniques used by the teacher.*

For example, a social studies teacher might write test items of this nature:

> 1. Who is the editorial page editor for the *Chicago Tribune?*
>
> 2. Write the names "Vietnam," "India," and "China" in the correct locations on the attached map.

Regardless of what this teacher *says* his objectives are, his students will soon learn that his tests are based on the *recall of knowledge,* and they will study for the course accordingly.

Another teacher might write the question like this:

> 1. Describe the editorial position taken by columnists A and B regarding the Vietnam conflict.

This question is based one step higher in the domain. The students will not simply be recalling information; they must show that they *comprehend* the position taken by this particular columnist. Once again, the students will see this teacher's objective as being learning of this type, and they will learn to comprehend what they read, and be ready to write synopses for their teacher.

If these two teachers were really interested in their students' ability to *analyze* the things that they read, the evaluation items should have reflected this concern. It seems reasonable that if critical analysis is the primary thrust of a course, the best critical analyzers ought to get the highest recognition from the evaluation devices. Once the students in the class realize that this is the criterion upon which comparisons will be made and grades assigned, each will try harder to concentrate on this skill.

PROGRAM OBJECTIVES OR BEHAVIORAL DIFFERENCES?

The business of the school is guiding pupils. As the student moves through school, both he and his parents have the right to expect changes to occur. Some of these changes will be beyond the control of the school—for example, those due to natural maturation and those due to the social pressure in his unique environment. The responsibility for bringing about other changes, however, is the responsibility of the school.

Most public schools attempt to fulfill this responsibility for causing the expected changes by implementing specific programs. The administration of the school, in conjunction with the other professional staff, must make important decisions about these programs. What is the responsibility of each staff member? How shall the students be organized? By age? By ability level? By performance level? By sex? When should science instruction begin? The teacher is most concerned about the program in his particular classroom. The mathematics coordinator is most concerned about the total mathematics program. Each professional staff member has a responsibility for a certain segment of the program. The ultimate goal of all of these programs is to bring about the changes in the student which the community expects will occur.

The planning of these many programs, then, should start with a statement of purpose. Since the school's very existence is a function of bringing about desired change in pupils, the statement of purpose must include a delineation of the expected changes in pupils due to this particular program. We submit that wherever it is possible to do so, these expected changes should be stated in terms of student behavior. That is, what will the student be *doing* differently as the result of each program?

Suppose we develop this point further, in the context of the program in a teacher's classroom. On the first day of school, the teacher (who is actually a program director) should have the entire year's activities outlined, at least in general. The program objectives assume varying degrees of specificity, depending to a certain extent on the instructional area involved. The tenth-grade typing teacher's objectives can be more specific than those of the seventh-grade science teacher; but this science teacher's objectives are probably more specific than are those of the teacher in a self-contained second-grade classroom. The year's activities might range from a vague blueprint in the mind of the teacher to an elaborately printed booklet carefully prepared by a committee of many.

Even if the statement of objectives for the year's activities is vague, it is safe to conjecture that some type of learning is envisioned. In the broadest sense, the objectives and the course outlines define a program of learning, and the teacher is the program director.

The teacher and all other program directors (the superintendent, the principal, the math coordinator, etc.) have three responsibilities which should be fulfilled before the first day of their programs. Each must first answer this question:

> *What behavioral changes should and can we expect in the members of this group, due to their tenure in this program?*

In other words, what student changes justify this program's existence? Next, the program director must answer this question:

> *What strategies will be most effective in bringing about these changes?*

The decision regarding strategy involves factors like cost, time, effort, and probability of success with competing techniques. Finally, if the program director really intends to bring about student change, this third question follows quite naturally:

> *What is the best method available for determining whether the year's classroom experience did, in fact, result in the hypothesized behavioral changes?*

Where are we going? How can we best get there? How can we tell if we really made it? These are the questions each program director must ask.

The answer to the first question is essentially identical to a statement of the objectives of the new program. However, the phrase *behavioral changes* is purposely used in place of *program objectives*. Too often the objectives listed for a program are so general, so nebulous, that evaluation of resulting changes in behavior is totally impossible.[2] Not only does an emphasis on behavioral changes keep the program planner's eyes sharply on the ultimate purposes of the school (bringing about desired behavioral changes in students), it also works to answer the third question posed above. That is, when objectives are stated in terms of behavioral changes, the techniques for evaluating the degree of goal attainment are clearly implied.

Behavioral changes deal with the things the student does. They deal with his actions which are overt and observable. Statements of behavioral change use verbs like "attends," "recalls," "recognizes," "distinguishes," "predicts," "computes," "diagrams," "composes," "completes," "justifies," "verifies," or "categorizes." Each of these involves an observable act on the part of the student. Each can be measured.

Objectives stated in nonbehavioral terms use words like "learn," "understand," "appreciate," "really appreciate," "have a deep understanding of," or "know." These words seem acceptable enough on the surface. Suppose we try out the first in a specific statement: In this unit, the student should *learn* about pendulums. Will that statement suggest

---

[2] One of the authors, while working on the evaluation design for a sex education program, asked the director what his objectives were for the program. The director looked him right in the eye, and with a straight face replied that his objective was to "make the world a better place to live in." The writer commented that the change might be a little difficult to measure.

comparable instructional strategies for different program directors? Will it suggest comparable evaluation strategies for all program evaluators?

What are some ways that a student can "learn" about pendulums? Well, the student might simply *recognize* one when he sees it. He might be able to *draw* a picture of one. He might be able to *label* a diagram with the terms "bob," "arc," and "length." To do this, he might also have to *recall* the terms from memory; or the terms might have been presented for him to *recognize*. Perhaps he might be able to *use* a pendulum to *measure* its period. He might be expected to *define* the term period; or he might be expected to *demonstrate* that a change in length of the pendulum alters the period. The list is incomplete. There are many other relationships, formulas, and principles which could have been in the program director's mind when he stated that the student should "learn about pendulums."

The point is that the use of the verb "learn" without supporting statements simply does not communicate in an unambiguous manner. Each of the statements in the paragraph above has an action verb. It communicates something specific to the teacher. The teacher's strategy will depend upon the specific outcome he is trying to effect. Each action verb clearly implies how the evaluation will be carried out.

Evaluation tied to the specification of behavioral changes is a recurring theme in this book. The topic will be discussed at some length in chapter 6, about evaluating in-service education programs, and in chapter 9, about evaluating teacher effectiveness; and it is closely allied with the discussion of most of the other chapters as well.

Some will object to our preference for behavioral changes rather than program objectives on the grounds that not all the objectives of a program can be stated in behavioral language. The point is well taken. As will be discussed in chapters 6 and 9, it is true that the more abstract an objective becomes (and, oftentimes, the more important a goal becomes), the more difficult it is to state that goal in behavioral terms. Examples include objectives such as "building character" and "developing good citizenship." We believe, however, that (a) a very large proportion of the goals of the school can be stated in behavioral terms; (b) the fact that not all goals can be so stated does not negate the usefulness of stating the maximum amount in behavioral language; and (c) fulfilling the behaviorally stated goals might be looked upon as stepping-stones to the fulfillment of those more abstract goals, which could not fit into behavioral language.

THE COSTS AND BENEFITS OF MEASUREMENT

Generally, decision-makers deal with existing programs, facilities, teachers, and space. Decisions are often based on past experience. *Did* the programs work? *Were* the facilities adequate? *Was* the staff performance satisfactory? *Did* we run out of space? There will be exceptions to this statement, but *generally,* decisions for change are increments from the existing condition. Next year's budget is based on this year's budget, with incremental changes; planning for next year's staff begins by studying this year's staff; and space allocations are projected from current use, based on present programs.

The school decision-makers should be in a position to plan the future of the operation, rather than to simply "put out fires"; they should control events when possible, rather than react to them.

Heavy dependence upon planning from present conditions means that projections about the future are based on *input* measures. The buildings, the teachers, the administrators, the curriculum, and the instructional devices are all inputs. The *outputs* may be more difficult to define and measure; *but they represent the very reason for the school's existence.* Output measures deal with changes in the students served by the school, and trends in the factors which are most closely linked to these student changes. Has the school fulfilled the cognitive objectives at a satisfactory level? Do the students know what the community thinks they should know? Do they comprehend the events around them? Can they analyze events, trends, causes, and effects? Has the school helped them become independent decision-makers? Some *outputs* are affective. Are students interested in knowledge and in furthering their learning both formally and informally? Are they good citizens—do they respect the rights of minorities, for example, and do they recognize that responsibility goes with freedom? Has the school fulfilled its primary responsibility—preparing the graduate to be a self-sufficient, satisfied, functioning adult citizen?

Basing next year's staff and budget figures on those of last year does give continuity to the school's program, and that is good. It also encourages inflexibility and a "hardening of the arteries" for those budget lines which do exist. New programs are added, but old programs die hard.

Short- and long-range plans (call one or two years short-range, and three to ten years long-range) are generally made by the administration and school board of a district, sometimes in conjunction with groups of teachers or taxpayers. They use both input and output measures in the decision-making process, which is admittedly a complex thing. However, the input measures they use are based on hard data—this many dollars, that many fourth-grade teachers, so many square feet of floor, ABC & Co.'s reading series, and so forth. The output measures all too often are based on data which are difficult to comprehend and generalize. For example, "It seems to me that the students are not as good in mathematics any more," or "Kids just do not seem to like to read any more," or "Although our standardized reading scores are down, this is because the norm group has inconsistencies in the . . ." The planners usually do not have detailed, reliable information going back a reasonable amount of time to show trends in the important *output* measures.

Can all of the desired outputs be defined and accurately measured? Of course not! Should we quit trying? An answer to that is another question: Have we even started yet? A large proportion of the important objectives could be stated in terms of expected behavioral changes. This does not mean a half-page statement of platitudes; we are talking about thick booklets of objectives for each instructional area, and for each grade level. These objectives *are* generally measurable, and could be reviewed by the school's ultimate directors—the people who pay for the schools with their taxes. If the objectives were stated by the school's decision-makers, agreed to by the school's benefactors, and were measurable—would not this be the kind of quantified information which should go into these planning sessions? This would be the needed hard output information.

This book includes discussions of both input and output measurements. But the emphases are on *planning before crisis, trend analysis of results,* and *direct specification and measurement of objectives.* Continuous assessment is suggested; that is, we want the decision-makers to keep gathering data in each important part of the school's program—not to prove a point or to diagnose an existing problem, but rather to use in making plans for the future. We suggest the measurement of teacher effectiveness through student output. This suggestion, by the way, is prefaced by a strong plea to be far more specific in telling the teacher what the community expects from him. The clear specification of objectives, coupled with the most appropriate technique for measuring objective attainment, is a recurring theme in this book.

Comprehensive manuals of specific measurable objectives at each grade level and in each instructional area generally do not exist in the typical school district. Furthermore, the typical district would probably have to initiate programs of continuous assessment of student achievement and attitude, staff and community attitude, and other important output aspects of the school's overall program. What will all of this cost?

The cost of continuous assessment. In chapter 10, it is suggested that a regular, periodic sampling program be set up to survey the attitude of the community toward the school's program. Suppose such a program involved a sample of one hundred households, sampled at random from the community at large. What would such a program cost?

The *initiation* costs would occur only once. Someone on the school staff, or a consultant called in, would have to develop the scope of the questionnaire, the interview technique, the procedures for selecting the sample, and the methods of handling the data. To handle the actual interviewing, the school might use housewives who would be willing to work twenty or so hours per week for a short time. Suppose, for example, that a typical interview would take about an hour. Then an interviewer needs some time moving from one place to the next, so about one and a half hours might be appropriate to estimate for each complete transaction. At this rate, 100 interviews would require 150 hours, which at about $3.00 per hour would cost less than $500. This amount depends on the charge by the interviewer, the length of the interview schedule, and the distance the interviewer needs to travel between visits. The cost could also be reduced by simply having fewer interviews, which would reduce precision, but not eliminate the usefulness of the system. That is, the continuing cost might go as low as two or three hundred dollars per sample. Samples might be spaced six weeks or two months apart.

If the planning efforts were complete, the data handling should be nothing more than a clerical chore. That is, responses to the interviewers' questions would be coded by the school staff in a manner which would make the overall results and trend information most useful to the school decision-makers.

We believe the investment in this approach toward hard output data will lead to the strengthening and support of effective programs, and the eventual elimination or reduction of weak ones. We are not suggesting that procedures currently used for planning are totally incorrect, inadequate, and inefficient. But changes occur rapidly, and an additional emphasis on output measures will allow the district to diagnose existing "soft spots" in the school program and to better articulate future needs. Present practices need not be abandoned; but we would hope for additional emphasis on output measures to offset the overdependency on input measures. The cost of these measures would be a new "line item" in most school budgets, to be true. But we contend that the actual *cost* would be minimal when the potential *benefits* of such a system are considered.

THE TIME SCHEDULE IN EVALUATION

As was stated earlier, the director must decide before the program begins what behavioral changes are expected, what strategies to use to reach them, and what devices could be used to measure the level of objective attainment. We have stressed that in the classroom the emphasis used in assessment is an important factor in setting the learning climate. One sure way for the teacher to avoid failure in the classroom—failure in terms of the nonfulfillment of objectives—is for him to set the objectives at such a low level that the class has reached that stage before the first day of class!

Consider separating the time continuum into four discrete periods. Each is important to the program director. These are:

1. The time immediately preceding the beginning of the program, before the imposition of the experimental conditions. The evaluation term which first comes to mind is *pretest*.

2. The time during which the experimental conditions are in operation.

3. The time immediately following the cessation of the experimental conditions. Here the most common evaluation term is *post-test*.

4. The time which follows, to continue as long as the experimental conditions are thought to still have an effect.

The categorization is trivial, and seems obvious. Nevertheless, it is included because the great proportion of research carried out in education, including most doctoral studies, course evaluations, or small research projects concentrates on the third of these categories, or the first and third categories taken together. These most common designs use period 1 to set a benchmark for possible change, and period 3 to find out if the change did occur. Measurements at time period 2, covering the course of the project, are often of critical importance to the active project administrator, as we will point out in chapter 3. Measurements during time period 4 might be termed *validity* measures, for they tell whether the project's effects were lasting. We might, for example, teach fourth-grade students a foreign language, and find in our post-test that the group had made significant changes. If, however, three years later this group were compared to a similar group of students who were untrained in the language, and no difference resulted, we must wonder about the ultimate value of the original program.

OVERVIEW OF THE BOOK

Tests, standardized and unstandardized, represent one important measurement technique in education. Testing is usually done in the classroom. Measurement in a classroom setting is important, but we will not concentrate on it to the exclusion of other topics. Topics ranging from community attitudes to staff morale, and from homogeneous grouping to continuous assessment will be included in the chapters which follow. The quantitative methods which will be suggested for these diverse situations will range far afield from tests alone.

Chapter 2 will describe a specific *outcome* experiment, and the methodology of this type of assessment. An outcome experiment focuses on time periods 1 and 3 as described in the previous section, or perhaps only on period 3. That is, it is a pre- and post-test design. The chapter is written in the context of an administrator's attempt to evaluate the effects of a specific secondary-level course. An illustration of behavioral changes will be given, and a distinction will be made between "real" and "statistical" significance. In the data analysis suggestions, two types of criterion variables will be used. One of these is frequency counts; the other is achievement test scores. Both of these are common techniques for measuring an effect in a school situation. A final step for statistical analysis is suggested: the determination of the strength of association among the variables.

Chapter 3 introduces an approach to assessment which has wide-ranging applicability. The chapter introduces *continuous assessment,* with which measurements are gathered throughout the period that an educational program is in operation. Continuous assessment is more than a technique to be used to evaluate a particular program, however. We have suggested that all of the important aspects of the school program be made part of a regular sampling schedule under a continuous assessment design. Using this device, the school's decision-makers could keep track of trends as they develop, rather than waiting to react at some critical moment.

The continuous assessment approach is based on five principles, which are introduced in the chapter. Of additional interest is a unique approach to student evaluation and pupil progress reporting, based on these five principles. Entitled the *individualized corridor approach,* this technique has the advantage of being a method with which a student competes with his own record rather than with other students. It is designed for the modern-day realities of assessing achievement.

The topic of chapter 4 is the use of achievement tests. The widespread use of standardized achievement test batteries makes this topic important to the school decision-maker. The discussion begins with the question of *why* districts use achievement testing programs. A few answers are suggested, and then the most appropriate reporting systems are developed for each given reason. Grade equivalents, as shall be seen, are appropriate for one testing purpose, but are a poor choice for others. Likewise, percentiles can be used effectively for some purposes, but are difficult to interpret elsewhere. The reporting system chosen by the school administrator should be *a function of the purpose for testing* in the first place. The chapter ends with some suggestions for techniques of reporting scores to teachers, the public, parents, and students.

Pupils are assigned to the schools and the school administration has the task of sorting them into classes. Many options exist for this sorting process. Some classes are grouped heterogeneously. Other times, the administration sees benefits in grouping the students homogeneously (or, as we shall see, less heterogeneously). Very often in homogeneous grouping, pupil assignment rests heavily upon educational measurement. Chapter 5 discusses homogeneous grouping and the test scores upon which it is usually based.

After a brief review of the extensive literature dealing with homogeneous grouping, it is noted that there are three dimensions which should be considered before deciding upon an ability grouping scheme. First, *appropriateness*. That is, the procedure might be excellent for high school geometry, but detrimental in third-grade social studies. Next, we point to errors which occur in assignment to groups, for instance, errors of measurement. We believe it is important for the decision-maker to be aware of the extent of these errors. As many as one out of five students may be in the wrong group, due to measurement errors alone. At least as important as these unbiased errors are errors of bias inherent in certain educational measurements. These measurement devices are thought to reflect differences in the socioeconomic standing of the pupil. We have dealt with this topic quite completely, for the authors believe it is of critical importance to the school administrator.

Chapter 6 deals with evaluating in-service programs. Times change; so do methods and content. Old jobs are eliminated, and new jobs appear. If they are to keep in tune, school districts must operate programs of in-service education for their staffs. Often someone—the school board, the community, or some outside funding agency—is interested in knowing whether a given program is effective. This suggests evaluation. The behavioral objectives approach has usually been concentrated on classroom learning situations. In chapter 6, we attempt to show how the director of an in-service program can specify the objectives of a program in behavioral terms. Once this is done, the evaluation of the level of objective attainment is not difficult. One of the behavioral changes described deals with attitude changes by the staff. We have made extensive comments at this point about the possibility of disagreement between expressed attitudes and behavior, and the causes of this disagreement.

Chapter 7 deals with the measurement of staff attitude and morale, which is difficult from the *measurement* point of view. Much research has been done, but it is hard to translate the results into specific suggestions for the school decision-maker. Nevertheless, the topic belongs in this book, and we have mined the available research for specific measurement suggestions. After these discussions, a specific technique for surveying staff morale and attitude is introduced. This is one area where a continuous assessment design is appropriate, and we have sketched a design for such a program.

Chapter 8 is another one difficult to handle from the educational measurement viewpoint. But one of the most important decision points for the school administration is that of the selection of faculty, and their retention after selection. Again, the research has been reviewed with an eye toward extracting the measurement suggestions from the results. We have noted that there are two general groups of factors to be considered; namely, those which are obvious and which operate almost independently of the local conditions, as contrasted with those which are district-specific and which may be controlled by the local administration. The discussion includes techniques whereby the data on applicants can be accumulated efficiently, as well as some suggested decision-making models. The discussion of teacher retention focuses on plotting "survival curves" which are designed to delineate certain of the district-specific factors.

The topic of chapter 9 is evaluating teacher effectiveness. We have noted that concentration on one or two predictor variables ignores certain very important interaction effects. It ignores the interaction of certain teacher characteristics with highly variable classroom environments, as well as the intra-teacher interaction of variables. In discussing the use of personality measures to determine teacher effectiveness correlates, we comment that the results are very situation-specific. That is, the results obtained depend heavily upon the situation which the respondent perceives himself to be in. For this reason, and because the reliability of personality measures is often very low, we are not optimistic about their use. We do strongly urge the use of student output measures as a basis for determining teacher effectiveness. Superimposed upon this suggestion, however, is the necessity for the detailed specification of the things the district expects of teachers. We have suggested extensive listings of the important behavioral changes expected, so that the teacher knows quite clearly what is expected of him. These lists could then be the basis of the measurement of teacher effectiveness through pupil changes.

Chapter 10 is built around a hypothetical situation in a community faced with the need of money for a building program. A bond issue is called for. The example which is used centers on the superintendent's attempt to determine whether his community would pass a bond issue for a new school. The chapter includes sections on selecting a sample, preparing a questionnaire, determining proper sample size, testing a hypothesis, and making a decision. Also included is a rather detailed series of suggestions for choosing the most appropriate sample size for given conditions. Each topic discussed has applications far beyond the example given.

Chapter 11 is directed toward the role of educational measurements in school desegregation decisions. It appears that educational measurements are becoming one of the primary targets of court litigation in this area. Progress toward integration of schools has been slow, and our attempt has been to trace some of the steps in this progress since the original decision directing the schools to integrate "with all deliberate speed." The chapter is intended to be a supporting chapter for the information presented in chapter 5.

REFERENCES
Bloom, Benjamin S., ed. *Taxonomy of Educational Objectives.* New York: David McKay, 1956.

OUTCOME EVALUATION

An Example of Outcome Evaluation

Specifying Behavioral Outcomes

The Control Group

Measuring the Four Outcomes
Outcome No. 1: An achievement test
Outcome No. 2: Longitudinal investigation
Outcome No. 3: Student attitudes
Outcome No. 4: Frequency counts

Statistical Significance and Predictive Association
Strength of predictive association
Measures of association

This chapter will focus on many of the issues which arise when a program is assessed by outcome evaluation. Outcome evaluation generally involves measures made only at the beginning and end of a program. If the resulting data indicate that changes have occurred, *causality* is often inferred. That is, the program director infers that the observed changes occurred *because of* the imposition of the program. Inferential statements must be made with great care, however, for the changes may have been a matter of chance, or they may have been due to forces related in an unknown manner to the experimental conditions or program.

AN EXAMPLE OF OUTCOME EVALUATION
Anderson High School District No. 161 is located in a blue-collar area of a large city. About half of the graduating seniors do not continue on to college. The administration and faculty have become alarmed about certain characteristics of the student body. Of special concern is the apathy of the students, which is most noticeable in the lack of student participation in school events. To determine the reasons for the students' apparent lack of interest in school, the guidance department conducted many interviews with both former and current students. These interviews led the guidance department to conclude that one of the primary causes was a perceived lack of relevance in the school program. The students argued that their high school courses did little to prepare them for specific problems as they became workers and parents after high school.

The faculty decided to attack the problem of relevance by introducing a new two-year social science program for the tenth and eleventh grades. The program, entitled Contemporary Problems I and II, included units ranging from Income Tax, which included specific instructions on filing properly, to Political Participation, in which the students were introduced to techniques for joining and participating in both local and national political organizations. Other topics included loan agencies, investigation of the local and national employment situations, and studies about how national economic changes such as inflation have affected the population near Anderson High School. Newspapers, periodicals, and paperbacks were the media for instruction.

SPECIFYING BEHAVIORAL OUTCOMES

The entire program is to be evaluated. Before we specify behavioral outcomes, it might be well to outline the situation with a diagram (Figure 1).

The journey from initiation to action involved intermediate steps, some of which include more than one idea. All assumptions, both explicit and implicit, should be tested. Based on the diagram, a list of evaluation points should include the four outcome statements which follow.

First, the new program will attempt to emphasize topics relevant to people living near Anderson High. It is essential that the students *do learn* this material. An achievement test is implied. It is also important to know how well students in the old program do on the same achievement test. Perhaps the new course simply has a new name, but the same old course content. A behavioral outcome for this evaluation need could be stated as follows:

> **Outcome no. 1:** *Students in the new program will manifest their increased understanding of the information*

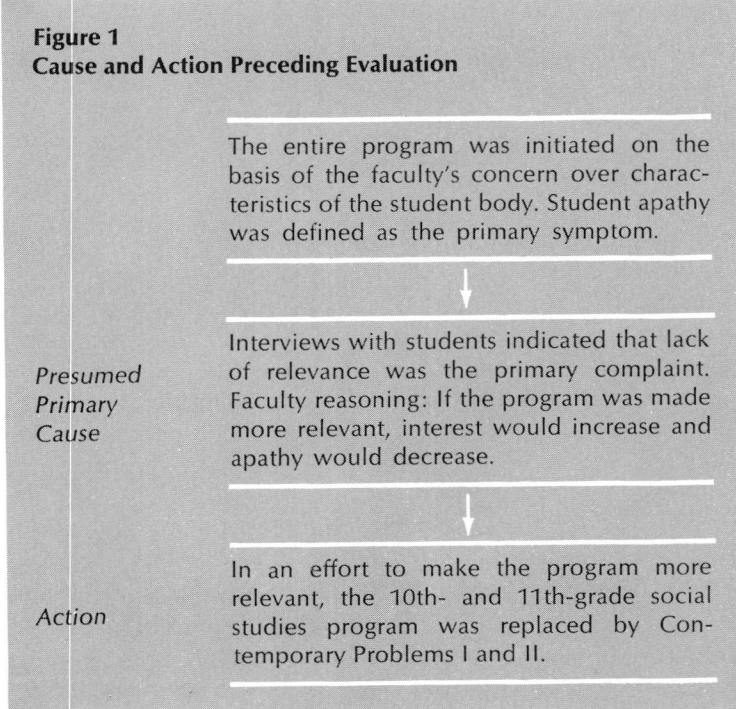

Figure 1
Cause and Action Preceding Evaluation

	The entire program was initiated on the basis of the faculty's concern over characteristics of the student body. Student apathy was defined as the primary symptom.
Presumed Primary Cause	Interviews with students indicated that lack of relevance was the primary complaint. Faculty reasoning: If the program was made more relevant, interest would increase and apathy would decrease.
Action	In an effort to make the program more relevant, the 10th- and 11th-grade social studies program was replaced by Contemporary Problems I and II.

covered by performing satisfactorily on a comprehensive achievement test on the information, and by better performance on such a test than that of previous students.

This statement approaches behavioral language, but does fall a little short. To be completely behavioral, the term "satisfactorily" must be defined. "Satisfactory" could be defined as "reaching the 90 percent correct level" or some other level; or it could be a variable mastery level, based on the incoming scores of the students. In addition, if the statement is to be behavioral, the "comprehensive achievement test" must be spelled out completely. When a test is based on behavioral statements, each item fits a particular expected outcome. Thus it can be seen that this particular outcome should be considerably expanded in a real situation.

Outcome no. 2: *The students involved in the new program will use their knowledge through more effective participation in the adult world.*

Again, the statement only suggests the behavioral terms which would ultimately be used in a real situation. The people involved in designing the new program would need to specify precisely how they expected the new information to help the school's graduates. If one part of the program dealt with obtaining the best kind of loan, a statement about the student's expected behavior in a loan-seeking situation would be made under the general heading of outcome no. 2.

Outcome no. 1 dealt with knowledge. The program was not designed to stop at the knowledge level alone; it was designed to make the school relevant. Thus outcome no. 2 is appropriate, because it translates the knowledge into expected action. But there are further steps in the chain.

The program was devised to correct a perceived lack of relevance in the high school curriculum. It has been assumed that lack of relevance was a primary cause for student apathy. It is important to evaluate the relevance issue—do the students' attitudes regarding relevance change after implementation of the new program? The general statement of this expected outcome can be stated as:

Outcome no. 3: *Once the new program is under way, the attitude of the students regarding the relevance of the curriculum will improve.*

The statement is not in clear behavioral terms, for it does not specify the attitude statements about which students will be surveyed, nor does it mention the specific techniques which will be used to evaluate these attitudes. In a real situation, the program director would use this general statement as a starting point, and make an exhaustive list of the types of attitudes which will be evaluated, and the techniques to be used.

The final point requiring evaluation is the relationship between lack of relevance and student apathy. If the new program is more relevant, does it follow that student apathy will decrease? Since apathy was especially apparent in the low level of student participation in school activities, the following expected behavioral outcome applies:

> **Outcome no. 4:** *The improved attitude of the student body will be shown by a higher level of student participation in school activities.*

This outcome communicates fairly well in behavioral terms. It also should be followed by a listing of the school activities under consideration, however.

The situation in which an administrator must evaluate the merits of a new program of instruction is common in education. Usually these investigations compare two or more things—for example, an old program and a new approach; two (or more) methods of presenting a concept; television instruction and regular classroom instruction; graded classrooms and nongraded classrooms; ability grouping and heterogeneous grouping; and lecture instruction and laboratory instruction—all are examples of common alternative approaches. This kind of decision will continue to be among the most important made by the educational administrator.

The point of this evaluation study at Anderson High School is not to *prove* that the new program is better than the old one. Professional educators, using their best judgment as well as the opinions of former students, have specified a group of concepts to be used in this program. The evaluation study has been designed to measure the extent to which these concepts have been attained. If the evaluator is only interested in determining whether the new program is better than the old, he might unknowingly be comparing a bad program with one that is worse. The ideal program has been prepared by the professional staff, and the comparison should be between the ideal program which was envisioned and the degree to which its objectives were met, and not between the attainments under the old program versus the attainments under the new. The goals of the program are not dependent upon the relative merit of this particular Contemporary Problems sequence as compared to the program that existed before. Each is compared to a standard set by the staff. The relative performance of one compared to the other is only of passing interest.

The changes expected from the new program at Anderson High School are quite broad—decisions which educational administrators make are certainly not always this sweeping in their implications. A decision might simply involve alterations in the qualifications required of the school bus driver.

Who does the specifying? Whenever a new program is undertaken, the specification of expected behavioral changes is the responsibility of those who administer the program— the people who decided that some aspect could be improved and who have designed a new program to correct a deficiency. To be sure, an educational measurement specialist can be consulted about the wording of the proposed outcomes, and asked to comment on the measurability of each. However, no one knows what to expect of a new program better than the people who originated it.

If the reason for the new program has substance, an attempt should be made to translate this reason into measurable terms. The content of the four outcomes mentioned above should be illustrative of the *non*mathematical nature of the task. The responsibility for this translating should not be left to a consultant, and it should not be ignored. The program's initiators *can* do it; the program's initiators *should* do it. Someone with experience in this line of work can be brought in to help, but not to direct. The people behind the new program must ask themselves questions like these:

> What behaviors did we object to, or did we see as needful of improvement? What was wrong with the old way of doing things?
>
> Exactly what experiences have we designed for the students? What will they experience now that they did not experience before?
>
> What changes can we reasonably expect in student behavior, due to their participation in the new program?

After the program's originators have answered these questions, the specialist can be of service in two ways. First, he can make sure that the specified outcomes are stated in a manner which makes them measurable. Second, he can help the district find or develop appropriate measurement methods to see whether the program actually operates in the expected manner.

The administrator might do well to consider the techniques used by the Exploratory Committee on Assessing the Progress of Education (the National Assessment). In this program, before items could be written about a certain concept, the concept had to be acceptable to three screening groups. *Educators* had to agree it was the school's responsibility to include the concept; *experts* and *scholars* had to agree that the concept was important; and thoughtful *citizens* were asked to pass on the concept's desirability. These considerations could be paraphrased for the situation at Anderson High School: Does the faculty agree that the units covered in the new program belong in the school curriculum? Do social studies experts agree that the topics are important? Do thoughtful lay citizens—in this case, graduates of the school —feel that the topics are desirable?

THE CONTROL GROUP

A large body of research in education and psychology is carried out through the use of a control group in addition to an experimental group. At the beginning of the experiment, two groups are defined which are comparable at that time (except for the unavoidable error inherent in sampling). Each group is exposed to a prescribed series of experiences, with care taken to keep the experiences of the two groups exactly alike except for the experimental conditions. At the end of the experiment, measurements are obtained to find out whether the different experiences resulted in different levels of performance on appropriate criterion measures. If the two groups differ in levels of performance, and it can be shown that it is highly unlikely that such differences were due to chance factors alone, the experimenter usually concludes that the levels of performance differed *due to* the presence or absence of the experimental conditions.

Should a control group be used in the Anderson High School situation? This is a large school, and it would be possible to define half of the tenth- and eleventh-grade classes as Control, and the other half as Experimental. However, consider two ramifications of such a procedure.

1. If a control and experimental approach were used, the new program would be carried out only with the experimental group, and the control group would not have the benefit of any of the new content. Suppose that after five months of the new program it is clear to the educators involved that certain important aspects of the new program make it far superior to the old. The administrator of the program is wearing two hats—educator and researcher. As an educator, he must feel committed to a policy of providing for all students the program which, in his considered judgment, is the best possible. If the administrator and his staff feel that the new program is superior, can they conscientiously refrain from contaminating the experiment by altering the control group's program?

On the other hand, the administrator as researcher realizes that contamination resulting from exposing the control group to experimental group experiences reduces the possibility of clear differences in the final measures. For clearest results, the prescribed experiences should be maintained until the final measurements are taken and decisions made.

2. The hypothetical dilemma in which the administrator has been placed may be entirely academic, however. The control group may be indirectly exposed to the experimental conditions in ways he cannot control. Experimental teachers have informal communications with Control teachers. The same teacher, in fact, may teach both types of classes. Administrators talk with other administrators, and the informal communication lines within the student body are very efficient. It may be impossible to isolate one program from the other.

A control group has not been included in the evaluation design envisioned for Anderson High School. Note that the term *evaluation design* is used rather than *experimental design*. Professionals have diagnosed the problem and prescribed the medicine, and the motivation for tampering with the program has not been just intellectual curiosity. The motivation was the considered belief that the new program is superior to the old. This is no experiment; therefore, evaluation is the proper word. Does the new program operate in the manner predicted? Methodological as well as philosophical arguments against establishment of a control group can be set forward.

This is not to say that control groups are never acceptable or practical. The prevailing conditions should dictate the evaluation design. In the Anderson High case, use of a control group does not seem to be justifiable. Absence of a co-existing control group does not excuse the administrator from careful evaluation. Statistical treatment of results can still be carried out by comparing what *is* happening under the new program with what *did* happen under the old.

MEASURING THE FOUR OUTCOMES

OUTCOME NO. 1: AN ACHIEVEMENT TEST

Under the first outcome, the staff hoped that the new program would arm the students with increased understanding of and knowledge about the topics included. The statement of the objective suggests an achievement test.

A discussion of techniques of writing achievement test items is inappropriate here—such a topic needs a book of its own. But two general principles should be stated.

First, the concepts to be surveyed by the test should dictate the types of items to be written, and not the other way around. The test writer should not begin by requiring a multiple choice format, for example, and force everything into this form. Instead, the topics to be covered should be specified, and the format which fits them best should be used. Some items may require special media for presentation. For example, a contrived situation on tape or film may fit some concepts best, while another item requires oral presentation. The situation comes first; the technique follows it.

Second, time should be allotted for a pilot run on the test. Much is written about writing and polishing items so that the test measures what it was intended to measure. This polishing phase requires a tryout period, so that ambiguous items and items which do not serve a useful purpose can be corrected or eliminated before the actual evaluation begins.

A time schedule for the achievement test. Suppose a representative achievement test has been developed. The concept attainment measured by the test should represent the primary concerns of the new program. The test should have gone through a tryout stage. The next decisions: Who should be tested? What comparisons are of interest? What should be the testing schedule? Refer to the schematic diagram (Figure 2) and the comments which follow for an outline of the required steps.

Block A. A control group was not included so that measures of student performance under the old program should be taken before the beginning of the new program. Although the new program involves only tenth- and eleventh-grade students, it would be well to use the achievement test with tenth-, eleventh-, and twelfth-graders in the spring of the school year before the new program is implemented.[1] The results of this first testing will answer two interesting questions even before the new program begins.

The concepts included in the new program—and tested with the new test—were considered by the staff to be relevant and important for this student body. In the new program, a conscious effort has been made to include these topics. To what extent did the student body learn these concepts before a conscious effort was made to include them? Is it possible that the new program will be just the same old stuff under a new name?

A second interesting result centers on performance changes as measured by the test. Do eleventh-graders know more about the concepts than tenth-graders? Do the twelfth-graders outscore the eleventh? If the three groups have approximately the same average score, it would seem to indicate that they are not growing in these concepts as they move through high school. A decrease in performance with age might indicate that the topics are covered in earlier years, but not reviewed in high school, and are subsequently forgotten.

Block B. At the end of the first year of the new program,

---

[1] As will be pointed out in chapter 3, to test *all* of the students in these grades at the same time is probably wasteful, since it would yield more accuracy than the test can stand. A random sampling would utilize these students more efficiently.

Figure 2
A Schematic Diagram of the Evaluation Schedule

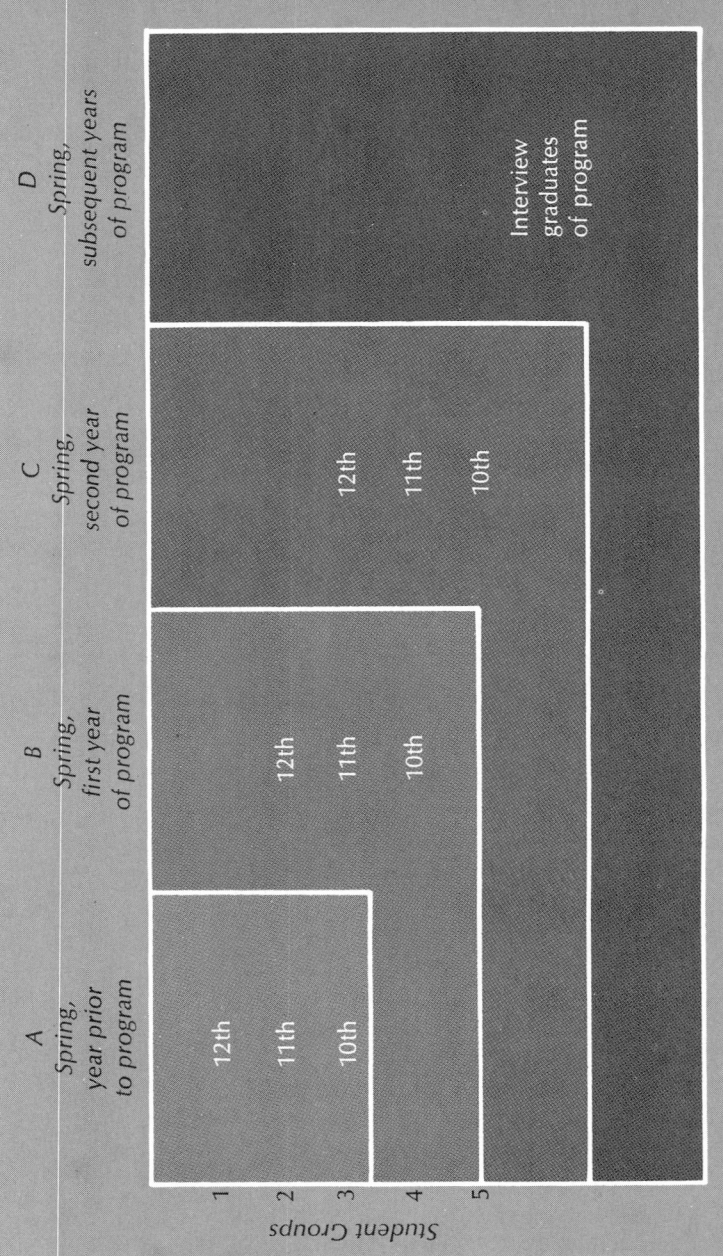

the same three classes (or a representative sample thereof) should again be tested. The performance of the tenth- and eleventh-graders after one year of the new program should indicate the extent to which these groups have mastered the concepts. Tenth-, eleventh-, and twelfth-grade before and after comparisons should also be made. The tenth and eleventh grades will each have one year of the new program under their belts, so that direct measures will be available. Neither of the two twelfth grades (spring of year before program and at end of first year) will have had the new program themselves, but the second group of twelfth graders will have been in school when the new program was operating. It would be interesting to see if any runoff occurred to raise this group's average achievement level by an appreciable amount.

Block C. At the end of the second year of the new program, the tenth, eleventh, and twelfth grades can be examined again.[2] The mastery level of the tenth and eleventh grades (without any comparison to past performance of similar groups) is important. The twelfth-grade scores will indicate the amount of forgetting which occurs in one year, since the Contemporary Problems sequence would end in eleventh grade. In terms of comparisons, the performance level of tenth-graders, under the old and new programs, is obtained for the second time; the performance level of eleventh-graders with two years' training in the new program is compared to eleventh-graders under the old program.

Block D. By the end of the second year, the major questions associated with the total evaluation of outcome no. 1 will have been answered. Feedback from both student and teacher groups will probably cause certain changes in the basic program, so that continued evaluation will be necessary in subsequent years.

The statistical handling of each of these questions is straightforward and the techniques are well documented elsewhere. To compare the pre-test performance of tenth-,

---

[2] If the same test is used, and all the students are examined each year with this test, the problem of "learning the test" will become a real one. However, parallel tests could be made, or, more realistically, samples could be taken from the class each year, so that the likelihood of multiple testing of the same students with the same instrument would be low.

eleventh-, and twelfth-graders, the Simple Randomized Design in the Lindquist (1953) notation, or a "fixed effects, one-way analysis of variance" following Hays (1965) could be used. The statistical hypothesis would state that there is no difference in the performance level of the three groups, and that any differences that did occur could be explained as chance variations. To reject the hypothesis of equality implies that the observed result should not have occurred *if* the three groups really were equal—chance variations in performance could not account for the observed differences. A fairly thorough (and heuristic) discussion of the sequence of steps in the testing of hypotheses is included in chapter 10, with the discussion of the bond issue data.

The statistical treatment for Blocks B and C is somewhat more complicated. The data are now more than "one-way." There are certain main questions (Are there meaningful changes in average performance levels for different years?) as well as specific smaller questions (At the twelfth grade for the first two testings, is there a change?). Lindquist and Hays are both sources for analyzing these data. A technical discussion of each of these techniques is out of place here, for this book is not meant to supplant a statistical handbook. If the administrator feels insecure in the area of selection and application of statistical methods, and the accompanying interpretation of results, he should seek advice from a specialist. A high level of methodological sophistication is not a prerequisite for all educational evaluators and researchers. Research should not be restricted to the mathematical treatment of data by measurement and statistics specialists. The most difficult parts of a research program or a new program come in defining the problem, prescribing corrective actions, and finding measures that will tell whether the corrective measures are working. These steps do not require a mathematical orientation, only a problem-solving orientation. The expert can help polish things as the program develops, and apply the mathematical principles where appropriate.

OUTCOME NO. 2: LONGITUDINAL INVESTIGATION

The most difficult to measure is outcome no. 2, which requires longitudinal investigations of post–high school activities of graduates. The questions which should be asked of the graduates are clearly implied by the units in the new program, and by the statement in outcome no. 2 that the participants will ". . . use their knowledge through more effective participation in the adult world." If one unit of the new program deals with types of loans and their merits, the interviewer would see whether the participants used their knowledge to procure the best possible loans. If a unit deals with political participation, the interviewer would see whether the program participants used their knowledge to a higher degree than had previous years' graduates. The problems involved in measuring outcome no. 2 are certainly not unsurmountable—the measurement itself would not be as difficult as locating the graduates and asking the questions.

OUTCOME NO. 3: STUDENT ATTITUDES

Outcome no. 3 deals with student attitudes. The process of attitude measurement is similar to the process of achievement measurement—both involve the initial step of clearly specifying what changes are expected. This list of expected changes then dictates the method to be used in measuring the student attitudes. We will note later (in chapter 7) that expressed attitude is often situation-specific—that is, a person's attitudes depend on his expectations and perceptions of his situation. We will delay further discussion of this topic until later.

OUTCOME NO. 4: FREQUENCY COUNTS

The fourth behavioral outcome is based on the presumption that if the students' attitude toward the school improves, this improvement will be manifested by increased involvement in school activities. Remember that the student characteristic which caused the administration to institute the new program was apathy toward the school, and that the new program is directed toward the cause most often expressed by graduates for this apathy.

School activities range from class plays to sports events, and include club activities, class elections, dances and other social functions. Any or all of these could be used to check on the last behavioral outcome. The activities could be categorized under the headings of sports events, social events, and academic events. The only real evaluation requirement is that data be gathered in the spring before the new program is begun, so that these results are available for comparison one and two years after the new program goes into effect. This type of data collection is simplified by the fact that much of this information is a matter of record—attendance at the prom, for example, can be inferred from the number of tickets sold.

Note that all of these results will necessarily be based on frequency counts. It would be a little absurd to think of "attendance at the prom" in evaluative terms, unless a scoring formula is derived—based, for example, on the quality of formals, plus a factor for age of automobile used, and minus a factor for hair length. Our best bet is to find out if a reliably larger proportion of the class attends the prom after the new program is introduced, which may indicate that the new, relevant program does create a more positive attitude toward the school. Of course, only through an accumulation of such measures, to include frequency counts of participation in school elections, clubs, plays, sports events, and others, could the administrator determine if outcome no. 4 has actually been achieved.

Since data collection based on frequency counts is so often encountered by the school administrator, it might be worthwhile to follow through a typical investigation under outcome no. 4. Assume data for two years are available. Call the year prior to introduction of the new program *Year 0*, and the first year of the program *Year 1*. The object of inquiry is membership in clubs—Science Club, Home Ec Club, Nurses Club, etc. Some of these would be sports clubs, some social, and some academic. The sophomores and juniors for the two years are categorized in one of three cells, namely: no club memberships, member of one or two clubs, or member of more than two clubs. The data could be shown as in Table 1.

Table 1
Club Membership Frequencies Before and After the New Program

	Year 0	Year 1	Totals
Member of more than two clubs	50	150	200
Member of one or two clubs	150	250	400
Member of no clubs	200	200	400
Totals	400	600	1000

For the two years, 200 students out of a total of 1,000 belonged to more than two clubs. Forty percent of this 1000 total were counted during Year 0 (400/1000), and 60 percent (600/1000) during Year 1. Now—if attitude toward joining clubs did not change, the 200 in row 1 should be divided up in proportion to class size. That is, 40 percent of the 200 (or 80) should have come from Year 0, and 60 percent (or 120) should have come from Year 1. These figures—80 and 120—are the "expected" frequencies. Obviously, these are not the numbers which occurred, since the numbers in row 1 are 50 and 150. Of course, it is important to remember that normal sampling errors can account for small variations in cell frequencies.

The steps, therefore, are: First, assume that students participate no more in Year 1 than they did in Year 0. Second, determine what frequency count can be expected if this is so. Last, decide whether the observed numbers differ so drastically from the expected numbers that they cannot be attributed to chance variations in responses. For row 1 of Table 1, the data look like this:

	Year 0	Year 1
Member of more than two clubs	observed 50 expected 80	observed 150 expected 120

The difference in each case is 30; for Year 0, the observed number is 30 too low, and for Year 1, it is 30 too high. Is this far enough from expected in each case so that it can be said that this would probably not occur if there were no basic change in attitude? This question can be answered in the probability, or statistical, sense.

First, for each of the six cells of the table, find the squared difference between expected and observed frequencies. Remember that the expected frequencies are found by dividing up the row total in proportion to the class size. The 200 in row 1 are allotted by taking 40 percent (400/1000) for Year 0 and 60 percent (600/1000) for Year 1. The 400 total for row 2 is allotted 40 percent for Year 0 and 60 percent for Year 1. The *expected frequencies* for row 2 are, therefore, 160 and 240. Since the total for row 3 is the same as row 2, these expected frequencies are also 160 and 240. Thus the squares of the differences of all six cells are indicated in Table 2.

Table 2
Squared Differences Between Observed and Expected Frequencies

	Year 0	Year 1
Member of more than two clubs	$(50 - 80)^2 = 900$	$(150 - 120)^2 = 900$
Member of one or two clubs	$(150 - 160)^2 = 100$	$(250 - 240)^2 = 100$
Member of zero clubs	$(200 - 160)^2 = 1600$	$(200 - 240)^2 = 1600$

The size of the squared difference noted in Table 2 is in a very real sense determined by the size of the frequency count in the cell. It seems logical to find an average squared difference. To obtain this average squared difference, the squared differences of Table 2 are divided by the expected cell frequencies, to obtain the results shown in Table 3.

Table 3
Average Squared Differences Between Observed and Expected Frequencies

	Year 0	Year 1
Member of more than two clubs	$900/80 = 11.250$	$900/120 = 7.500$
Member of one or two clubs	$100/160 = 0.625$	$100/240 = 0.417$
Member of zero clubs	$1600/160 = 10.000$	$1600/240 = 6.667$

The sum of these six numbers is 36.459, or about 36.5. Fortunately, mathematicians have provided tables which tell us the approximate probability of such a sum, under the assumption that nothing systematic is happening between years 0 and 1. These are called chi-square tables. These tables are very common and can be found in almost any statistics text. For a problem like the one described above, where the table has three rows and two columns, the following statements of probability can be made:

> *If nothing systematic is happening between years 0 and 1, you would obtain a sum of average squared differences larger than 5.99 only about 1 time in 20.*

If nothing systematic is happening between years 0 and 1, you would obtain a sum of average squared differences larger than 9.21 only about 1 time in 100.

If nothing systematic is happening between years 0 and 1, you would obtain a sum of average squared differences larger than 13.82 only about 1 time in 1000.

The sum of average squared differences was actually as large as 36.5. It is *highly unlikely* that the assumption that nothing systematic is happening is correct. In fact, it is so unlikely (less than 1 chance in 1000) that we are forced to throw the assumption out. Something systematic must be happening—that's the only way we can reasonably explain our observed result.

To summarize, then, what has been done:

1. Start with the statement of the statistical hypothesis—that students of the two years had the same average propensity to participate in club activities.

2. Based on that assumption, determine the frequencies which can be expected in the cells of the table.

3. Find the sum of the average squared difference between observed and expected frequencies.

4. Find out if this sum is beyond the range of what can reasonably be expected if the assumption that nothing systematic is happening is true.

5. If this sum is within the realm of what can reasonably be expected, retain the assumption. If the observed sum shows that the assumption is highly improbable, conclude that the assumption must have been incorrect, and that the contrary is true.

STATISTICAL SIGNIFICANCE AND PREDICTIVE ASSOCIATION

Significance, as the term is used in educational measurement, is related to probability. A "statistically significant" result is one that could not have been expected through the operations of chance alone—something systematic was operating. The researcher should not assume that this "something systematic" is necessarily important in the real world. There may be a statistically significant weight difference between the ten-year-olds of Minneapolis and Saint Paul, but if the real difference is 64.3 pounds for Minneapolis and 64.2 pounds for Saint Paul, one would not expect a grocery wholesaler to include this fact in his decision-making machinery. In groups of human beings, no attribute is exactly the same for two groups, nor are any two attributes of a given group completely independent of one another. But are these differences meaningful? *That* decision is not the responsibility of the quantitative specialist, but rather of the practicing researcher in the field. When the specialist reports to a superintendent that a new algebra program "reliably increased the average performance level on the comprehensive achievement test," he is not saying by implication that the new program should be immediately implemented. It is the responsibility of the superintendent to find out from his mathematics staff whether the degree of increase is meaningful, and whether the payoff is worth the changes involved.

Methods are available to quantify the degree of relationship between attributes. These are usually based on the concept that an outcome (dependent variable) can be best predicted when certain input information (independent variables) is known. Take this question: To what extent will John Smith support a bond issue proposal? If nothing is known about Mr. Smith the answer could be anything from "damn little" to "completely." Now suppose it is further known that Mr. Smith is young, has four children in the school system, has a political philosophy which strongly favors local control of educational policy, and is fairly wealthy. Each of these input facts tends to reduce the range of possible answers—to use the jargon, they account for a lot of the variance in support level. When a statistician says he has "accounted for a lot of the variance," he means that the range of possible outcomes has been considerably reduced. That is, knowing these things about Mr. Smith, it is possible to make a fairly intelligent guess about the extent to which he will support the bond issue.

Two attributes may be significantly related without accounting for a substantial percentage of variance. Thus, whenever possible, it is best to report the results of an experimental situation in terms of both the significance of the results and the proportion of available variance accounted for.

There are two closely related reasons for desiring to know the proportion of variance that has been accounted for by the independent variables (that is, to know the degree of predictive association). Most often, the researcher is simply interested in knowing how certain variables relate to one another. Prediction is not necessarily implied. Suppose a researcher finds that males do very poorly in a certain math program, but that females do quite well—that is, the dependent variable (performance) is related to the independent variable (sex of student). The information is important, and the school might alter the program so that it accommodates the males as well. However, the information is not particularly important in the *predictive* sense, since the administrator probably would not just predict poor male performance and leave the program as it stands. He would alter the program, based on such knowledge.

Sometimes, however, information of this type *is* important in the predictive sense. School administrators often must make predictions, more often called *projections* of the future. School buildings and school programs require long-range planning, and the administration must use current information to predict future situations. More confidence can be placed in a projection when the predictive association is strong.

STRENGTH OF PREDICTIVE ASSOCIATION

Necessary decisions often deal with the future needs of a school or district. When this is the case, the technique of measurement of predictive association can be very important to the school decision-maker. Suppose we use an example to illustrate:

Assume that a certain school district has an excellent vocational education program, but that the facilities are becoming inadequate because of increasing enrollment. The district's planners must inaugurate a design which will be completed five years in the future. How shall they predict how much additional space will be needed at that time? Inaccuracies in the estimate would cost the district money, not to mention confusion and embarrassment.

The most obvious approach for estimating the size of the enrollment five years in the future is to look at the enrollment trends in vocational education for the past five or ten years, and project them five years in the future. Obviously the trend has been upward, or the facilities would not have become overcrowded.

Suppose enrollment data are available for the past eight years, and the data are as given in Table 4.

Table 4
Enrollments in Vocational Education over an Eight-Year Period

Year	Enrollment	Year	Enrollment
1	127	5	118
2	101	6	160
3	113	7	179
4	108	8	165

The question is: How much space will be required five years from now? The answer requires an estimate. In cases like this, it is always a good idea to start with a graph of the information, as has been done in Figure 3.

Year 8 on this graph is the current year, and year 13 is five years after the current year. This is the time that the new facilities are scheduled to be done.

Once the data are summarized on the graph, it is possible to make an "eyeball" projection, as shown. Any thin, straight object will help here—we have shown a very thin knitting needle. The pointer has been placed so that there are as many points above the line as below, with an attempt to equalize the distances from point to line above and below. Using this "eyeball" technique, the pointer crosses year 13 at about 182 or 183.

An obvious problem exists with this approach, however. It is likely that each person would place the pointer in a slightly different position. To avoid this ambiguity, the following placement rule is generally adopted: The line shall be placed so that the sum of the *squared deviations* from the line will be a minimum. One of the deviations, for year 4, can be seen in Figure 3. The deviation at year 4 (the distance from the point to the line) is 24; the squared deviation is 24 squared or 576. To get the sum of the squared deviations, this amount would be added to the squared deviations for the other seven points. The line will be placed where this total sum is as small as possible.[3]

---

[3] This rule is called the *least-squares* condition. Besides removing ambiguity in the placement of the line, this placement rule has other mathematical properties which make it a most fortunate choice.

Figure 3
Plot of Vocational Education Enrollment Data Showing "Eyeballed" Projection Line

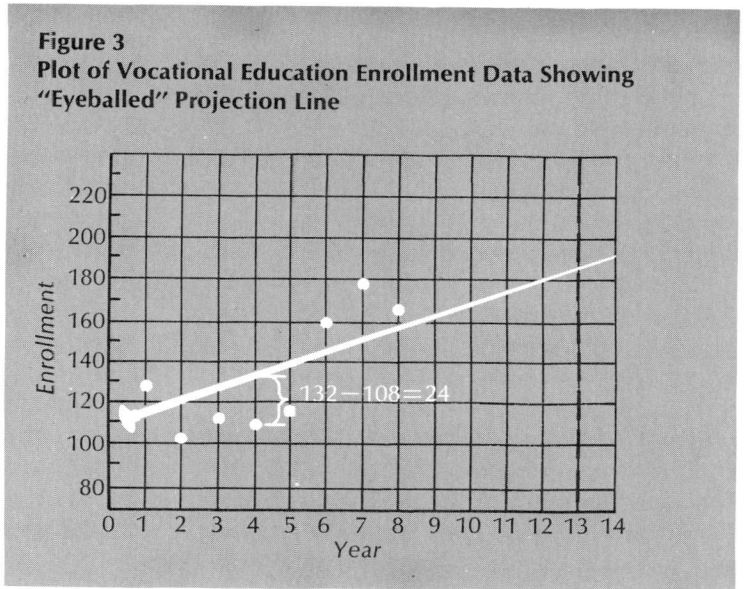

The line could be placed quite accurately through a trial-and-error method. It would be possible to find all eight squared deviations for many different placements, and use that placement which gave the smallest sum of these. There is, however, a mathematical technique for finding this best-fitting line. In Figure 4, the line has been placed on the graph to have a minimum sum of squared deviations.[4]

This best-fitting line crosses the year 13 at a different point than did the first attempt at an eyeball fit. Using this second line, the projected enrollment five years hence is approximately 216.

The precision of the estimate: Even the best-fitting line

---

[4] This book is not meant to be used as a statistical methodology handbook. The line, however, takes the form of $Y = aX + b$, where

$$a = \frac{\Sigma(X_i - \bar{X})(Y_i - \bar{Y})}{\Sigma(X_i - \bar{X})^2}$$

$$b = \bar{Y} - a\bar{X}$$

where X_i and Y_i are the year and the enrollment that year, respectively, and $\bar{X}$ and $\bar{Y}$ are the average year and enrollment, respectively. The a is often called the *slope* and the b the *intercept*. For these data, $a = 9.61$ and $b = 90.6$. (For a detailed presentation, see Blommers and Lindquist, 1960.)

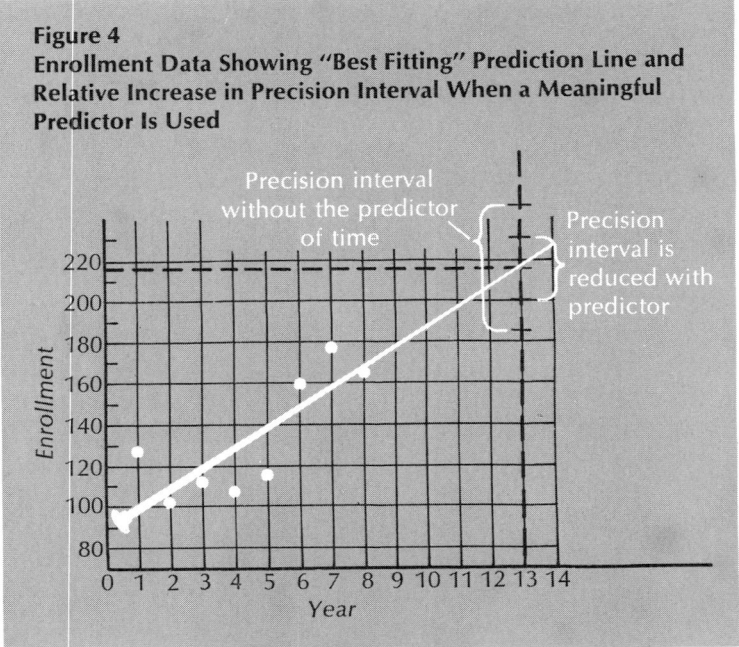

Figure 4
Enrollment Data Showing "Best Fitting" Prediction Line and Relative Increase in Precision Interval When a Meaningful Predictor Is Used

does not fit the eight points precisely. In fact, it does not fit any one of them precisely. It seems reasonable that the estimate for five years hence is also not precise.

The most common measure for variability of scores is the standard deviation.[5] For these eight scores the standard deviation is approximately 29.7, or, rounded off, about 30. If the decision-maker chooses an interval one standard deviation above and one standard deviation below the estimate, the interval will span from 216 − 30 to 216 + 30 or from 186 to 246.

This precision interval can be reduced, however, by the presence of a meaningful predictor variable. The precision interval becomes *smaller* as the relationship between the

---

[5] The formula for the standard deviation is:

$$s = \sqrt{\frac{\Sigma(X_i - \bar{X})^2}{n-1}}$$

where the X_i stands for the eight enrollment scores, and $\bar{X}$ is the mean of these.

predictor (in our example, time in years) and the criterion (in our example, enrollment) gets larger. This relationship, or correlation, can be perfect (in which case the correlation is +1.00 or −1.00). If there is a total lack of relationship between the two variables, the correlation is 0.00.

When the correlation between predictor and criterion is something other than 0.00, it is common to say that the "predictor accounts for some of the variance in the criterion." For our example, this statement can be paraphrased to say that there is certainly variation in the enrollment figures, and some of this variability is accounted for by the passing of time.

If the predictor variable accounts for most of the variance, there will be little variance left over, due to unknown or undefined factors. This small amount of leftover variance would lead to a very small precision interval. The estimate of 216 could be pinned down pretty accurately.

However, if the predictor is not effective in accounting for much of the variance in the criterion scores, the precision interval is not much smaller than when computed using the standard deviation of the eight scores. As the predictor (or in some cases the predictors) accounts for more and more variance, the estimate becomes more and more precise.

For our example, approximately 63 percent of the variance is accounted for, and the interval is reduced from about 60 to 36.[6] These two intervals, with and without the presence of a predictor, are shown in Figure 4. The relative reduction in size indicates an increase in the precision of prediction.

The discussion of this section has included some terms and formulas which may be quite unfamiliar to some readers. Two general concepts are important to practicing school decision-makers, even if some of the specifics are subsequently forgotten. These are:

---

[6] The most commonly used correlation coefficient is the *product-moment correlation*, and the amount of variance accounted for is the square of this value (see Blommers and Lindquist, 1960). The reduced standard deviation is given by the formula

$$\text{Reduced standard deviation} = \left(\text{Old standard deviation}\right) \sqrt{1.00 - \text{proportion of variance accounted for}}$$
$$= (29.7) \sqrt{1.00 - 0.63}$$
$$= 18$$

The reduced interval is twice the reduced standard deviation.

1. When projections are to be made into the future, it is often very helpful to make point estimates of needs at a future time, based on straight line fits to data from previous times.

2. The precision of the projections can be calculated, and is a function of the relationship (correlation) between the predictor and the predicted (or criterion).

The illustration is now complete; but suppose we go one step beyond completion, and try to apply some systems analysis–type thinking to our results. What enrollment should the district's administrators plan for? Should they use the estimate 216? That decision depends on balancing the cost of underestimating against the cost of overestimating.

What will be the cost of underestimating? Well, in five years' time, new facilities would again be needed. These would have to be constructed on a crash basis, and if the economy is in a period of inflation, at a higher cost per student. This is not to mention the "cost" to the students from overcrowded facilities, or the "cost" to those students who might have to be turned down.

On the other hand, what would be the cost of overestimating in the enrollment projection? This is pretty obvious: if you plan for 216, and only 108 show up five years from now, you have invested a lot more capital outlay on this part of the school district's program than you needed to.

Suppose, after carefully considering all of these factors, the district estimates that it will cost $10,000 per student for underestimating, and $5,000 per student for overestimating. If this is true, the district would probably try to err on the side of overestimating.

We have tried to illustrate here that (a) there are methods for making these projections in at least a quasi-scientific manner; (b) that the accuracy of the estimate is important, and can be increased by finding an independent variable which accounts for some of the variance in the dependent variable; and (c) that often there is a marked difference between the *cost* of under- and over-estimates.

MEASURES OF ASSOCIATION
When the dependent variable is based on frequency counts.
Earlier we discussed the statistical treatment of data when the dependent variable, regarding club membership, was

in the form of frequency counts. If there is really no relationship between club membership and the presence of the new program, were the observed frequencies likely to have occurred? This is a statistical question. In the present section, the question under consideration is: How strong is the relationship between club membership and presence of the new program; that is, is the relationship strong enough to have any real meaning?

A number of different measures of association have been developed to answer the question. Only two will be discussed here. First, the *phi coefficient* will be introduced using the data reported in Table 1. The phi coefficient is a measure of statistical association. The value obtained for phi is somewhat difficult to interpret, and for this reason, a measure of *predictive* association will also be introduced. The interpretation of the value obtained from this second index will be somewhat analogous to the "reduction in variance" principle discussed in the previous section.

To compute the phi coefficient, the chi-square value, the number of subjects, and the number of rows and columns are needed. The relationship is

$$\text{phi} = \text{square root of} \left(\frac{\text{chi-square}}{N(L-1)} \right)$$

where L is the *smaller* of the row and column dimensions. Thus, in the example of Table 1, which had three rows and two columns, L would be two. For the example, then,

phi = square root [36.459/1000(2 − 1)] = square root (.036459) = 0.19

The "reduction in variance" concept has a meaning which is directly interpretable. A phi coefficient, however, has no such common-sense meaning. Without a number of other phi coefficients obtained for similar situations for comparison, it is difficult to decide whether 0.19 is a very low, low, average, or even high value.

For this reason, a second coefficient will be introduced. The coefficient is a *measure of the predictive association* of two variables. To illustrate it, consider again the example of club membership, where the dependent variable is club membership, and the independent variable is the year. You are given the name of a student, and asked to predict how many clubs he belongs to. If you would be *greatly helped* in this task by knowing whether it was Year 0 or Year 1 (the independent variable) then the index of predictive association would be high. If it would help *very little* to know this student's position in terms of the independent variable, then the index of predictive association would be low. The index measures the reduction in the probability of making an incorrect prediction. If the index is 1.00, knowledge of year would allow you to say, without error, the number of clubs the student belongs to. An index of 0.50 indicates that your errors *with knowledge* of the independent variable will only be about half as large as without such knowledge.

The index is derived in Hays (pp. 606–610). The working formula is given by:

$$\text{Reduction} = \frac{(\text{sum of largest frequency in each column}) - \text{largest row frequency}}{\text{number of students} - \text{largest row frequency}}$$

For Table 1, the largest frequency in column 1 is 200, the largest frequency in column 2 is 250, the largest row frequency is 400, and the number of students is 1000. Thus the *reduction* in the probability of a prediction error is given by:

$$\text{Reduction} = \frac{(200 + 250) - 400}{1000 - 400} = 50/600 = 0.08.$$

Knowledge of the independent variable (year) results in only an 8 percent reduction in the probability of making a predictive error.

Significant relationships. In the example involving club membership, the statistical tests for two important situations were outlined. The first dealt with quantitative independent variables, the second with frequency counts in this role. The question to be answered was "Were the observed results likely to have occurred by chance?" If the answer is no, the researcher assumes that something other than chance is operating. A "statistically significant" relationship has been shown.

But "significant" relationships may be meaningless in terms of real decisions. For this reason, the measures of association have been included. These indices deal with the question, "How *strong* is the relationship between independent and dependent variable?"

As an illustration of this point, consider the data of Table 1. Based on a chi-square test, it was concluded that there is a statistically significant relationship between year and club membership. A reader might conclude that after only one year, the new program was having a profound impact on club membership. But the reduction in predictive error measure shows only an 8 percent reduction, given the year of the student. It does not really help *much* to know which year the student belongs to. Use of only the significance test, without the subsequent measure of association, leads to a deceptive conclusion.

The authors would be seriously remiss if a word of caution were not added at this point. This measure of predictive association has been criticized in the past, and again recently (Lindquist, 1953; Glass and Hakstian, 1969). The primary criticism rests on the fact that the size of the index is quite sensitive to the range of categories in the independent variable. If the study of our example were extended to the next five years, it is possible that the index of predictive association would be increased.

In a certain sense, however, this same criticism applies to a correlation coefficient; and researchers have found this index a useful one for conceptual purposes. Sometimes a correlation of 0.95 is *too low,* if, for example, it is the correlation between height measurements of the same group of students made by two nurses. Sometimes a correlation of 0.30 is very high, if it is the relationship between two variables previously considered to be independent. Test publishers are aware that one way to obtain a high correlation between age and achievement is to use a wide range of ages.

The need for caution in interpretation and the susceptibility of these indices to misinterpretation do not justify dispensing with their use. We caution the school decision-maker to seek a bench mark for comparison, if possible. That is, in interpreting the 0.08 reduction in our example, he might find that when sex is used as the independent variable, the reduction was 0.30—which gives both values some additional meaning.

REFERENCES

Blommers, Paul, and E. F. Lindquist. *Elementary Statistical Methods in Psychology and Education.* Boston: Houghton Mifflin, 1960.

Glass, Gene V., and A. Ralph Hakstian. "Measures of Association in Comparative Experiments," *American Educational Research Journal* 6 (May 1969): 403–414.

Hays, William B. *Statistics for Psychologists.* New York: Holt, Rinehart & Winston, 1965.

Lindquist, E. F. *Design and Analysis of Experiments in Psychology and Education.* Boston: Houghton Mifflin, 1953.

CONTINUOUS ASSESSMENT

Five Basic Concepts of Continuous Assessment

Individualized Continuous Assessment
The individualized corridor approach
How many corridors?
Using the computer
Interpreting the computer printout
Will this freeze the curriculum?
Will this freeze the student's placement?

Other Uses for Continuous Assessment

In the last chapter, we pointed out that much educational evaluation is properly called outcome evaluation. In outcome evaluation, the status of a group after certain conditions have been applied is compared with that group's status before the conditions were applied. However, in some situations it would also be appropriate to obtain measurements while the experimental conditions were operating. This would be a kind of continuous assessment. This kind of assessment still measures the same thing: whether the outcomes behind the imposed conditions are in fact being met satisfactorily.

Continuous assessment has other applications, one of the most important being measurement of attitudes and opinions (see chapters 7 and 10). Used in this way, continuous assessment can either measure attitudes toward a specific innovation (such as student attitudes toward the new Contemporary Problems curriculum in chapter 2), or it can be used by an administration to keep a finger on the pulse of the student body and community about issues affecting the school. This chapter will deal with continuous assessment as it applies to classroom use. In the classroom it is employed both to give teachers and administrators a picture of how the group as a whole is progressing, and to define how individual students are doing.

FIVE BASIC CONCEPTS OF CONTINUOUS ASSESSMENT

Continuous assessment combines five basic concepts. None of these five is new to the educational scene, but taken together they represent an orderly system for attacking some of the difficult evaluation problems in educational programs.

> **Concept no. 1.** *The evaluation must decide whether the question requires group or individual measurement.*

Every four years, just prior to presidential election time, the public opinion polls receive much national attention. The Gallup or Harris polls and their like obtain fairly accurate estimates of voter preference by contacting only a small percentage of eligible voters. This total number may be as small as twelve hundred. The pollsters are not interested in the individual preference of each eligible voter—their interest is in *group* preferences.

Many of the evaluation questions faced by educators are also not individual, but *group* considerations. For instance: What is the attitude of the student body toward a certain administrative policy? The measurement of the attitude of each student is not necessary. It is the attitude of the student composite which is of interest. What is the attitude of the students in eleventh grade toward the law? What is the attitude of the staff toward a merit pay schedule? What is the attitude of the community toward a busing proposal? These are all group questions. They do not require that each individual in the group be measured; a sample, random or stratified, would be adequate.

On the other hand, some measurements are obtained primarily for their individual use. A major function of elementary school achievement tests is to influence decisions about individual students. The teacher receives independent measures for each pupil, which he can compare with his own more subjective perceptions. A random sample is not appropriate in such situations.

Many educational measurements are obtained for both reasons: they have value both as group and individual measures. For example, the superintendent is interested in testing each pupil with an achievement battery for individual diagnostic purposes. But he may also be interested in knowing the average performance level of fourth-graders in arithmetic, or of third-graders in reading.

Concept no. 1, then, requires that the evaluator make a rational decision about what he is trying to find out—is it the group, or each individual, that is the primary object of this evaluation activity? The proper decision here may avoid wasted effort and ambiguous results.

Concept no. 2. *The sample size should correspond to the accuracy of the test.* **Corollary:** *A sample too large is wasteful.*

Educational researchers are often like a woman buying shoes—if a 6B is comfortable, a 5AAA is what she buys. In educational research, if a sample of fifty is adequate, it is assumed a sample of five hundred is better . . . ten times better, at that. Such reasoning is usually incorrect. The point is best illustrated with an example.

Suppose two elementary schools, equivalent in every other way, including their having exactly the same objectives for their science programs, differ in their presentation of the science material. School T uses a traditional approach, and School E uses an experimental, innovative approach. The question is: Which program does the better job of reaching the objectives? The diversity of new approaches to the teaching of science makes this a less than totally hypothetical question.

Assume further that a 100-point test, to assess the degree to which the objectives of the program have been obtained, is available and that this test has a standard deviation of about 12—a reasonable figure for a 100-point test. Suppose School T, at the end of a year, has an average score of 55, while School E has an average score of 56. The difference in average scores is one point, which, if more than a thousand students are involved at each school, is a statistically significant difference, at a commonly accepted level of significance. The researcher might be led to conclude that the experimental program was superior to the traditional one.

This type of mistake should be avoided. The mistake might be illustrated with this crude example: Estimate the height of the room in which you are sitting. Without using any sort of measuring device—without even getting up from your chair—suppose you estimate eight feet. Unless you are very experienced at estimating heights, your estimate is probably only accurate to the nearest foot. Now suppose you are asked what one-third of the height of the room is. You would divide 8 by 3 and get 2.66667. The division is accurate and is rounded properly at the last digit, but the answer gives a distorted picture of the accuracy of your measurement. The measurement is really only accurate to the nearest foot, but the reader will think you have obtained accuracy to the nearest hundred-thousandth.

This is a good analogy for the test situation. The difference of one point is statistically significant, but the real accuracy of the difference depends on the accuracy of the test. On this particular test, how big does the difference between the two means have to be before it can be said that one program is actually better than the other? If Charlie is 69" tall, and Peter is 68", it can be concluded that Charlie is taller than Peter. But if Charlie scores 69 on a vocabulary test and

Peter scores 68, can it be concluded that Charlie's vocabulary is better? Probably not. If Peter's score had been 21, we would be more sure of our judgment in favor of Charlie.

In assigning grades for a course, teachers usually list the total scores for all pupils, ranked from highest to lowest, and divide the group at certain points for letter grades. Most teachers acknowledge the problem of test accuracy by trying to find points of division which have at least a three-point gap between obtained scores; one-unit division points are generally avoided.

If the differences in the mean scores of School T and School E had been 45 and 55, in favor of the E school, most would agree that this difference is real. But as the gap between means decreases, our reticence to judge one program more effective increases, even though the differences continue to be statistically significant. The researcher in the field, in conjunction with the test author, must decide how accurate the test really is. Suppose they decide, for the situation at hand, that any difference of five points or more in the mean scores is a "real" difference.[1]

In such a case, the original sample of more than one thousand students per school was far too large. Based on the notion that the difference must be five points or more before it is considered important, and using some well-known computational techniques (see Blommers and Lindquist, 1959, pp. 297–301), a sample of 150 per school would have been large enough. The extra 850 per school represented what a colleague has called a "statistical overkill."

The underlying consideration of Concept no. 2 is that the real accuracy of the test should be determined by the researcher in the field, after consulting the test's author. The sample size used at any one time should then be gauged by the accuracy of the test. Using a larger sample makes inefficient use of the subjects.

> **Concept no. 3:** *If the proper sample size (based on Concept no. 2) does not utilize all of the subjects available for the evaluation, use the remaining subjects at a different time.*

---

[1] Note that the difference then must be at least five points and, in addition, the difference must be statistically significant.

Concept no. 3 follows directly from the last statement in Concept no. 2. Consider once more the district that is attempting to evaluate its science program. Suppose this district has 3,000 students available for this study—1,500 for the new program, and 1,500 for the old. Suppose also that the researcher and the test writer agree that 150 in each group is an adequate sample size, based on the accuracy of the test. The test accuracy is the limiting factor here, and a sample of 1,500 is no better than a sample of 150. Does that mean the other 1,350 available subjects are not used at all in the evaluation of the science programs? That would also be wasteful. But the other 1,350 could be randomly assigned to nine other groups of 150 each ($9 \times 150 = 1,350$), and one of these could be tested each month over the course of the academic year. That is, the evaluator could obtain an estimate of group ability September 1, October 1, and so forth, for every month of the year. This is the *continuous* part of continuous assessment. Instead of a snapshot, the evaluator has a motion picture—admittedly with a rather low frame frequency. With a continuous evaluation design, at the end of the year the evaluator will know not only which program is better, but also the pattern that each group followed in reaching its final level.

> **Concept no. 4.** *The spacing of the testings should be based on considerations of the time required for meaningful changes to occur.*

How often should the testings occur? This is best answered by a second question: How much time is required for meaningful and measurable changes to occur? Of course, the time required for change depends upon what is being measured. For example, if arithmetic achievement is being evaluated, and the group spends an hour each day working on arithmetic, it is not unreasonable to expect meaningful and measurable changes in the group's ability each week. Weekly measurement would allow the evaluator to follow trends in mathematics achievement.

However, in many cases longer intervals would be required. A deep-rooted attitude probably cannot be altered in a week of intensive indoctrination. The attitude of high school students toward the police is such a deep-rooted attitude, since these attitudes have been developed through years of interaction with family and community. If school officials feel that a certain attitude of the group is undesirable, and attempt to change this attitude, the school could not expect its success to be measurable weekly. Such changes —if indeed it *is* possible to bring them about—require time, and the evaluator of such a program might decide that monthly measurement would be satisfactory.

It should be reiterated that the specification of weekly or monthly measurement does not imply that the entire group will be tested that often. The weekly measures would cover samples large enough to produce an accurate picture (as limited by the test) of the group's position at that time. All of the students would be measured at fixed intervals, but not all at the same time.

> **Concept no. 5.** *The administration should determine which areas of the district's program need continuous assessment for proper decision-making; and continuous sampling programs should be initiated in these areas.*

This last concept might seem out of place in a list with the first four, which were all measurement-oriented. They dealt with sample size, test accuracy, and timing. Concept no. 5 states the measurement philosophy of action before crisis. The idea is to decide, in calm times, the areas in which continuous measurement would be helpful; these measurements would then be available in a time of stress.

For example, it is too late to start worrying about student attitudes after students go on strike or take over the administration building. The reality of such a demonstration of overt student unrest is irreversible, and makes alleviation of its causes very difficult. School administrators who have a strike on their hands should have known for some time that students were restless about a number of social issues, of which civil rights is a primary example. If the administration had carefully considered the entire program, looking for areas in which continuous measurement would aid decision-making, they could not have bypassed student attitudes toward important social issues. Continuous measurement of these attitudes—as infrequently as monthly or bimonthly samples—might have allowed the administration to detect changes such as increased militancy.

A wide variety of other examples could be given. An inappropriate or inefficient mathematics program should be identified as quickly as possible—in six months, for example, instead of three years. Six months of trend data, when compared to student performance under previous programs, would make an informed decision possible. The area of faculty-administration relations is another example. When the faculty votes to have a union act as their bargaining agent, it is too late for the administration to attempt to set up satisfactory relationships with the independent local faculty organization. This administration should have been obtaining continuous measurement of the faculty's attitude. A faculty which looks outside for organization probably did so only after deciding that the internal organization could not achieve the desired goals. With a program of continuous assessment, the administration would have had warning of faculty dissatisfaction. If the administration wanted to head off unionization, steps should have been taken long before. The "action before crisis" philosophy might help avoid such a crisis.

INDIVIDUALIZED CONTINUOUS ASSESSMENT

It would be incorrect to say that the schools are just beginning to look more closely at programs of individualized instruction. Schools have always tried to teach the pupil as an individual, but recently there has been a much stronger emphasis on the idea of a totally individualized program of instruction.

Three aspects of the individualized approach to instruction are important from the measurement viewpoint. One aspect is *individual evaluation:* Is this student ready for the next step? Is more review necessary? To what degree have the concepts of the present lesson been mastered?

The second aspect is closely tied to the first, but is a little broader. This second aspect is *individual diagnosis*. Using individualized continuous measurement, individual diagnosis is carried out primarily through trend analysis techniques. Are there trends in the pupil's performance which seem atypical for him? Has he changed from his typical performance level?

The third primary aspect of this approach deals with *pupil progress reporting*. If the program of instruction is to be individualized, the method of reporting should also be individualized to show his progress in each area measured. A graph of some sort is the best device to use, and could be used to report to the student himself, his teachers, and his parents.

The authors wish to emphasize the importance of individualized continuous assessment because it is particularly effective in making evaluation an integral, continuous part of the learning process. There are three central reasons for this conviction.

The first reason is that there is an increased emphasis on true individualization of instruction. If a teacher is to individualize a student's program, he must make day-by-day (even moment-by-moment) decisions regarding the next step for that student. Has the student's performance been slowly deteriorating, so that an intensive review is necessary? These decisions demand frequent evaluation. The results of these frequent evaluations must be available quickly, and presented to the teacher in a form which will allow for quick and accurate interpretation, without intensive training in data analysis techniques.

The second important reason for the development of these procedures is more philosophical. Most evaluation systems currently in use are explicitly based on a student ranking system, from top to bottom. Grades (A is better than D), grade equivalents (5.2 is better than 3.8), percentile ranks (88 is better than 64), and test scores (11 right is better than 7 right) are but a few examples. By using reporting systems which explicitly suggest "rank in group," we are encouraging between-student competition. Competition between students is not appropriate to the philosophy of individualized instruction. The student's competition should be *with himself*—to continue to learn and improve at *his own performance level*. The evaluation system, then, should be designed so that the student competes with himself, or at least competes to maintain a growth trend comparable to that of others *at his performance level*. Learning, not competition, should be the primary focus of our instructional programs. It is axiomatic that in any group, only a small proportion can be at the top. In a society which places heavy emphasis on achievement and success, we should not ignore the implications of the continued failure of the larger proportion of students to be at the top. To be sure, we cannot completely eliminate between-student comparisons. Even first-graders will know quickly that the Bluebird group reads tougher material than the Cardinals do. But it does not necessarily follow that we should foster these comparisons by using a reporting system based upon such comparison. Far better, it would seem, to develop an evaluation and reporting system adaptable to the individual and an individualized instruction program.

The third reason for recommending individualized continuous assessment is technological. As each generation of computers becomes more sophisticated, the potential for their use in educational programs increases. The technique we will now describe is computer managed, and firmly links the incredible speed and accuracy of the computer to the interpretive skill of the teacher.[2]

THE INDIVIDUALIZED CORRIDOR APPROACH

This system was developed, as described here, in a pilot study carried out by John Wick during the 1967–1968 and 1968–1969 school years. The study involved all of the third grades of one school district, with a total of 300 third-graders. The 300 students were divided into six testing units of about 50 students each. In the pilot study, each testing unit was examined four different times at intervals of approximately eight weeks. At each testing, students were given eight short tests, covering most of the curricular areas for third grade.

Since the testing units were tested at different times, at the end of the year there was a sample of the average performance level at 24 times of the year. Testing unit no. 1 was examined during the 1st, 7th, 13th, and 19th testing times; testing unit no. 2 was examined during the 2nd, 8th, 14th, and 20th testing times; and so forth, so that testing unit no. 6 was examined during the 6th, 12th, 18th, and 24th testing times. Four different but presumably parallel test batteries were used for the testings. The fact that the batteries were not exactly parallel in every case is not of primary importance in most cases, because of the computation methods used.

---

[2] One might argue that most schools do not have a computer. While this is becoming less true each year, we should add that it is not essential for the district to have a computer *on the premises*. Remote links to computers located many miles away are commonplace.

In order to use the corridor technique, achievement information from the district must be collected for one year, using a collection design similar to the one just outlined. These normative data can then be displayed in a series of graphs having time as the independent axis (abscissa) and achievement level as the dependent axis (ordinate). These normative data then make it possible to compare a student's achievement with that of a substantial number of other students (a) at his own level, and (b) at the same time of the year. For example, when a certain individual takes a mathematics test on, say, March 15, the teacher will know how comparable students from that district have done on that test during the previous year.

Since educational measurements are known to have a certain amount of random error associated with them, the student cannot be expected to perform at exactly the average level of the similar students who preceded him; on the contrary, a certain amount of variation is known to occur. The measure of random variations most often computed is the standard error of measurement. Using the standard error of measurement, a confidence interval can be determined, centered on the average score, and giving an upper and lower limit from the average. The range of values is set to include most of the scores which vary from the average in a random manner. When a score falls below or above the confidence band, it is considered to be an event which was unlikely to occur by chance; some other factor probably caused the wide variation between actual and expected performance.

This is the spirit of individualized continuous assessment. The two most important features of this approach are (1) that the teacher has a dependable *pattern of achievement* (corridor) upon which to base his expectations for each student; and (2) that expectations for a student's performance are *self-defined*.

Corridors of achievement based on past scores. The teacher using this method has available graphically plotted patterns of expected achievement for any given level of student in his classroom. These are formed by plotting the confidence intervals of past years' series of tests to form a rising corridor within which the scores of a student at this level may be expected to fall. Each time a student is tested, his score is plotted on the "achievement level versus time" axis. If his score places him within the corridor for his level, it can be assumed that he is achieving as expected. If it falls outside, however, it is a warning to the teacher. It is likely that something besides chance caused the changed performance. Inquiries into the cause should be initiated.

Self-defined achievement level. It is well known that wide ranges of individual differences do occur at each grade level, and in every important area of the curriculum. It is illogical to determine the expected level of a very good or very poor student in terms of the average performance of the entire group. A far more defensible approach would be to compare the performance of a student with that of students in the past who were most like him. For example, if a student finishes third-grade arithmetic work at the sixtieth percentile level, compared to his local peers, we should expect him to perform at about this level in fourth grade. When he is tested in fourth grade, his expected performance is computed on the basis of the average performance of students at about the sixtieth percentile in previous years. The student's past performance determines the level of future expected achievements, so that he does not compete with the better or worse students in his peer group. He only competes with himself to *at least maintain* the performance level which he had set for himself.

HOW MANY CORRIDORS?

At this point another problem presents itself: If a student completing a year's work at the 63rd percentile were compared only to previous students who were at exactly the 63rd percentile, there would be too few subjects and too little range for validity. Thus it follows that it is necessary to group the students to some extent. How many levels are appropriate to this approach? It would be possible to have only three, but the definition of a larger number seems necessary if the expectancy for achievement is really to be fitted to the individual. At the other extreme, if too many levels are defined, differences between levels will be essentially meaningless. The pilot study mentioned earlier settled on nineteen levels, and this number was found to be adequate while maintaining meaningful individual differences. These nineteen were defined as shown in Table 5.

Table 5
Suggested Corridor Groupings

Corridor Number	Percentile Ranks
1	1– 7
2	8–12
3	13–17
4	18–22
5	23–27
6	28–32
7	33–37
8	38–42
9	43–47
10	48–52
11	53–57
12	58–62
13	63–67
14	68–72
15	73–77
16	78–82
17	83–87
18	88–92
19	93–99

Now, suppose a student entering fourth grade has the following third-grade percentile ranks (compared to the other students in that district who are entering fourth grade):

Language	44
Mathematics	60
Science	66
Social studies	50

His corridor assignments for fourth grade will be:

Language	9
Mathematics	12
Science	13
Social studies	10

Not only will his fourth-grade performance be compared with students from other years whose performance levels were most like his own, but the technique allows for the student's differing performance in the many curricular areas.

USING THE COMPUTER

The procedures depend on a computer-managed system with minimum input-output data handling by the classroom teacher. The scheme demands an elaborate array of normative data, so that all of a student's scores are quickly compared to the results obtained by similar students at that time of year, and these comparisons are computer-plotted to provide the teacher with a diagnostic tool which can be quickly and simply interpreted. A flow diagram of the system is given in Figure 5.

Figure 5 is a flow chart for the entire input-output system. It shows test information being obtained from the classroom, passing through a series of computer-managed steps, and being returned to the classroom in a useful form. A few comments on this figure seem appropriate.

A multiple choice format for the test items has been implied heretofore, but such a format is not essential to the system. Other types, such as essay or oral examinations, can also be treated by this technique. The only real requirements are that a *score* can be attached to each examination, and that the test will be scored in the same manner in future years.

The $N \times S$ matrix shown in Figure 5 will be specific for each school district. The N indicates the number of students in the district, and the S the number of subtests in the battery administered. The sequence of input-output events envisions the program attaching to a given student's test scores the appropriate corridor assignment for each subtested area. The corridor assignments which are stored for a given student will be based on that student's past performance levels in each of the areas tested.

The normative data must be stored in a three-dimensional array, as indicated in Figure 5. Whenever the teacher administers the battery to the class, three important aspects must be considered. Each class has students in most, or all, of the corridor levels; it is assumed that the battery has a number of subtests; and the expected performance level of a student depends on the time of year that the testing took place. To illustrate the use of this information, suppose a fourth-grade student is examined during the 18th week of the school year. For the language subtest, his corridor assignment is 9. At the position defined by Corridor 9, Subtest

**Figure 5
Flow Chart of Input-Output System for Corridor Approach**

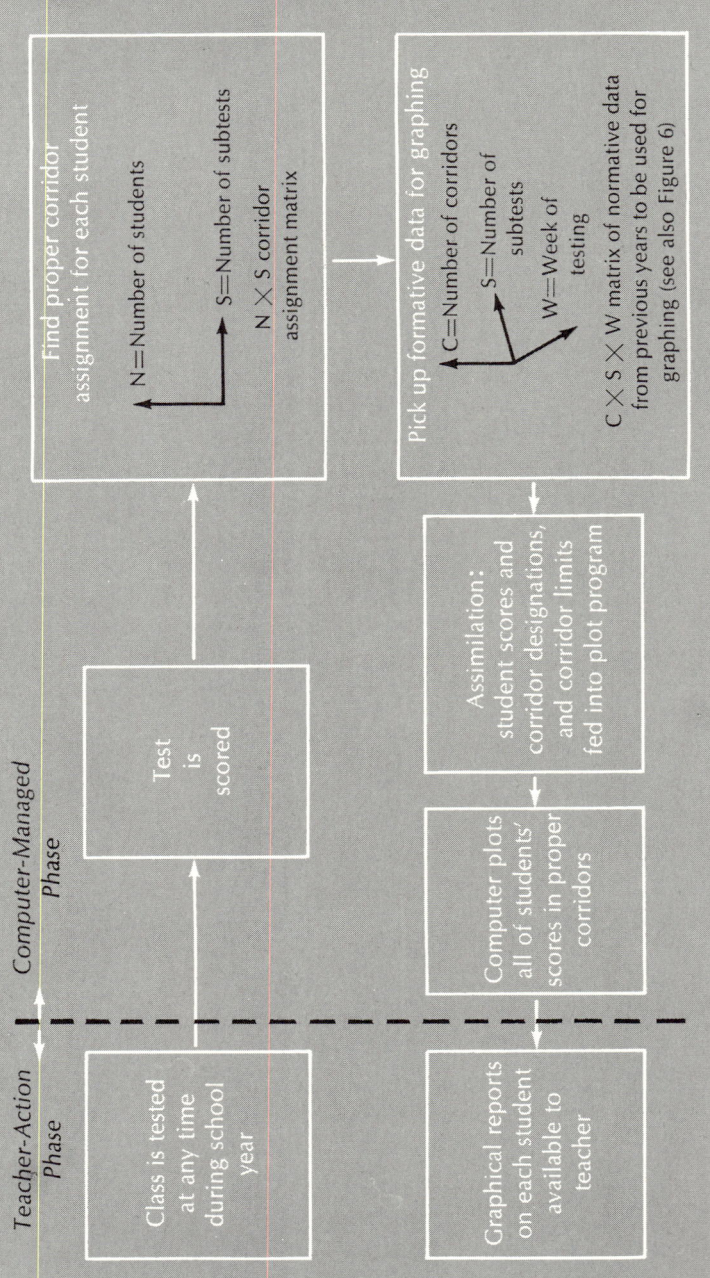

L, and Week 18, the computer has stored the expected performance level of corridor 9 students in previous years. A deviation score is computed by comparing the expected performance level to the student's actual performance level.

By this point, the computer has (1) taken the current and past obtained scores for each student on a particular battery of tests, (2) determined which corridors the student has been assigned to, based on past performance, (3) for each subtest, and for the week of the testing, found the expected performance levels, and compared these with actual performance levels. Stored with the expected performance levels in the $C \times S \times W$ matrix is the information needed to plot the confidence bands, or corridors, on the student graphs.

Finally, the computer plots a time versus achievement graph for each of the subtests that the students took. The points plotted are in terms of deviation from the expected. If the student's actual performance is somewhat below expectation, a point is plotted below the center of a corridor. The edges of the corridor are determined on the basis of probability statements. A 90 percent confidence corridor would be associated with statements such as: "Given a large number of testings, this student's scores could be expected to fall into this band about 90 percent of the time, if his *real* performance level is as expected."

Each student has at least as many graphs as there are subtests. Besides one graph for each subtest, composite measures might also be computed. The computer output for the teacher could take on a variety of appearances, but one possible form is illustrated by Figure 6. Four graphs fit on one computer output page. The reporting form, as can be seen, lists student name, class, the subtest, and his corridor assignment.

This last piece of information, corridor assignment, may be desired by certain school districts, but is not in line with one of the major philosophical reasons for devising this technique. Many educators (including the present authors) feel that the present level of between-student competition, especially at the elementary school level, is in the long run detrimental to a large proportion of the students. The graphical printouts do not need to have any indication of the student's level assignment in the different subtests. This information

Figure 6
Eight Corridors for Peter Smith

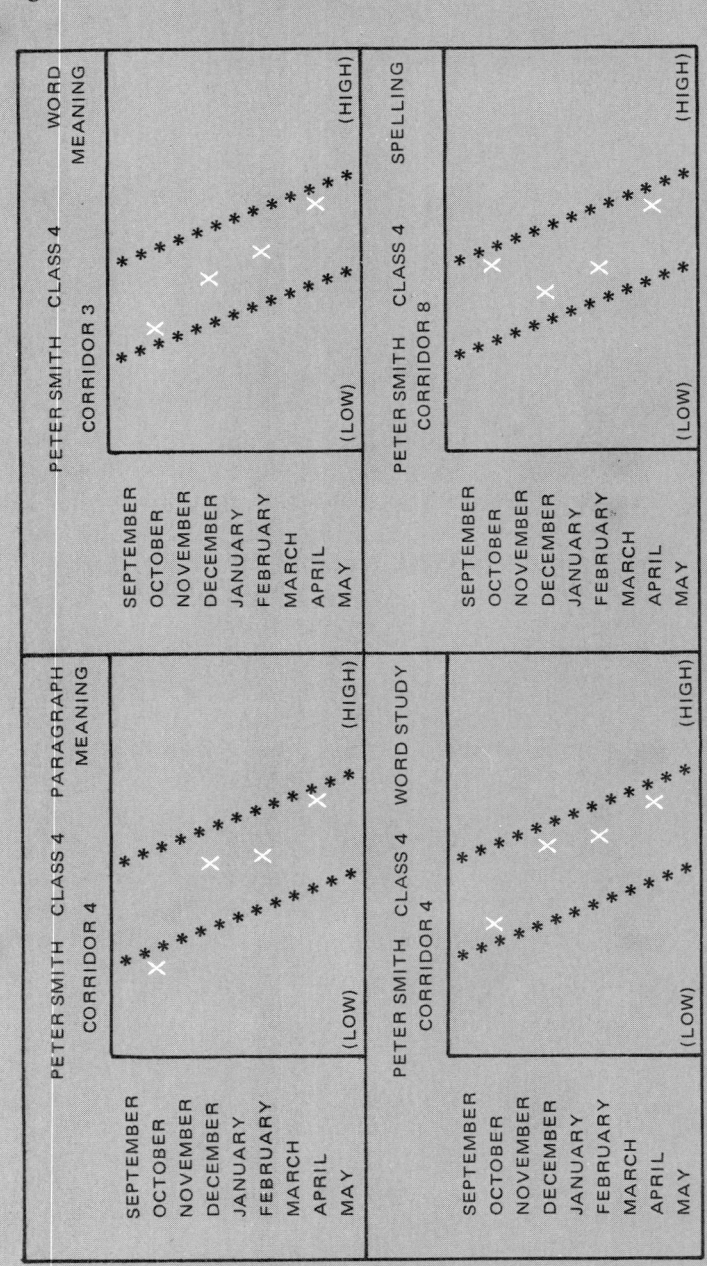

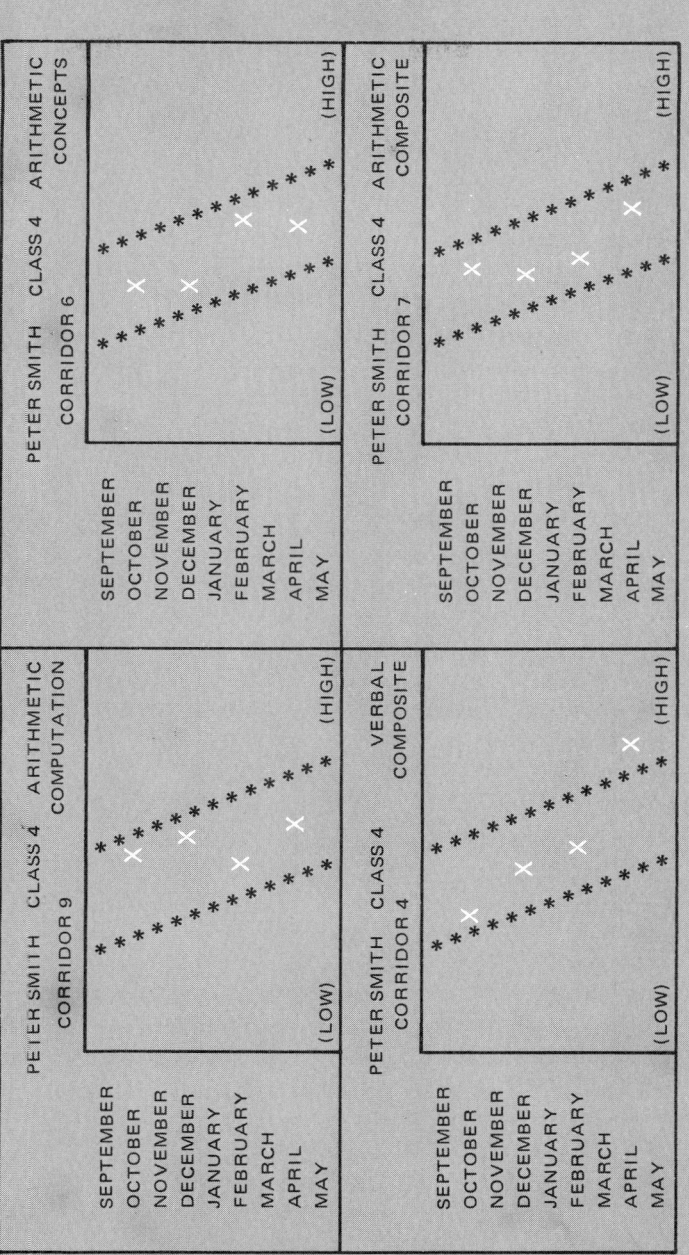

should, of course, be available to the teacher, and it may be made available to parents, preferably during conference periods. Some districts may not adhere to this particular viewpoint regarding the reduction in between-student competition, and will want to have the corridor level printed on the computer output.

Along the side of the sheet is the time of year of the testing, and to the right of this time axis is the expected corridor for that performance level on that subtest. The expected performance level is at the center of the corridor. The student's deviation score (deviation of actual performance from expected) is plotted by an X.

One of the primary purposes of the system is to allow the teacher to quickly spot trends in the student's performance. To facilitate this purpose, all of this student's *previous* testings should also be plotted on this graph, at the appropriate time positions.

INTERPRETING THE COMPUTER PRINTOUT

The graphs shown in Figure 6 belong to a real student who participated in the pilot study (although the name Peter Smith is fictitious). He is not typical, but belongs to a small but noticeable subpopulation which we have dubbed the "upward mobile" group. The typical student in the pilot study group has very few scores outside of the corridors. In this study, each student had four test scores for each of eight subtests. Our findings were that about 75 percent of the students had two or fewer scores out of the corridor (out of a possible thirty-two).

We have chosen not to show a typical student, but to use the illustration of "Peter Smith" because it shows the type of diagnostic information which can be obtained from these graphs. Note that the members of the upward mobile group are not necessarily high achievers to begin with, but show a definite tendency toward accelerating growth as compared to their classmates. The growth pattern for Peter is in the verbal areas. Some of this group show the accelerated growth in the math tests, and not in the verbal. In the total group of students, quite a few examples of this syndrome occurred, and it was felt that Peter typified this subgroup.

The corridor assignments for Peter are:

Subject	Corridor
Word Meaning	3
Paragraph Meaning	4
Word Study	4
Spelling	8
Arithmetic Computation	9
Arithmetic Concepts	6
Verbal Composite	4
Math Composite	7

This list, in conjunction with the X's plotted on the eight graphs, suggests the following series of comments:

1. This is not a top student. His appropriate corridor assignments range from a low of 3 to a high of 9. On the other hand, he has not manifested the kind of results which would tend to get the attention of the teacher. That is, he is not among the high achievers and he is not losing ground with respect to his peers. The teacher might have the tendency to pay little attention to him.

2. Three of the graphs, however, show an unmistakable upward trend in this boy's test performance. These are Paragraph Meaning, Word Meaning, and Word Study. The Verbal Composite graph also indicates this upward trend. This means that he is learning faster than other children at that performance level. He is accelerating, and this rapid growth is coming in the areas where his performance has been lowest.

3. His Spelling and Arithmetic Computation corridor assignments have him at a higher performance level. These are apparently proper placements (at least for this year), since his performance matches the corridor each time.

4. This may be a very important time for this third-grade student. Some extra help and encouragement from the teacher during this period may maintain the accelerated rate until he at least reaches the level of his spelling and mathematics computation work. Or perhaps these are both being depressed by his low performance on the concepts tested by the Paragraph Meaning, Word Meaning, and Word Study subtests.

5. The point is that this acceleration is happening over an entire year's time. With the problems of the other twenty-five children also pressing for attention, this rather subtle change in performance for Peter might be missed, and the extra help and encouragement may not be offered. Is this critical? Will his growth rate and ultimate maximum performance level be the same regardless of whether or not he is diagnosed as upward mobile in time to give him extra encouragement? The question is difficult to answer; but it is not inconceivable that this type of child needs special encouragement at a critical moment, and that when the moment passes without the boost, the results are irrevocable.

6. This is not a top student. However, when these graphs are shown to him, to his teacher, or to his parents, it can be reported that his progress has been perfectly satisfactory, based on his self-defined achievement levels. As we have noted earlier, there is no need to have the corridor levels marked on the graphs at all. Thus, each student, regardless of his relative position in the group, can be "rewarded" with graphs of this type, as long as satisfactory progress is maintained.

WILL THIS FREEZE THE CURRICULUM?

To operate, the evaluation program as described requires the presence of normative data from the previous year. Certain parts of the instructional program change each year, however, and this constant change is important. The evaluation system should not operate to stifle such changes. Continuous assessment procedures *can* be used quite simply without discouraging necessary change.

In a normal situation, the amount of the instructional program which changes from one year to the next is far smaller than the amount which does not change. Rather than start from scratch each year, the planners take that which exists and attempt to improve it. The instructional program in a given district has a great deal of inertia. On the average, it is likely that not more than 5 percent of the entire instructional program changes from one year to the next.

During the first year in which a new concept is introduced, normative data will not be available for that segment. This small segment could simply be excluded from the evaluation reports. Data would be collected, however, for use in the following year. All of the normative information would be updated each year to conform to the instructional program which exists at that time.

WILL THIS FREEZE THE STUDENT'S PLACEMENT?

The answer to this question has been implied previously, but needs reiteration. Remember that as the teacher receives the computer output from testings, a student's scores can do one of three things: (a) they can tend to be above the corridor; (b) they can basically be in the corridor; or (c) they can tend to be below the corridor.

If a student's scores tend to be above the corridor, the teacher should be alerted. The student might be manifesting a growth period when some special encouragement might even accelerate the process. In any event, the student's corridor assignments should be quietly raised. Recall that the graphs all look the same, and changing the corridor assignment upward requires no fanfare. The goal, of course, is to encourage each student to eventually have the highest possible corridor assignment.

The teacher should be especially alert to those students whose scores tend to fall below their previously self-defined corridor level. When this happens, it means the student cannot maintain the relative performance level he was previously able to handle. Such an event should signal the teacher to look for the cause. Is there some particular part of the instructional program which is stifling growth in all other areas? Is there a social problem for this student in the classroom? Has there been a profound change in his home environment? Is there a personality conflict between student and teacher? A reason will probably not be found in every case, but the earlier the teacher is signaled to begin the search, the greater the probability that the primary cause will be found and ameliorative action prescribed.

OTHER USES FOR CONTINUOUS ASSESSMENT

In the last section, the emphasis was on the individual student. The data from the students would be gathered primarily for the purpose of providing individualized evaluative and diagnostic information. However, there would be *group* benefits as well. In an achievement testing program which tests only once per year, the staff receives a good picture of the performance level of the group, but at one-year intervals. The continuous assessment design outlined in the last section would give the staff a good estimate of group performance twenty-four times over the course of the year, spanning the time from September through May. Consider the possible uses for such information:

1. Do pupils learn at different rates during the year? Are there times, say in the fourth-grade language arts program, when the learning curve flattens out—when no gains seem to be made? Does the high group in the fifth-grade mathematics class seem to reach its highest performance level in mid-March, and make no further gains thereafter? Such a result would indicate either that the test was inadequate for measuring growth, or that the curriculum needs beefing up with additional content after mid-March. Once-a-year testing cannot provide information of this type.

2. With information on group performance which spans the entire year, the administration will be capable of comparing each year's performance with preceding and subsequent years. Because information will be available for the entire year's work, the administration can compare learning *curves,* instead of learning accumulations. Two programs of instruction might both bring students to the same performance level at the end of the year; but the program which brought them to that point most quickly seems like a better bet.

3. Data gathered continuously can be used to check the impact of certain gross external situations on the learning curves. Some trends in learning growth might be caused by metamorphic occurrences outside the school—that is, occurrences which are gross and nonrecurring. The assassination of a beloved public official, or the switch from a graded to a nongraded administrative structure are both examples of nonrecurring events. There might also be cyclical trends in the learning curves. Such events could be expected to occur each year. The February–March doldrums, for example, when the food tastes bad, rooms seem drab, and nerves are a little more raw than usual is illustrative of an event which occurs yearly. This event probably affects student performance, attitude, and interest in a wide variety of ways.

4. The discussion of the corridor technique centered on one important area in the school's program where the continuous assessment philosophy might be an improvement over current techniques. The emphasis was on the students, where the schools' primary interest should be. There are other topics dealing with students besides the achievement-oriented ones. To be sure, a primary reason for having the children in school is to present subject-matter topics such as arithmetic, social studies, and science; but this is not the only reason. Besides these academic goals, there are practical goals, which include vocational goals, self-realization and other more personal concepts, and value goals, through which the ethical values of our society are transmitted. The degree of emphasis placed on each of these four kinds of goals will vary considerably between school districts, but each district must include each to some extent. Continuous assessment can be applied in each of these areas, to determine the present and changing status of the student body.

For example, it should be important for the school district to determine the attitude of the student body toward both school and non-school matters. (The term *attitude* is defined more carefully in chapter 7.) What is the attitude of the student body toward extracurricular programs, the counseling services, administrative programs, and communication channels between students and staff? Each of these is an example of a school-based attitude. The administrator should not wait until a problem develops, but should be gathering information on these attitudes in order to head off impending storms. In this time of increased social awareness on the part of the students, non-school attitudes are also important. The attitudes in the student body concerning the topics of drug use, the law and legal system, and many others could be of much use to the school's decision-making bodies.

The teaching and administrative staffs, through their formal and informal contacts with the student body, have formed their own opinions about student attitude on each of the questions mentioned above. Attitudes change, however, and sometimes the changes are slow and subtle—almost imperceptible on a day-to-day basis. The trend over a period of time might be very important. The administrative staff could first define the attitudes which are important (and the ones listed above are only a partial listing), and then regularly, perhaps monthly, *sample* the attitudes of a random group of students.

5. The administration is also interested in the attitudes and morale of the school's staff, including the teaching staff, associated professional staff, and nonprofessional staff. Staff attitude and morale is discussed in chapter 7.

6. Finally, the administration should be actively interested in the attitude of the community served by the school. In chapter 10, techniques for ascertaining community attitude are outlined. Community attitudes can be measured on a continuing basis, using small samples, to keep track of the trends in community support of and knowledge about the school.

REFERENCES

Blommers, Paul, and E. F. Lindquist. *Elementary Statistical Methods*. Boston: Houghton Mifflin, 1959.

Coughlan, Robert J. "Dimensions of Teacher Morale," *American Educational Research Journal* 5 (March 1970): 221–235.

USING ACHIEVEMENT TESTS

Primary Uses of Standardized Achievement Tests

Using Norms for Comparison

Conversion of Raw Scores
Grade equivalents
Percentile norms
Standard scores

Using Achievement Tests to Measure Growth

Using Achievement Tests for Fixed Time Interpretations

Reporting Test Results
Reporting to the teachers
Reporting to the public
Reporting to parents
Reporting to the student

Suppose some clever systems analysis–type person asks the school administration one day "What does your achievement testing program cost?" Implied is the additional question, "and what are you getting for that cost?" The school administrator would start with the cost of the test booklets and answer sheets, and include the cost of the scoring service. But these are probably not the most important costs. Someone decided which tests to use, when they should be administered, and who should score them. Someone set up the test schedule; someone proctored the test; and someone made arrangements for proper interpretation and dissemination of the results. These are the costs which can be translated to dollar values quite quickly. There are other costs as well—like the "cost" of time to the students; if they had not been tested, some other activity could have been planned. It stands to reason, then, that the school administration should attempt to get the maximum mileage out of its investment in a standardized testing program.

When he considers his school's testing program, an administrator should begin by answering this question: Why are you currently administering a standardized achievement testing battery to your students? If he cannot say why, it might be a good idea to eliminate the battery for a year to see if any decisions become more difficult to make.

On the other hand, the decision-maker might answer that the tests are given to:

(a) aid in individualized instruction through their use as diagnostic measures;

(b) help determine whether students are growing at an acceptable rate;

(c) spot weaknesses in the instructional program—for example, to detect areas where the group is relatively low compared to national norms; or

(d) help in making instructional decisions—for example, choosing the difficulty levels of instruction materials.

PRIMARY USES OF STANDARDIZED ACHIEVEMENT TESTS
To indicate present status. Achievement tests have been constructed primarily to help educators answer questions regarding the present status of pupils. The following are questions of present status:

> *How does this child's performance in mathematics compare with that of the other children in this room, or to that of all children of a similar age in the country?*
>
> *Which level of reading test is most appropriate to the performance level of this class?*
>
> *In which sections of the school's instructional program is this student's performance atypically low, or atypically high?*
>
> *Is this student's low performance in mathematics computation due to certain specific and identifiable problems?*

The first question asks for the comparison of an individual to a group—a problem of ranking. The second question also is somewhat comparative in nature, since the performance level of the class would be based on comparisons with other classes. The third question compares an individual's own achievement in his various subject areas. The final question also involves individual performance, but it is directed at specific problems within a single instructional area.

To indicate growth. Another major use for achievement test results is to indicate pupil or group *growth*. Achievement tests are not written primarily for this purpose, but most test publishers provide techniques for interpreting two or more scores, separated in time, to obtain a measure of pupil or group growth.

The questions we have raised involve comparison of a student with a local group and with some normative group, comparisons of a class to a local or normative group, comparison of a student's scores in the various parts of his school program, diagnostic statements about one student's problems in one subject, and comparison of a student's growth over a period of time to the growth of other students. That's five different uses for achievement test scores, and other examples might be given.

USING NORMS FOR COMPARISON

A *norm* is a series of statistical facts about a defined group of people. Norms should not be confused with *standards*. Norms tell us what *is;* standards tell us what *should be*.

When the purpose for administering the test is that of comparison (individual with group, group to other groups) it is appropriate to ask "Comparison with whom?" Test publishers generally report the results of national normative studies. That is, the publisher of a third-grade reading test might administer the test to a cross-section of third-graders in the country (say about 1 percent of them); and his norms report the results of this testing. Are these national norms appropriate to all schools? Certainly not! Just as there is no "average American" (with 1.3 cars, 2.7 children, etc.), there is also no typical school. There are, however, a large number of schools that have students whose parents are mostly neither rich nor poor, that have instructional programs with many common elements, and teachers that each face about thirty pupils who behave in a manner commonly regarded as "acceptable." Decision-makers in such districts may feel that comparisons with a national sample would be helpful.

Suppose, however, that the practices of the local district differ significantly from those in the "average" school. Suppose the students are predominantly from one minority group, and the school's instructional program has been constructed to reflect this culture. National norms are not satisfactory for such a district; separate norms based on that district and others like it should be constructed.

What of a district whose administrators have decided to delay reading instruction until the child has reached age eight, and where they have replaced the reading emphasis with a heavy emphasis on socialization of the child? What of a district which believes that children should not be introduced to science and mathematics until grade six? Are national norms appropriate in reading for the former case, or science and mathematics in the latter? Of course not; districts in the national cross-section do not usually use these approaches.

Although national norms may not be appropriate for some districts—and they are probably not *completely* appropriate for any district—this does not mean that standardized achievement testing batteries are useless to them. Local norms can be derived to replace the national norms; and growth information as well as individual diagnostic information will still be available.

Summary: National norms are useful to a local district only when the national norming group is reasonably appropriate for comparison with the district. And when the national group is reasonably appropriate, differences between local and national performance levels must be evaluated in terms of the standards which the local educators have set for this district.

CONVERSION OF RAW SCORES

For comparative purposes, a raw score by itself hasn't much meaning. To allow educators to make comparisons, raw scores are converted to convenient scales. The most popular of these are grade equivalents, percentiles, and standard scores. *Grade equivalent norms* are obtained by administering the same test to samples at a number of different grade levels. The time span for the norming sample can be three or four years. *Percentile* and *standard score norms,* by contrast, are generally obtained for single grade levels. That is, a test appropriate for fourth-graders is normed on a sample of fourth-graders. The time span for such norms is one year.

GRADE EQUIVALENTS

The uses and misuses of grade equivalents become apparent when we consider how such norms are constructed. Suppose a publisher has a reading test which he believes is appropriate for the mid-elementary grades. The publisher would define a satisfactory cross-section of students in grades two, three, four, five, and six across the country, and administer his test to the sample, say, for example, in November (the third month of the school year). Suppose the average scores for his sample, from grades two through six respectively, were 12, 22, 32, 40, and 45. The publisher could construct a graph like the one shown in Figure 7 to determine the grade equivalent norms.

With a grade equivalent graph such as Figure 7, it is possible to equate a child's performance on this test with the average performance of a grade group. For example, see the dashed line on Figure 7. A child takes the test, and scores 25 correct. This score translates into a grade equivalent of approximately 3.6. That is, this child has scored as many correct as the average third-grader who is six months into the school year.

The testing was done in November, and these are the scores the test publisher is sure of. To obtain grade equivalents corresponding to the scores *between* 12 and 22 (average scores for second- and third-graders in November) test publishers *interpolate* (assume that the increase has come about in a linear manner). The school year is considered as

Using Achievement Tests 83

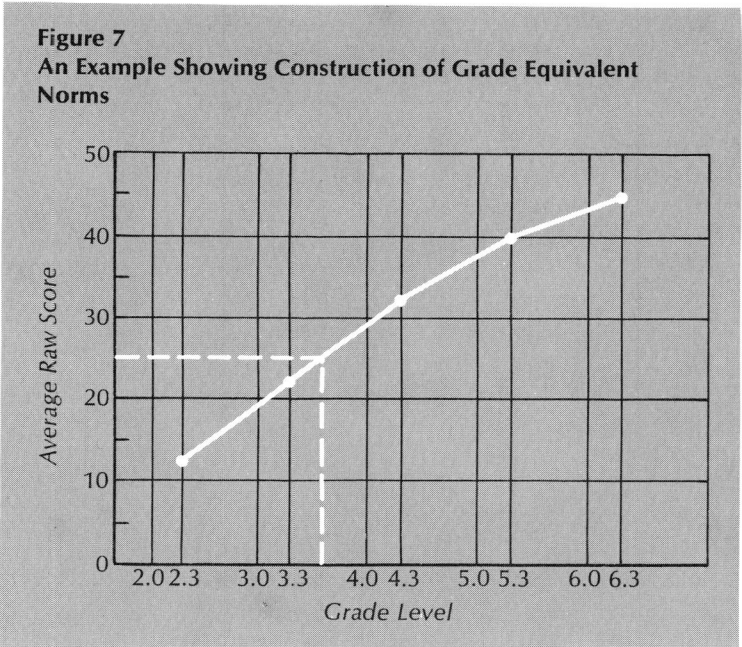

**Figure 7
An Example Showing Construction of Grade Equivalent Norms**

having ten parts—one for each month from September through May and one for the summer. Thus 5.4 (sometimes just given as 54) stands for average performance at the end of the fourth month of fifth grade (December).[1]

PERCENTILE NORMS

Percentile norms are primarily a within-grade measure. To assemble a table of third-grade percentile norms, the test publisher would test a cross-section of third-graders in the country. A percentile rank could then be given for each possible score.

The percentile rank of a score corresponds to the percentage of people in the reference group who scored at or lower than the given score. If a third-grader scores 23 correct on a test, and the percentile rank of that score is 74, it means that 74 percent of the people in the standardization sample scored 23 or lower. Statements like this, however, require that the reference group be appropriate for the student.

---

[1] Beggs and Hieronymus (1968) have seriously questioned this assumption, but it continues to be used in the testing industry today.

As a matter of fact, the same score, 23, can have many *different* percentile ranks—if we change the reference group. The score 23 will have a *low* percentile rank if the reference group is a selected sample of high-achieving third-graders, or a high percentile rank if the reference group consists of mentally retarded third-graders. In fact, this dependency on the appropriateness of the reference group makes comparison of two percentile ranks obtained from two different reference groups very hazardous. *Therefore it is imperative that any statement of percentile rank be accompanied by a description of the reference group.* "My son is at the ninety-ninth percentile in reading" is not enough; but "My son is at the ninety-ninth percentile in reading when compared with boys who dropped out of school" tells us something.

In the same manner, *equal* percentile ranks, obtained from different groups, cannot be equated. Clint might have a percentile rank of 95 in his arithmetic class, and Johnny might also have a PR of 95 in his class; but this does not mean the boys have performed equally. If Clint's class was brighter than Johnny's, Clint probably scored higher.

Percentile ranks are very appealing because they are almost universally understood. They have a serious limitation, however. They should not be used in any mathematical operation—adding, subtracting, multiplying, or dividing. This limitation results from the fact that the score patterns of most school-related groups are bell-shaped—that is, a lot of people bunch up around the middle scores, and fewer people score very high or very low. Thus, at the middle of the scale, it is relatively easy to jump past 10 percent of the people and have a PR increase of ten points. At the extreme ends, the people are more spread out, and to jump past 10 percent of the people, a person must have a relatively large increase in his score.[2] Scales which exhibit non-equal interval characteristics are sometimes called "rubber scales."

STANDARD SCORES

To make it possible to carry out arithmetic operations on reported scores (and for some other reasons as well), test publishers often report *standard scores*. Standard scores are based on a reference group within each grade, and are there-

---

[2] Contrast this to measures of weight, for example, where the difference between 40 and 50 pounds is the same as the difference between 90 and 100 pounds.

fore subject to possible misuse resulting from an inappropriate reference group.

Test publishers obtain standard scores by transforming raw scores into another scale which has more pleasant characteristics. If your height is 5'-11", you might consider transforming that height into 71". You have not become taller or shorter—you have only transformed it because saying "seventy-one inches" takes a shorter time than saying "five feet, eleven inches." That is, the second scale has more pleasant characteristics. Some of the "more pleasant characteristics" of standard scores include the fact that mathematical operations can be performed on them; and transformed means and standard deviations are numbers that are convenient to work with. The transformed mean and standard deviation of the CEEB (College Board) examination are 500 and 100 respectively. This is an example of a standard score.

Stanine scale. One very popular standard score is the *stanine* scale. This is a nine-point scale from 1 through 9, with a mean of 5 and standard deviation of 2. The word *stanine* is derived from "*st*andard *nine*-point scale." Stanines reflect a philosophy that nine groupings are enough for most decision purposes. That is, regardless of the number of items in the test, only nine levels of performance are reported, beginning with 1 (the lowest) and through 9 (the highest). Most other standard score scales report far more levels of performance. Stanine advocates might say, "But why have fifty levels of performance when nine are enough?"

Two different stanine scores cannot be compared unless the *same* reference group is used in both cases. Stanine comparisons and individual stanine interpretations are just as sensitive to the reference group as are percentile rank interpretations and comparisons. Stanines and other standard scores have the additional limitation of not being universally understood. Most laymen do not have a working knowledge of standard scores, and will have difficulty visualizing the implications of a "stanine 7" score. If stanines, or any standard score, are to be reported to the uninitiated, adequate time should be set aside for training in correct interpretation.

USING ACHIEVEMENT TESTS TO MEASURE GROWTH
Growth within a grade level. A common use of achievement tests is to determine how much growth has occurred during

a school year. This requires the administration of achievement tests twice—first in late September or early October, and again in late April or early May of the same school year.

Which of the converted scales is most appropriate? The scale should be capable of reflecting growth in an understandable way. Of the three scales we have discussed (percentile ranks, grade equivalents, and standard scores), grade equivalents would be best for this use.

If the same test, or an equivalent one, is administered to a child at times separated by seven or eight months, and if he has grown in the concepts measured, this growth will be seen in a higher raw score at the second testing. Suppose a particular child obtains a raw score of 23 in the September testing, and 34 in the May testing. Without converting these scores to any other scale, we know he has grown in this instructional area.

But raw score scales have some unhappy characteristics. The means and standard deviations change across tests, and it may be more difficult to jump two points from 24 to 26 than from 14 to 16. The child mentioned earlier gained 11 points, from a 23 to a 34. Should we cry or cheer? Unless the teacher has years of experience interpreting such changes, or has completed normative tables of his own, the change is difficult to interpret.

If, however, this child is in fourth grade, and if the two tests have been administered to samples of third-, fourth-, and fifth-graders on a national basis to obtain grade equivalent scales, the two raw scores can be converted to a scale which indicates growth in a very direct manner. If the raw score of 23 converts to a grade equivalent of 3.5 (the average third-grader after five months in third grade gets 23 correct), and the 34 converts to a 4.3 (average performance for a fourth-grader in November), the student has an estimated growth of 0.8 years (4.3–3.5) for the eight-month period. The word *estimate* is used, for all educational and psychological measurements are subject to some error.

Growth across years. Many elementary schools administer a complete standardized achievement battery each year. One of the purposes of such a program is to determine whether each child is growing in the expected manner. Once again, grade equivalent scales are designed to reflect growth.

When the child is tested and later retested in a school year, the grade equivalent conversions for the two tests are based on the *same* test and the *same* standardization sample both times. If a child is measured in one grade, say third, and then again in fourth, the test and/or standardization sample will probably differ. Although the test publishers try very hard to equate grade equivalent scales even when these differences occur, some error of interpretation can result. If a child in third grade takes the third-grade test and obtains a grade equivalent of 3.9 and a child in fourth grade takes the fourth-grade test and obtains a grade equivalent of 3.9, we are not absolutely sure that the two 3.9's mean the same thing because of the difference in test and standardization samples.

Why not use standard scores to determine growth? Grade equivalents can be badly misused by those who are not aware of certain idiosyncrasies in these scales. Why not just use standard scores, and eliminate grade equivalents?

If a child has a percentile rank of 75 in third grade and a percentile rank of 75 in fourth, the teacher knows only that his relative performance is the same both years. Without additional information, such as whether the reference group changed, the teacher will not know whether this student has grown. If a student scores at the 89th percentile in October and the 75th percentile in May, does this mean the student has not grown at all or that the student has actually gone backwards? Or does it mean that the student simply has not been holding his own—learning, but not as fast as the reference group?

Standard scores have these same limitations with respect to growth measurements. That is, percentile norms and standard score scales do not directly reflect growth. The situation is pictured below:

Child: P.J.

Raw score in Nov., 3rd grade	26	converts to	grade equivalent of 3.3 percentile rank of 50 stanine of 5
Raw score in Nov., 4th grade	38	converts to	grade equivalent of 4.3 percentile rank of 50 stanine of 5

Only the grade equivalent scale directly reflects the growth.

USING ACHIEVEMENT TESTS FOR FIXED TIME INTERPRETATIONS

The use of standard scores. One important use of standardized achievement tests for individuals and groups is to find the group's strengths and weaknesses. Diagnostics for each student across subject areas can be useful to the teacher. For example, if a child seems to perform better in mathematics and science than in social studies and reading, the teacher might use the strengths to improve the weaknesses. A young child who does better in arithmetic and spelling, in which little reading is required, than in any other area is probably having trouble reading.

When interpretation will be based on a single test administration, the reference group will be the same for all of the subtests in the achievement test battery. Since both percentile ranks and standard scores are rank-in-group conversions, both would be appropriate for these diagnostics. Most people have an intuitive feeling for percentile rank meanings, and this is a strong point in favor of these scales. Because it is a "rubber" scale, discussed earlier, interpretations must be made with great care. A difference of twenty points between percentile ranks of 99 and 79, for example, is more meaningful than a difference of twenty points between 60 and 40. To a certain extent, standard scores get around this problem. Their weakness is that most laymen and teachers do not understand the meaning of standard scores.

Misuse of grade equivalents. Grade equivalents *should not be used* for comparing individual performance across subject areas. Suppose we illustrate. Consider two frequently tested areas—mathematics computation and paragraph meaning; and assume we are preparing grade-equivalent scales for the fourth grade. Mathematics is a cumulative sort of discipline, and most children do most of their mathematics learning in school. Consequently, second-grade children will not do well on a fourth-grade mathematics test, for they have not had much experience with these concepts; and the fourth-graders will have some difficulty competing with sixth-graders. Because the distribution of scores has a narrow range, a fourth-grade student whose percentile rank is 5 may still be better than the average beginning third-grader; and a student in fourth grade whose percentile rank is 95 may be only as good as the *average* beginning sixth-grader.

Reading is a different matter, however. The range of performance in reading is far wider within a grade. It is not too surprising to find second-graders who read better than the average fourth-grader; and it is not surprising to find fourth-graders who read better than the average eighth-grader. Our 5th and 95th percentile performers in fourth grade might have grade equivalents in reading of 2.2 and 8.0, for example.

Now if grade equivalents are used for individual diagnostics, here is what can happen. Our friend P. J. might be a 95th percentile performer in both areas; that is, compared to the same reference group, his rank is the same in paragraph meaning and in mathematics computation. Because the distribution of scores is wider in reading than in mathematics, his converted grade equivalents are 5.9 for mathematics and 7.9 for paragraph meaning. He takes these two figures home to Papa, and Papa gives him a tongue lashing (or worse) for falling down in arithmetic—when he has done relatively as well in both! Fathers are not the only ones who make such errors; a few teachers and counselors have been guilty of the same thing.

The uninitiated can also misinterpret a grade equivalent by implying that this figure tells the grade the child should be in. At the beginning of fourth grade, P. J. may obtain a grade equivalent of 5.9 in mathematics. Does that mean he should be immediately boosted into fifth grade? Of course not. It simply says that he is very good at applying *fourth*-grade mathematics concepts; better, in fact, than most fifth-graders are. The performance does not say anything about his ability with fifth-grade concepts, since fifth-grade concepts should not be in the fourth-grade test. Some fourth-graders may perform better on a fourth-grade reading test than does the superintendent of schools; but that does not mean they are ready or able to handle his work.[3]

REPORTING TEST RESULTS

Most districts have their tests scored by a scoring service—often one provided by the test publisher. Some districts with access to scoring equipment within their own district may analyze their own results. Regardless of how the scoring is handled, someone must eventually decide how the results will be reported. As the authors have stressed before, the types of scores used depend on the primary purpose for the testing. The testing industry has done an excellent job of

---

[3] Some laymen may quarrel with this statement.

preparing different ways in which test results can be reported back to the school systems. For example, results can be reported for individual students, individual classrooms, individual buildings—and in terms of school district norms.

Suppose the district wishes to use the tests for both growth determinations and immediate diagnostics. Both grade equivalents and standard scores (or percentile norms) should therefore be reported. Percentile norms should be reported especially if those who will use the test results are not sophisticated in the use and misuses of standard scores. If the district is one of those for which comparison to national norms is inappropriate, then the results should be reported in terms of state or local norms. Both the reporting scale and the norm group should be chosen as a function of the unique characteristics and purposes for testing in the local district.

REPORTING TO THE TEACHERS

Which of these scores should be made available to the teachers? The answer depends on answers to two other questions: Which of the results are useful to the teacher, and which kinds of results can the teachers properly interpret? Someone must make the decision about which results will go to the teachers, and the decision is important. It makes little sense to clutter up meaningful results with figures the teacher does not need. It is even more important to avoid assuming that all teachers have sufficient training to interpret different scales and comparative groups properly.

It is the opinion of the authors that teachers should obtain all results that relate to their particular classroom and to the students within the classroom. If the administrator is not sure that the teachers are able to correctly use the results, he should schedule in-service talks by experts in the field—possibly people on the test publisher's staff. Administrators must make provisions for training teachers to interpret the scores so that they can make group and individual diagnostic statements. The administrator should not wait for the teachers to *ask* for help; it should be provided in large amounts. If the tests are not used properly in the classroom, one of the primary uses for the test has been eliminated.

The teacher should keep cumulative profiles of each student. These profiles allow him to see how a student is changing as the years go by. The test results can also give the teacher an impartial outside evaluation of the students in his class, and the teacher should be interested in determining how these rankings differ from his own.

REPORTING TO THE PUBLIC

The school district should routinely prepare a comprehensive summary of the results of each year's testing. This report, or sections and summaries thereof, would be passed on to interested groups such as the school board, parents' organizations, special interest groups in the community, as well as the professional staff of the school. This reporting must be done carefully, for the public cannot be expected to have expertise in test interpretation. Five important suggestions follow:

1. Graphical displays are preferable to tables of numbers. Both graphical presentations and tables *can* facilitate interpretation, but they will be misunderstood unless certain pitfalls are avoided. For example, there is a strong tendency to attempt too much with a single graph. Too much information tends to confuse rather than inform.

A common mistake is the use of partial vertical scales. A graph displaying percentile ranks of a class in the district, for example, should show the entire range of possible percentiles from 0 to 100. If only the percentiles from 30 to 70 are required to display the district's information, there is a temptation to eliminate 0 through 29 and 71 through 100 on the vertical axis. This accentuates small differences and creates a distorted interpretation.

2. The type of converted score used must conform with the audience's interpretive ability. Generally speaking, most lay groups can be expected to understand percentile norms. When standard scores or grade equivalents are used with lay groups, the administrator must allow time for adequate instruction in interpretation.

3. More than just the median or average performance levels should be reported. Because the school is interested in the success of its program with all students, the performance of those at the highest and lowest levels should be reported as well. The graphs and tables might illustrate performance

of the students at the 25th, 50th, and 75th percentiles, for example. It would not be too confusing, if done carefully, to add the 5th and 95th percentiles to this list, since special education candidates come from these ends of the scale.

4. Most displays should be comparative in nature. That is, the layman should be given a bench mark so that he sees the local district's performance in the proper perspective. The need for an appropriate reference group has been mentioned earlier. These comparisons might be to national or local norms; they might compare *present* performance levels; they might compare performance across special socioeconomic or geographic classifications; or they might be comparisons of achievement in different areas of the instructional program.

5. Most districts have a yearly testing program, and the administration should include past results in summaries of the current testing. To be sure, the most current results will dominate the yearly report; but past performance should be included for proper perspective.

Figure 8 is the kind of diagram which could provide useful trend information to the school administration and its public. It deals with a five-year time period; it deals with three of the most important instructional areas; and it is reasonably easy to interpret.

Following are some interpretive comments:

1. The vertical axis is the national norm bench mark. If we assume that the same test battery has been used with this class over the five-year period, the national norm sample will be a reasonably unchangeable reference group over the five-year period.

2. The markings on the graph refer to *local* norms. For example, refer to the first vertical bar for second-grade reading. The top line refers to the local 95th percentile scorer. This line is at the 99th percentile nationally, meaning that a student whose *local* percentile rank is 95 will rank 99th nationally. Likewise, a 25th percentile scorer locally (see the top line of the lower large box) scores at about the 32nd percentile nationally. In other words, the students in this district tend to score a little higher than the students of the national sample.

Figure 8
Test Performance in Three Instructional Areas over a Five-Year Period for This Year's Sixth-Grade Class

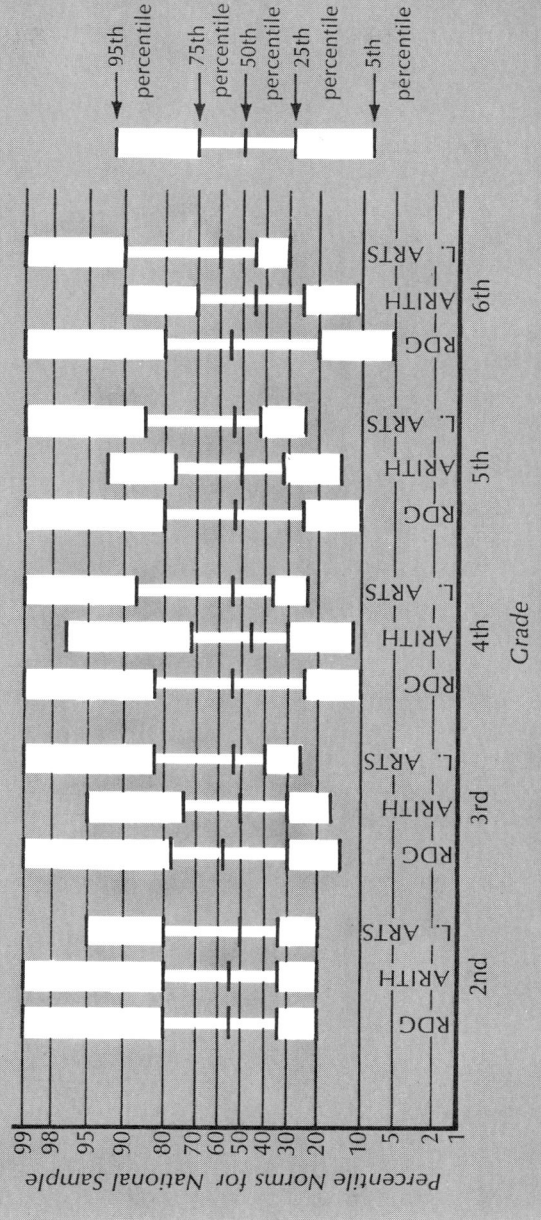

3. The fact that ten of the vertical bars (out of fifteen possible) reach the 99th percentile mark nationally indicates that this test is too easy for the best students in the local district. If the students at the 95th percentile are topping out the test, how can the students in the 99th percentile locally possibly show their potential?

4. Over the five-year period for this class, there has been a relative increase in language arts performance at all levels. The 95th percentile performers went from the 95th to 99th percentile nationally and stayed there. (Who knows how much better they could have done had the test allowed further growth.) The 75th percentile performers locally grew steadily from the 80th to the 90th percentile nationally. This same trend is indicated at the 50th, 25th, and 5th local percentiles. Apparently something in this district makes this particular group of students relatively better in language arts than the national normative group.

5. Now look at the trend in the reading scores, and we will see the purpose of plotting five different local percentile levels. The reading scores at the local 95th, 75th, and 50th percentile levels are fairly constant. However, the students at the local 25th and 5th percentiles have been steadily falling over the five-year period. A school administrator who sees a result like this, showing a selective decrement for one group of students, should look very carefully at his current reading program. There is a strong possibility that it is simply inappropriate for the students at this performance level, and that other materials and programs may be necessary.

6. A careful study of the chart will also show a general downward movement in arithmetic. This downward movement is at all levels. Such a result has more than hypothetical interest, for many districts have recently been faced with very similar outcomes. A school administrator faced with such results should carefully consider two things. First, he should study the relationship between the existing curriculum and the test. If the local district has a program emphasizing modern math concepts, whereas the test has a rather traditional orientation, it is not difficult to understand the decrements in performance at all levels locally. If the test does conform to the local curriculum reasonably well, then

the school administrator must take a critical look at the local arithmetic program.

However, we do not wish to give the impression that any time there is a decrement in test performance or the local district performs relatively lower in one part of the test battery than in others, immediate steps should be taken to correct these seeming failures. National norms are not chiseled in stone; they are not sacred. *They are norms, not standards.* Arithmetic scores may be falling because of a rational decision on the part of the school administration—for instance, that more instructional time should be spent on reading and language arts at the expense of arithmetic drill. Or they may have felt that it is more efficient to stress arithmetic at the junior high level. The point is that test results should be available to help the school's decision-makers, but they should not be allowed to dictate district policy.

REPORTING TO PARENTS

In most school systems today the administration and teachers are responsible for making information about a student's academic growth available to the parents. In many instances this includes comparative results—comparing their child to other children in the classroom and to children in the nation as a whole.

Of particular concern to the decision-maker is the appropriate manner in which test results of low achievers are reported to their parents. Reporting grade equivalent scores to such parents—which indicate how poorly the student is doing—would not be a useful approach. It would be much more constructive to discuss the *growth* of the child in the achievement areas rather than his low standing at the time of the test. It would seem imperative that the test counselor, psychologist, or guidance counselor should attempt to interpret test results to the parents in a positive manner so that they will understand and look favorably upon testing.

At the present time it would seem that the grade equivalent or grade placement scores should not be reported to the parent, simply because this concept is so easily misunderstood. If the parent demands this information, then of course he has a perfect right to see it, but in that case, the administrator should be adamant in requesting that the parents spend time in discussing what the scores mean. Grade equivalents are commonly misinterpreted by parents, who often assume that the grade equivalent score can be interpreted as the grade the child should be in.

The percentile rank of a student's score can be interpreted to parents in a very meaningful way. It is of utmost importance that the teacher or administrator interpret such percentile ranks to the parent. More than one percentile rank for the child's attained scores—that is, the percentile rank for different reference groups—should be reported. Two such reference groups could be the student's class or grade and a national norm group.

REPORTING TO THE STUDENT

In any testing program it is important that the school provide feedback, as quickly as possible, to the students who were examined. A point of concern, though, is how to present this necessary information to the student. It is the opinion of the authors that caution is necessary when numerical results are involved, especially for elementary school children.

No responsible test publisher or author denies that there are inevitably errors of measurement involved in these instruments. If only a single score is reported to the student, we are, in a certain sense, implying that this error of measurement does not exist. It seems better to report a range of scores to the student, indicating to him that no absolute measures have been obtained and that this score is really only an estimate. To a certain extent stanine scores represent ranges in this manner.

Especially for elementary school children, an appropriate reporting form would contain no numerical results at all. Refer once again to Figure 6 of chapter 3 and the discussion of the corridor concept. A student with such a report in front of him has a visual picture of his progress; he knows whether he is moving along at an acceptable rate. With this approach, the student is constantly comparing himself to others whose initial performance at that grade level was the same as his own in the past. Discussion of results between student and teacher can center on comparisons of the student's current and past performance, and need not emphasize his standing compared to others in the class or some national reference group.

REFERENCES

Beggs, Donald L., and A. N. Hieronymus. "Uniformity of Growth in the Basic Skills Throughout the School Year and During the Summer," *Journal of Educational Measurement* 5 (Summer 1968): 91–98.

Davis, Frederick B. *Educational Measurements and Their Interpretation.* Belmont, Calif.: Wadsworth Publishing Co., 1964.

HOMOGENEOUS GROUPING

A Brief Review of Research

Dimensions of Ability Grouping
Three factors in decision-making
Three assumptions of ability grouping

Placement Errors Due to Measurement Errors

Placement Errors Due to Infrequent Testing

Placement Errors Due to Cultural Bias
Scholastic aptitude tests and disadvantaged children

Errors Due to Use of IQ as Determinant

Effects of Misplacement
Teachers and the self-fulfilling prophecy
Administrative considerations

Summary

The teacher in a self-contained classroom faces a broad range of abilities among her twenty-five or so pupils. In an average fourth-grade class, it would not be unusual to find reading levels ranging from grade equivalents of 2.5 to 8.5. In order to provide for individual differences, teachers often establish three reading groups *within* a class.

Since the 1920's published research has suggested a tendency of school officials to extend this within-class grouping to between-class grouping, with the idea that a program of study for like students could be fitted to their common interests and abilities. Since the grouping has generally been done on the basis of ability, the term *homogeneous grouping* is often replaced by *ability grouping*.

In an ideal world, the authors would opt for an individually prescribed curriculum for each student—a curriculum which would best provide for individual cognitive, affective, and motor needs. Although large and well-financed investigations of individualized and computer-aided instruction are being done, educational consumers must admit that this ideal world has not been even approximated as yet. In this chapter measurement techniques and research efforts related to ability grouping will be surveyed, in the hope that school administrators might avoid mistakes if they understand how educational measurements can be misinterpreted. The revived interest of the 1950's in ability grouping suggests that the topic is one about which school administrators must make decisions.

Table 6 has been prepared as an illustration of some of the variety of homogeneous grouping schemes commonly used. As is indicated in the diagram, ability grouping is not the only kind of homogeneous grouping used in the schools. For example, students whose physical handicaps are severe enough to prohibit participation in the regular school program are grouped together. Schools begin age-grouping early by allowing children to enter kindergarten only after they reach a fixed age. Thelen (1967) has advocated what he calls "grouping for teachability," based on pupil-teacher interaction. The premise is that a given teacher might work well with one type of pupil, but not with others. Others have suggested that grouping might be based on primary abilities, instead of overall achievement or aptitude.

A distinction is made in Table 6 between ability grouping and tracking (or, to use the British term, streaming). Tracking

Table 6
Homogeneous Grouping Schemes

Grouping due to special handicaps	Grouping on the basis of scholastic ability		Some other suggested types of grouping
Physical handicaps—speech, vision, hearing, for example	Tracking: in which a student is at the same level in all parts of the instructional program. There might be a college prep track, a commercial track, etc.—and very little cross-tracking occurs	Variable placement grouping, in which a student can be at different levels in the various parts of the instructional program	Placing students together who fit the teacher's personal characteristics (grouping for teachability)
Mentally retarded			
Emotionally and socially handicapped			Grouping children together who have similar learning styles or learning problems
Learning disorders			

is generally a secondary school term, and implies a prediction for the post–high school vocation of the student. A student designated as college prep is given a different curriculum than one designated commercial or vocational. The tracks can be very independent, with only a small amount of cross-tracking. Ability grouping at the secondary level refers to grouping within a part of the total curriculum. Thus a student could conceivably be in group 1 in mathematics, group 3 in language arts, and group 2 in history.

A BRIEF REVIEW OF RESEARCH

This section will deal with selected research studies, mostly recent, which deal with homogeneous grouping, with an eye toward discovering elements common to many of the studies as well as those which often conflict.[1] We will limit our discussion to the reported relationships between grouping practices and (a) student achievement, (b) teacher attitude, and (c) student attitudes—self-attitude, attitude toward school, and interests.

Student achievement. If the school administrator believes that ability grouping *per se* will lead to an increase in the average level of student achievement, his thinking is contrary to the results reported by most reviewers of homogeneous grouping literature. For example, the reader is directed to the writings of Eash (1961) and Ekstrom (1961). The concept of little relationship between student achievement and grouping practice has been generally supported by the results of more recent large-scale studies on the topic. Millman and Johnson (1964), in a large study, failed in their attempt to find a relationship between range of ability and class achievement. An equally large study is reported by Borg (1965). In this study, one entire school system practiced homogeneous grouping, whereas the second system used heterogeneous grouping coupled with a well-defined enrichment program. In reading through Borg's report, one is forced to conclude that no consistent results relating student achievement to grouping practice were obtained. The study was centered primarily on the upper elementary grades, and is of particular interest because the curricula of the two systems were actually altered to fit the manner of grouping students. Failure to do this is a common criticism of too many other studies.

---

[1] The review which accompanies the study by Borg (1965) is quite exhaustive, and the interested reader is also directed to the first chapter of the book by Goldberg et al. (1966).

Finally, the study by Goldberg *et al.* (1966) should be noted. This study was carried out in New York City, with approximately 2200 fifth-grade pupils. The study followed these pupils through fifth and sixth grades. The researchers concluded that narrowing the range of ability in a class did not result in increased student achievement. On the contrary, the greatest achievement gains were made in the broad-range (heterogeneously grouped) classrooms. The researchers are quick to add, however, that a special curriculum had not been devised for the narrow-range classrooms, and that a specialized curriculum may be necessary for increased student achievement. The individual classroom teacher, it would seem, is ill-equipped to carry out this task. The teacher, after all, is in the front lines, and the heat of the daily battle may preclude his effectively defining the proper curriculum for each group.

Teacher attitude. The school administrator, in his role as decision-maker, must also be interested in the attitude and morale of his staff. Very consistent results have been obtained by researchers studying teacher attitude toward homogeneous grouping. Teachers are more comfortable teaching a class with a narrowed range of ability—a result which is without contradiction in the reported literature. For example, see reviews by Goodlad (1960) and Otto (1941), as well as in the reviews cited previously.

Student attitudes. In his summary of research studies dealing with ability grouping through 1961, Eash (1961) felt five generalizations were supportable. His fifth statement was:

Ability grouping as an organizational structure may accentuate the attainment of goals and symbols for goals of narrow academic achievement to the extent that other broader desirable behavioral goals and objectives are attenuated and jeopardized. The organizational structure of ability grouping may promote grouping norms which are antithetical to norms that foster societal cohesion and individual societal responsibility.

One might logically argue that a low-ability student's attitude toward himself and his ability might increase if he is not made aware each day that others perform at a much higher academic level. At the other extreme, the high-ability student's picture of himself and his ability might be slightly diminished in the absence of his low-ability peers.

This was in fact observed in the studies by Goldberg et al. (1966) and Wilcox (1961), and partially observed by Borg (1965) and Drews (1963).

When researchers have attempted to find a relationship between grouping practices and student attitudes toward school, the results have not been consistent. Goldberg et al. found no relationship at all, and in fact noted a decrease in interest in all areas except music over the period of their study. This result is in agreement with an earlier study by Wick and Yager, (1966). These results may, however, be simply idiosyncrasies of the measurement devices.

The basis for establishing groups. With the exception of the more recent and extensive studies, researchers seem almost hesitant to report the bases upon which they established their groups. One study (Howell, 1965) reports that "five rigorous criteria are applied to eligible candidates to select the membership for the honors group in grade nine," but we are not told what the five criteria are. When the bases for the grouping are mentioned, it is often limited to a cursory sentence or two.

However, the available literature does seem to indicate that grouping is currently based on three available measures, either singly or in combination. These are measures of achievement, measures of aptitude (generally an intelligence test), and teacher evaluations. In the massive study by Goldberg et al. (1966), the grouping was based on an IQ measure. An IQ measure plus achievement scores were used by Deitrich (1964) and Kincaid and Epley (1960). West and Sievers (1960) and Wick (1968) saw teacher evaluation plus achievement test scores as the primary basis. The large study by Borg (1965) was based on achievement test scores only, as was the work of Leton and Anderson (1964). Finally, studies by Kierstead (1963), Braun (1959) and Ellers (1964) all used a combination of IQ scores, achievement measures, and teacher evaluation. In his contribution to the 61st Yearbook of the National Society for the Study of Education, Anderson (1961) concludes that "usually the criterion has been a summary index of general intelligence and academic aptitude."

Of course, the ideal basis for the grouping is a measure which best approximates the behavioral goals for the class. Groupings for a typing course, for example, would be best based on some measure of finger dexterity or visual-motor coordination than on a measure of general intelligence. Given the presence of a valid algebra aptitude test, teacher evaluation for algebra grouping should not be used *in lieu of* this test.

DIMENSIONS OF ABILITY GROUPING

A massive body of research has been done in an attempt to link ability grouping to gains in student achievement. Although the hypothesized gains do not seem to occur consistently, schools continue to ability-group students. About 75 percent of American teachers approve of the practice, and the popularity of ability grouping is apparently growing (*Phi Delta Kappan,* 1969).

THREE FACTORS IN DECISION-MAKING

Perhaps one reason for this apparent paradox is the tendency of many educators to look upon ability grouping decisions as single-dimensional problems. However, there are three central considerations in such a decision. The authors, for example, might support ability grouping in mathematics in a high school which draws from a fairly homogeneous population, but will argue bitterly against attempts to group first graders from a very heterogeneous population for their reading instruction.

The three dimensions are fairly obvious. *Age or grade placement* is an important consideration. If grouping is begun too early, there is the possibility that a late-developing child will be placed in a low group and may never be reassigned to a higher level.

The *characteristics of the school population* are also important. If the district has very little racial or ethnic mix and if the students are all drawn from about the same socioeconomic level, the fear of cultural bias in placement procedures is not serious. If there exists considerable heterogeneity in the district's population and if the placement procedures do contain a cultural bias, then there is a distinct possibility that ability grouping will tend to perpetuate cultural inequities.

Finally, for a given grade level and underlying population, the *subject area* for which ability grouping is being considered is an important consideration. The school's role is broader than simply encouraging the students' best academic performance in all areas of the program. The society in which graduates will live is heterogeneous, and the school experience these students have should prepare them to live in mutual understanding with people who are different. At the high school level, entrance requirements for certain universities make it necessary for college-bound students to take mathematics and science. But the universities should not dictate the entire curriculum of the high schools, since a substantial proportion of graduates do not go on to universities. Even though a high school does have college prep science and mathematics courses, it may be worthwhile to have completely random assignment in the other subjects. Furthermore, the authors are convinced that heterogeneous grouping in all classes, with well-conceived enrichment materials for the hypothetically college-bound, would probably give all of the students a better preparation for their post-school years than a program of rigid ability grouping.

THREE ASSUMPTIONS OF ABILITY GROUPING

Many readers will have decision-making roles in districts which practice some form of ability grouping, and they should be aware of three fundamental assumptions implicit in such grouping.

In a system which is not ability grouped or tracked, it is argued that the gifted pupil will not be challenged, he will become bored and lazy, and his performance will be far below potential. On the other hand, the slow pupil will become frustrated and depressed because he is unable to keep up with the ongoing program. The remedy is seen in a policy which separates these student types, and gives to each a course of instruction which is commensurate with his maximum ability. The first implied but fundamental assumption of those who advocate an ability grouping or tracking system is that:

> *The school is capable of measuring, without racial or socioeconomic bias, the maximum ability of each pupil.*

If no attempt is made to determine the maximum performance levels of the students and grouping is done on the basis of their current performance levels, then the term would be "achievement grouping" instead of "ability grouping." No such assumption of capability of measuring maximum performance levels would be made in achievement grouping.

But achievement grouping cannot meet the promise—those who group students have promised to ultimately place each at his maximum performance level, and some students will not currently be working at their maximum ability levels. These students presumably would be placed in a group which will eventually not be challenging enough. There could be many reasons for this discrepancy between current performance and ultimate ability, and much has been written about the concepts of over- and under-achievement. The second implied and fundamental assumption of ability grouping is that:

> *The school system can and will work to bring students known to be working below maximum performance level up to this level.*

The statement implies that adequate compensatory and remedial programs will be available so that the underachieving student will quickly move up to his proper level. Leading quite directly from the second assumption is the third fundamental assumption, that:

> *As the student moves toward his maximum performance level, the system will be flexible enough to allow him to move up through the levels.*

No responsible educational decision-maker would advocate a system which pigeon-holes a student at one level. Most recognize that student performance is a changeable thing, and the system must have flexibility built into it.

These fundamental assumptions were successfully challenged by the plaintiffs in the *Hobson v. Hansen* case cited in detail in chapter 11, which involved a large school district (Washington, D.C.) having a wide variation in socioeconomic level of its students. The plaintiffs charged that the school was not carrying out the three fundamental assumptions just listed, and the court agreed with the plaintiffs. The implication for an educational decision-maker whose own district has wide variability among the socioeconomic levels of its students should be clear.

PLACEMENT ERRORS DUE TO MEASUREMENT ERRORS

An ideal world in which criterion measures are perfectly accurate does not exist. When administrators group students in social studies or language arts courses, less direct measures such as general aptitude, past achievement, and teacher evaluation are usually used.

In the following imaginary grouping problem, the facts are hypothetical but reasonable. Grouping is often accomplished this way. In a heterogeneous group of 75 students, an IQ range from 75 to 130 would be typical. The hypothesized distributions of error and ability as well as the techniques for measuring the amount of error are commonly accepted by measurement specialists. This example is presented to show how a simple grouping program is carried out and how much error in assignment will occur even under relatively ideal conditions.

The situation: A junior high school building has three seventh-grade units with a total enrollment of 75 seventh-graders. After a series of discussions, the English faculty agreed to implement ability grouping for two years on an experimental basis, after which a vote to reconsider this action would be taken. The seventh-grade English curriculum in this school covered a variety of topics, including vocabulary, composition, spelling, and dictionary and writing skills. With such great diversity, the number of available aptitude measures was limited, and the group felt that a very reliable mental ability test (more often called an IQ test) would be its best choice for a placement instrument. The IQ Test the group decided upon was the Otis-Lennon Mental Ability Test, Intermediate Level (Otis and Lennon, 1967). This test, according to the publisher's printed information, has a mean IQ of 100, a standard deviation of 16, alternate forms reliability[2] of .90, and a standard error of measurement[3] (in IQ points) of 5.1. The reliability and standard error are related mathematically. For a further discussion, see Cronbach (1960).

Table 7 shows approximately how 75 students with a mean IQ of 100 would be distributed, assuming a common standard deviation. As the figure indicates, most of the students are bunched around the middle. Fifteen have IQs between 97 and 103, and 40 have IQs between 90 and 110. True IQs

---

[2] The alternate forms reliability coefficient is a measure of the equivalence of scores obtained when the same group of students is tested with two different forms of a test.

[3] The standard error of measurement is an index of the variability of the scores. A low standard error indicates relatively stable scores, while a high coefficient indicates instability.

Table 7
Probable Distribution of True IQ Scores for 75 Seventh-Graders

Range of IQ scores	Frequency	Tally
125–131	5	𝍢
118–124	5	𝍢
111–117	7	𝍢 //
104–110	12	𝍢 𝍢 //
97–103	15	𝍢 𝍢 𝍢
90– 96	13	𝍢 𝍢 ///
83– 89	8	𝍢 ///
76– 82	8	𝍢 ///
– 75	2	//

are known only to an Authority Higher than mere school administrators, and the scores actually observed are subject to errors of measurement.[4] The errors are assumed to cancel one another out—that is, it is reasonable to guess there should be roughly as many positive as negative errors, so that the mean of all the errors can legitimately be assumed to be zero. The standard error of these is 5.1 (according to the publisher) and the distribution of the errors is again approximately normal. Table 8 shows approximately how 75 error scores with a published standard deviation of 5.1 would be distributed.

Note that the errors are centered on zero, which means they are totally random—as likely to be positive (meaning you would score a little higher that day than you would most other times) as negative. Again, most of the errors are near the middle of the distribution. About one-third (actually 23/75) are either +1, 0, or −1, and 40/75 are between −4 and +4.

Since the errors are assumed to be random, the highest true IQ score of 131 could be associated with any of the errors shown in Table 8. To obtain theoretical observed scores for these 75 pupils, we assigned the error scores to the true scores by drawing lots. That is, each of the 75 error

---

[4] These errors can come from many different sources. For example, the individual's rate of working varies from day to day; the specific sample of tasks (items) may or may not be favorable to him; and a whole range of attitudinal and motivational variations can occur moment-by-moment in a student.

Table 8
Distribution of Error Scores Associated with IQ Measures for 75 Seventh-Graders

Error (in IQ units)	Frequency	Tally
+8 to +10	4	IIII
+5 to +7	8	𝓣𝓗𝓛 III
+2 to +4	14	𝓣𝓗𝓛 𝓣𝓗𝓛 IIII
−1 to +1	23	𝓣𝓗𝓛 𝓣𝓗𝓛 𝓣𝓗𝓛 𝓣𝓗𝓛 III
−2 to −4	14	𝓣𝓗𝓛 𝓣𝓗𝓛 IIII
−5 to −7	8	𝓣𝓗𝓛 III
−8 to −10	4	IIII

scores was written on a slip of paper and placed in a bowl. Next, beginning with the first IQ score of 131, an error score was drawn from the bowl and associated with the IQ score to obtain an observed score. A −2 error score was drawn for this first true IQ score, so an observed score of 129 is noted for this pupil. The analogy between game and real situation should be clear. It is assumed that the 75 students do have the true IQ scores,[5] which are unknown to us. The only information we can ever obtain is the observed IQ scores—but these are subject to error, and it is important to inquire into the frequency of student misclassification.

Table 9 lists the observed IQ score, the error associated with it (that is, the error drawn from the bowl for that true IQ score), and the resulting true IQ score for each subject. The three columns in the table indicate the manner in which the groupings would be made, based on the only information available—observed IQ scores.

Table 10 shows the three-group classification of students *if* the true IQ scores had been known. Twenty-five students are placed in each group.

A total of fourteen errors in classification have been made, which means that about 18.7 percent of the 75 students were misplaced. Remember that the assignment of error scores to true scores was a random process involving drawing the error scores from a bowl. If the experiment were run again, perhaps fewer would be misclassified, but there might also be increased misclassification. The assumptions regarding

---
[5] Note that we did *not* say "true and unchangeable."

Table 9
Observed and True IQ Scores for 75 Seventh-Graders

Group 1

ID	Obs. Sco.	Error	True IQ	Comment
1	136	+10	126	
2	129	−2	131	
3	129	0	129	
4	129	−2	131	
5	126	+1	125	
6	122	+2	120	
7	118	+1	117	
8	118	−1	119	
9	117	−6	123	
10	115	−3	118	
11	115	+3	112	
12	115	+5	110	
13	114	−6	120	
14	114	+9	105	From 2
15	113	−4	117	
16	113	−2	115	
17	113	−2	115	
18	112	+1	111	
19	112	+3	109	
20	112	+4	108	
21	111	+1	110	
22	111	+7	104	From 2
23	110	+2	108	
24	110	+5	105	From 2

Group 2

ID	Obs. Sco.	Error	True IQ	Comment
26	107	+4	103	
27	105	−2	107	From 1
28	105	+4	101	
29	105	−9	114	From 1
30	105	−1	106	From 1
31	103	0	103	
32	103	+2	101	
33	101	+4	97	
34	100	+2	98	
35	99	−4	103	
36	98	−1	99	
37	97	0	97	
38	97	+5	92	From 3
39	96	+3	93	
40	96	−3	99	
41	95	−5	100	
42	95	+3	98	
43	95	+1	94	
44	94	−10	104	
45	94	−5	99	
46	94	−3	97	
47	94	0	94	
48	92	0	92	From 3
49	92	+6	86	From 3

Group 3

ID	Obs. Sco.	Error	True IQ	Comment
51	91	−9	100	From 2
52	91	−4	95	From 2
53	91	+1	90	
54	90	+8	82	
55	90	+6	84	
56	90	+1	89	
57	95	+3	92	
58	88	0	88	
59	88	−8	96	From 2
60	88	−5	93	From 2
61	87	−1	88	
62	85	−4	89	
63	84	−3	87	
64	84	+7	77	
65	84	−1	85	
66	83	−7	90	
67	83	+8	75	
68	83	−7	90	
69	81	−1	82	
70	81	+6	75	
71	80	−1	81	
72	79	−2	81	
73	78	0	78	
74	77	0	77	

Table 10
Classification of 75 Students Based on True IQ Scores

Range of IQ scores	Number	ID of students included
106–131	25	1, 2, 3, 4, 5, 6, 7, 8, 9, 10, 11, 12, 13, 15, 16, 17, 18, 19, 20, 21, 23, 25, 27, 29, 30
93–105	25	14, 22, 24, 26, 28, 31, 32, 33, 34, 35, 36, 37, 39, 40, 41, 42, 43, 44, 45, 46, 47, 51, 52, 59, 60
75–92	25	38, 48, 49, 50, 53, 54, 55, 56, 57, 58, 61, 62, 63, 64, 65, 66, 67, 68, 69, 70, 71, 72, 73, 74, 75

normality of IQ scores and error scores are generally considered to be acceptable approximations in a regular school situation. The standard error of measurement, based on alternate forms reliability of 0.90 is conservative—this figure probably should be a little more in a real situation. A larger standard error would result in *more* misclassifications over the long run.

PLACEMENT ERRORS DUE TO INFREQUENT TESTING

If we accept the premise that test scores are a major determinant of placement, then testing which is too infrequent has a detrimental effect on learning. Students grow at different rates and each child's rate of growth is irregular; also, a central assumption of ability grouping is that a student who is currently performing below his maximum level can be brought up to that level. Therefore, a grouping program should be flexible enough to allow a student to freely change levels according to his individual rate of growth.

If the tests are given at three-year intervals, or even one- or two-year intervals, it is entirely possible that this will be the only time teachers will seriously reevaluate their students' performances, with the result that many students will be frozen at a level that has become inappropriate for them.

PLACEMENT ERRORS DUE TO CULTURAL BIAS

The clever prime minister of a small country happened to be left-handed. It was his belief that all right-handed people are inferior beings—"childlike in their simplicity"—and that the major decisions should be made by the "portsiders." If the left-handers are to be in the major decision-making positions, they must receive special attention in the country's school system. Since the school system was a four-track affair, he wanted to insure that most of the left-handers got into the upper track.

So he devised a series of track placement tests to be administered at age nine. The first test was called the Southpaw Range of Ability Test, in which the primary measure depended upon the distance each nine-year-old could throw a round ball left-handed. Next, he devised the Manipulative Dexterity Test, in which the student, holding a pencil in his left hand, attempted to trace around a complex figure. The right-handed children tended to make the largest number of "reversals" (leaving the line more than 1.96 standard error units), and these "culturally deprived" students were placed in special "compensatory manipulation" classes.

We can assume that a satisfactory battery of tests could have been devised to separate the left-handers into the upper tracks, away from the right-handers, who were relegated to lower positions. If the prime minister and his staff of medical, biological, and psychological experts (all university affiliated, and each the recipient of a large research grant from the prime minister) really put their minds to the matter, a whole battery of instruments biased for left-handers could be developed. The left-handers would probably prevail in this country.

Is the analogy to the currently used homogeneous grouping procedures in our schools a direct one? The role of the left-handers is played by our culturally privileged children. The role of the right-handers is played by the culturally disadvantaged students, among whom the racial minorities are disproportionately represented. The prime minister represents all those who, wittingly or unwittingly, would seek to stratify our educational system, separating those who have been placed in an advantageous position at birth from those who were not so fortunate. It is the authors' fear that educational measurement specialists are playing the role of the medical, biological, and psychological experts. When "IQ tests" and "social maturity inventories" are used to group a heterogeneous population of students, their unfairness to the culturally disadvantaged might be just as blatant as the

Southpaw Range of Ability Test and Manipulative Dexterity Test were to the right-handers. The analogy of left-handers to culturally privileged and "right-handers" to culturally deprived seems clear, but we must ask if the testing situations are also parallel.

In the hypothetical little country, placement in the schools was dependent primarily on *physical* ability. Some might argue that placement in the "homogeneous" groups[6] formed by current practices in this country is a completely different matter. Placement is based on tests which measure the same skills that the students will actually use. It could be argued that the "well-known IQ test" and the "social maturity inventory" are fair tests of the student's mental ability to perform in a school situation; but that the physical tests were not fair indicators of mental performance. After all, the tracking system pays off for mental ability, and placement should not be done through an unrelated attribute of the student. To top that off, the student presumably has no control over what his "handedness" is.

In defense of the analogy, however, it should be stressed that a child also has no control over the economic status of his parents, nor over his racial mixture or ethnic background. The analogy to "handedness" is direct. Are the physical tests in the hypothetical situation any less fair to the right-handers? The physically based tests are inherently and unfairly discriminatory to the right-handed pupils; are the "well-known IQ test" and the "social maturity test" likewise inherently and unfairly discriminatory to the culturally deprived pupils? Could a clever superintendent attempt to relegate these "childlike in their simplicity" culturally deprived students to the lower tracks by careful selection of the tracking criteria? Have school officials attempted to do this? This is where educational measurement enters the picture. Are educational measurement specialists being used to legally perpetuate a caste system?

Many have said that our educational system mirrors the middle-class culture in this country. The definition of "middle-class culture" is a nebulous thing. Studies have shown that a large proportion of the people believe they belong to the middle class.

---

[6] The proper term would be "less heterogeneous," but this practice gets cumbersome.

It should be noted that basing the educational system on the middle-class culture is not necessarily a bad or reprehensible thing. This orientation mirrors concepts and values which are fundamental to our democracy. Changing the orientation of some of these fundamental concepts could result in changing the direction of the Great Experiment of this country—an experiment which has been remarkably successful over these past two hundred years. To be sure, the total educational system is far from perfect. Changes in curriculum, instructional materials, administrative organization, methods of financing, plus many others should be constantly made to keep the total program in line with the needs of society. We should look very closely at suggestions which would alter fundamental beliefs.

To say that the system is difficult for the disadvantaged child, then, does not necessarily imply that we must change the system fundamentally. It means that procedures must be changed so that they are no longer unfair for these children. Upon what should these procedures focus? How is the system unfair? In particular, how is the unfairness reflected in ability tests? It is possible that the tests are intrinsically biased because they employ concepts and a vocabulary unfamiliar to children raised in poverty and cultural isolation from the middle classes.

Some educators may have the tendency at this point to say, "But this does not apply to *our* system, since here it is the teacher's decisions which are most important—test scores only play a supplementary role." But the same educators are often heard to say things like, "He is two grade levels behind in reading," or "His ability places him in the second stanine," or some other measurement-based statement. Test scores are on file; they are a comparison to a common criterion. The opinions of the teachers are not generally on file, and each teacher has his own criteria. Unless the administrator has a truly atypical program, it must be argued that test scores of all kinds are the single largest determinant of student placement in an ability grouping program.

SCHOLASTIC APTITUDE TESTS AND DISADVANTAGED CHILDREN

The charge that scholastic aptitude tests are unfair to disadvantaged children is well stated in a court opinion delivered by Judge J. Skelly Wright (*Hobson* v. *Hansen,* 209 Federal Supplement 401, 1967, p. 484). "[The plaintiffs] charge that the disadvantaged child's handicaps . . . are such that standard aptitude tests cannot serve as accurate measurements of innate ability to learn. In Dr. Cline's opinion [a witness for the plaintiff] these tests are worthless. The evidence that this is so is persuasive."

The plaintiffs in the *Hobson* case alleged that the school authorities were incapable of fulfilling their promise of determining the maximum potential of the students. Achievement tests, designed to measure the amount a student has attained from a given course of instruction, were not seriously challenged by the plaintiffs, but scholastic aptitude tests were. The plaintiffs argued that these tests cannot provide accurate information about the particular population at hand—heavily weighted with students from lower socioeconomic levels and with black students; and that, largely because of the presumed inadequacy of test scores for this special population, these students are being shortchanged by the educational system—undereducated. These two arguments should be considered very carefully, for they apply not only to the Washington, D.C., schools upon which the *Hobson* litigation was centered, but also to every school district which has a fairly large discrepancy between the highest and lowest socioeconomic levels of the district—and that must be a large proportion of the nation's schools.

A scholastic aptitude test is designed to predict future academic performance. The skills measured correlate highly with later scholastic achievement. Some tests have nonverbal elements (geometric drawings and number series, for example), but the tests are essentially verbal. Even nonverbal items have a verbal component, for the student must somehow receive the directions, and must make a mark which indicates which choice he thinks is correct. The distinction between verbal and nonverbal tests becomes essentially immaterial to the question of environmental bias, however, when it is noted that the skills required for success in the test are *not innate,* but are learned.[7] A scholastic aptitude

---

[7] Most educators and psychologists have dismissed the earlier theory that intelligence tests measure a fixed and unchangeable intellectual process. Recently, however, Jensen has questioned this view in at least two major articles. See Arthur R. Jensen, "Social Class, Race, and Genetics; Implica-

test, in short, can only measure the student's current performance level in certain skills, and predict from these what his future performance level will be.

When a student does obtain a low score on a scholastic aptitude test, so that we predict a low level of future attainment for him, the reasons are complex. Three of the most important possible causes are these:

1. Innate ability cannot be ruled out—individual differences exist. A student may score poorly on a scholastic aptitude test because he has limited intellectual capabilities.

2. If the test measures a learned skill, and if this skill is more likely to have been learned in one environment than in another, the low score might simply mean that this student was not born into the "right" environment. If the student has had no opportunity to learn the skills required, he obviously cannot perform well on the test.

3. Even though a test is designed to measure cognitive capacity, the affective factors cannot be ignored. The extent to which test-taking arouses certain emotional and psychological responses in the student is important. If the student's motivation to succeed is high enough to overcome weariness and frustration, he will give more correct answers than if his motivation is low.

Suppose the above discussion is summed up in this manner:

Premise: *Performance in scholastic aptitude tests is based on learned skills.*

It follows that in the long run, students who have had the greatest opportunity to learn the skills will perform at the highest level. This does not contradict the assumption of individual and innate differences. Students with low opportunity but high intellectual capacity can perform at a higher level than students with high opportunity but low capabilities.

---

tions for Education," *American Educational Research Journal,* 5:1–42, January 1968; and Arthur R. Jensen, "How Much Can We Boost IQ and Scholastic Achievement?", *Harvard Educational Review,* 39, 1969, 1–123; as well as the rejoinders to this article in the *Harvard Educational Review,* 39, Spring 1969.

It does not necessarily follow from the first premise that scholastic aptitude tests are biased against all children from the lower socioeconomic levels. Is this next premise still viable?

> **Premise:** *Performance in scholastic aptitude tests is based on learned skills; and these skills are more likely to have been learned in the higher socioeconomic environments.*

The premise does not say that the skills are of fundamental importance for all citizens. In the long run, students with the greatest opportunity to learn the skills will perform at the highest levels; and these students will tend to be disproportionately from the higher socioeconomic levels. If the affective factors are now added in, primarily the factor of high achievement motivation for students from higher socioeconomic levels, the possibility of an *artificial* bias against the one group of students is clear.

Remember that cultural bias in tests is distinct from the errors of measurement discussed earlier in the chapter. Errors of measurement are considered to be random—color blind and free from prejudice. The decision-maker should keep in mind that the cultural errors are *in addition to* the measurement errors discussed earlier. A further discussion of cultural bias may be found in chapter 11, statement no. 6.

ERRORS DUE TO USE OF IQ AS DETERMINANT

In the example illustrating measurement errors, the 75 students were grouped according to scores made on a mental aptitude test. But Mental Aptitude is not the name of the course under discussion—the course will be called either English or Language Arts. The test does measure mental aptitude in a relatively reliable manner, but it does not necessarily follow that the student with the best mental aptitude will be most able to succeed in the language arts course, or that the student who is second best on the mental aptitude test will be second best, and so forth. That is, the correlation between the *true* IQ's and the ability to fulfill the requirements of the language arts course is not perfect (+1.00).

Most reasonable people would conclude that *some* relationship exists between observed IQ scores and ability to succeed in the course, but the strength of the relationship depends partly on the specific requirements of *this* course.

EFFECTS OF MISPLACEMENT

The reason for ability grouping in the first place is to put each student in the group at a level where he can best fulfill the behavioral goals of the course. We have now discussed four kinds of errors common in ability grouping: (1) errors of measurement in the placement test; (2) errors due to too infrequent testing, (3) errors due to cultural bias in the test, and (4) errors due to the use of mental ability scores to predict success in a specific subject area. Clearly, when all the sources of error are taken into consideration, the number of misclassifications will be even greater than the 18.7 percent in the example of measurement error. It is impossible to escape the conclusion that as many as one out of every four pupils will be placed in the wrong group, based on their true ability in a specific course—some will be placed too high, and some too low. Teachers and administrators *must* be made aware of the magnitude of the misclassifications.

TEACHERS AND THE SELF-FULFILLING PROPHECY

In recent research carried out by Rosenthal and Jacobson (1968), the concept of a self-fulfilling prophecy was investigated. The basic premise of this work was that a student will perform at the level of achievement expected of him by the teacher. That is, through teacher-pupil interaction, the student becomes aware of the level of the teacher's expectations for him, and consequently performs at that level. The book by these researchers, cited in the references for this chapter, summarizes the results of their investigations. The data are not reported in an impartial manner, and in many situations one has the feeling that the results are *over*-interpreted. Nevertheless, their basic premise is at least in part supported by the reported experimental data. Even without the data, it is easy to see ways in which the expectations of the teacher influence the performance of the student.

Students will be misgrouped—perhaps with a frequency as high as one in four. Teachers will not know which students are misgrouped, and will have a very natural tendency to expect each child to perform at the level of his assignment. The research reported above indicates the distinct possibility that students who are incorrectly *under*-assigned will perform at this lower level, partly due to teacher expectation. Teachers *must* be made aware of the high frequency of misclassification, and must be admonished to look upon the groupings at all times as very tentative. Teachers must not look upon a child's ability as corresponding to the level of his present assignment, but must demand from the child performance comparable to his real ability.

There is a second reason for attuning teachers of homogeneously grouped students to the large number of misclassifications which probably exist. The teachers themselves must be the principal agents of change. If the teacher is aware of this important role, he will *actively seek out* misplaced students, rather than passively watch for them.

ADMINISTRATIVE CONSIDERATIONS

The magnitude of the proportion of misclassified students and the resulting deleterious effects on their achievement suggest two important implications for the school administrator who employs a system of homogeneous grouping. The first is that a review panel can best determine which students need to be changed to another level. The second is that certain curricula patterns work better than others in homogeneously grouped classes.

Review panel. Little information is available on the amount of level-shifting which does occur in districts currently using homogeneous grouping, but it would be surprising if it affected 5 percent of the enrollment. (See the discussion of *Hobson v. Hansen* in chapter 11.) Most changing, especially after the first month of school, is probably downward. The level of shifting should conceivably be very near the level of expected errors—that is, as many as 25 percent of the total enrollment should be shifted from one level to another during the course of any one year. To effect this, the review procedures cannot be left to the initiative of each teacher. This is not meant to imply that teachers are incapable of such activity, but systematic changes in an individual can often be overlooked in the day-by-day activities of the classroom, as well as through an unfortunate teacher-pupil interaction. Information from outside the classroom, unknown to the teacher, could also be important in a decision to shift a pupil. A teacher alone might hesitate in suggesting such a change for fear it was not an impartial conclusion, but a review panel would have more faith in the common convictions of the members.

This review panel should meet at fixed intervals—perhaps every four weeks. The panel might contain only one or two people besides the classroom teacher. The performance of each student in the period of four weeks or so should be reviewed to decide which students should be moved and which students the panel should gather more information about so that a move might be considered for the next review. The outside members of the review panel might be selected from the other teachers in the system—this is a good way to use and reward outstanding teachers. Student service personnel and administrative staff are also potential members.

Curricula for flexible grouping. The second implication deals with the program of study for the homogeneously grouped students. Consider Figures 9, 10, and 11, which are schematic diagrams of possible ways the curricula might be organized in a three-level grouping. To interpret these diagrams, assume that any units having the same name—such as Unit A—have the *same content*. Unit A' indicates the same content as Unit A but with increased depth, and Unit A'' indicates even more depth of presentation—more enrichment than Unit A'.

In Figure 9 the differentiation of programs for the three levels is through pacing. The upper group simply goes through the material more quickly than does the middle group, which in turn moves more quickly than the low group. In Figure 10 pacing is still partly in the picture, but each level has some aspects of its program which are unique to that level. The last figure indicates programs which are essentially parallel—at any given time during the year, roughly speaking, students at all levels are discussing the same concepts. The high group, to be sure, is investigating the concept more thoroughly, but the same general principles are being considered.

The relationship between the program's structure and problem of changing a student's level upward should be clear. In the system diagramed by Figure 9, a change as early in the year as November first will be doubly difficult for the student. In the first place the student will leave known surroundings to assimilate a whole new class environment, with its complex social structure. On top of this, when pacing differentiates levels this student will have to catch up with the more advanced class. He will need to quickly learn those concepts already discussed by the higher class, since they are necessary prerequisites for going on. Moving a child down might not be so traumatic, except that material

Figure 9
Differentiation of Programs of Study Through Pacing

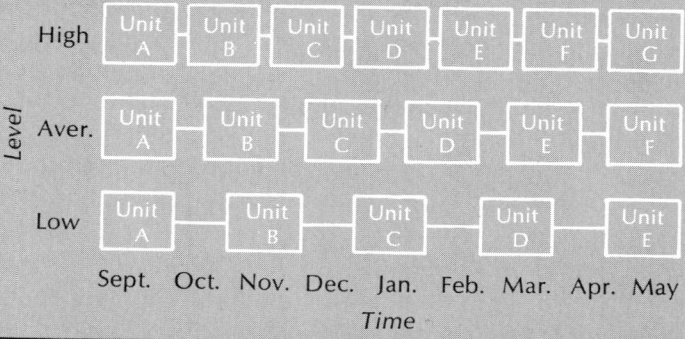

Figure 10
Differentiation of Programs of Study Through Pacing Plus Review

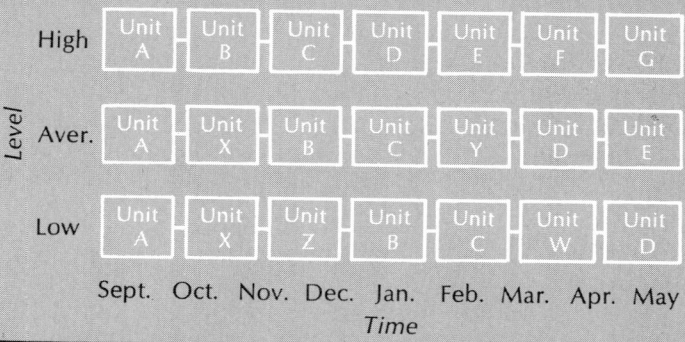

Figure 11
Differentiation of Programs of Study Through Increased Depth and Enrichment

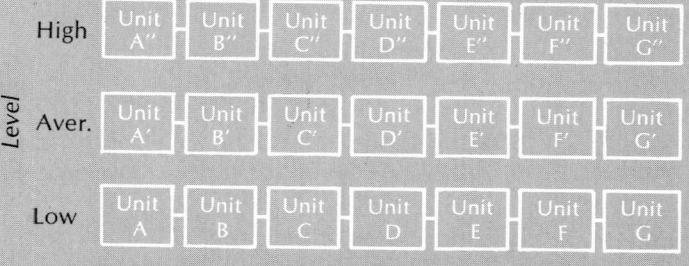

new to the lower group will be review for the shifted student. The program diagramed in Figure 10 has similar, although not as serious, restrictions for the student who would change levels. The seriousness depends upon the degree to which the heretofore unseen material is necessary sequentially.

If the school administrator admits that errors of classification will occur in homogeneous grouping and is willing to give more than lip service to the concept that continuous efforts will be made to have each student assigned to his most appropriate level, then the program of study outlined by Figure 11 is most appropriate. Here a student can move up or down one level without particular difficulty, since all levels are simultaneously working on the same general topics.

Of course, this program structure is more essential in courses which are quite sequential. Most mathematics programs are basically sequential, in that certain first steps must be passed before the next can be negotiated. This can also be said, to a lesser extent, of language arts programs, particularly at the lower elementary level. The curriculum structure schematized by Figure 11 is most essential when a course does have a sequential foundation, or when the teacher in the class requires that the incoming student be exposed to the material previously covered by the group.

SUMMARY

Ability grouping is one form of homogeneous grouping. This form of organization has been used extensively in this country at all levels of the school and in most instructional areas. Reports of research done in the area are sometimes confusing, even contradictory. A wag has said that a pro or con stand on any aspect of homogeneous grouping can be supported by research results. Teachers generally approve of ability grouping. The April 1969 issue of the *Phi Delta Kappan* reports that 60 percent of grade school teachers and 90 percent of high school teachers approve of ability grouping.

Each decision regarding ability grouping should be considered separately by the school's decision-makers. In each decision, the subject area, grade level of students, and degree of socioeconomic mix should be carefully weighed. School officials should carefully reexamine ability grouping in their districts since the possibility of detrimental effects on the student due to misplacement is very real.

In the reported research, placement procedures do not receive much emphasis, despite the fact that the placement procedures are the essence of the organizational structure. Errors will occur, and the percentage of such errors will be *much* larger than most administrators currently imagine. The errors will occur due to unavoidable measurement errors, too infrequent testing, cultural bias in the placement instruments, and inappropriateness of the criterion measures to a specific instructional program.

The school decision-maker should remember the three fundamental assumptions he is making when his district uses ability grouping, as outlined earlier in this chapter. Gross deviations in the district's ability to fulfill the assumptions can lead to harmful effects on certain subgroups of students, not to mention considerable unpleasantness for the school's administration.

It seems clear that teachers and administrators must devote more time and energy to finding misplaced students and getting them into the appropriate classrooms. To facilitate such shifting of students, it is suggested that the levels of study should be differentiated through greater depth and enrichment, and not through pacing. This suggestion need not be *rigidly* enforced from top to bottom, of course, since it will be a rare student who is misplaced by two levels, but adjacent levels should have programs which facilitate change. As an alternative to this, the school system could have teachers' aides available for tutorial help to students who are changing levels.

Finally, we would admonish the review panel not to adhere strictly to quantitative measures, especially in the face of an impoverished educational background. Although it has been difficult to document the extent to which cultural bias does exist in tests, a lack of evidence to the contrary does not prove the point. The committee should take socioeconomic background into consideration, to avoid the criticism that ability grouping is a cloaked form of economic and/or ethnic segregation. This concept is discussed from a legal viewpoint in chapter 11.

REFERENCES

Anderson, R. H. "Organizing Groups for Instruction," in *Individualizing Instruction*, Sixty-First Yearbook of the National Society for the Study of Education, 1961.

Borg, W. R. "Ability Grouping in the Public Schools," *The Journal of Experimental Education* 34 (Winter 1965): 1–97.

Braun, R. H. "Homogeneous Grouping and Acceleration," *Bulletin of the National Association of Secondary School Principals* 43 (January 1959): 255–257.

Conant, J. B. *The American High School Today*. New York: McGraw-Hill, 1969.

Cronbach, Lee J. *Essentials of Psychological Testing*, pp. 129–130. New York: Harper & Row, 1960.

Deitrich, F. R. "Comparison of Sociometric Patterns of Sixth-Grade Pupils in Two School Systems: Ability Grouping Compared with Heterogeneous Grouping," *Journal of Educational Research* 57 (July–August 1964): 507–513.

Drews, E. M. *Student Abilities, Grouping Patterns, and Classroom Interactions*. East Lansing, Mich.: Office of Research and Publications, Michigan State University, 1963.

Eash, M. J. "Grouping: What Have We Learned?" *Educational Leadership* 18 (April 1961): 429–434.

Ekstrom, R. B. "Experimental Studies of Homogeneous Grouping: A Critical Review," *School Review* 69 (1961): 216–226.

Ellers, A. "San Angeles Three-Rail Program," *American School Board Journal* 149 (1964): 11–12.

Goldberg, M. L., A. H. Passow, and J. Justman. *The Effects of Ability Grouping*. New York: Teachers College Press, 1966.

Goodlad, J. I. "Classroom Organization," pp. 223–225 in C. W. Harris, ed., *Encyclopedia of Educational Research*. New York: Macmillan, 1960.

Howell, W. J. "Influence of Curriculum Enrichment in a High School Honors Group on College Board Examination Scores," *Journal of Educational Research* 59 (November 1965): 113–114.

Kierstead, R. "A Comparison and Evaluation of Two Methods of Organization for the Teaching of Reading," *Journal of Educational Research* 56 (February 1963): 320–321.

Kincaid, D. J., and T. M. Epley. "Cluster Grouping," *Education* 81 (November 1960): 136–139.

Leton, D. A., and H. E. Anderson, Jr. "Discriminant Analysis of Achievement Characteristics for Multi-Grade Grouping of Students," *Journal of Experimental Education* 32 (Spring 1964): 293–297.

Millman, J., and M. Johnson, Jr. "Relation of Section Variance to Achievement Gains in English and Mathematics in Grades 7 and 8," *American Educational Research Journal* 1 (1964): 47–51.

Otis, A. S., and R. T. Lennon. *Otis-Lennon Mental Ability Test.* New York: Harcourt, Brace & World, 1967.

Otto, H. J. "Elementary Education—II, Organization and Administration," pp. 439–440 in W. S. Monroe (ed.), *Encyclopedia of Educational Research.* New York: Macmillan, 1941.

Phi Delta Kappan. "Ability Grouping: Good, Bad?" 50 (1969): 499.

Rosenthal, R., and L. Jacobson. *Pygmalion in the Classroom.* New York: Holt, Rinehart & Winston, 1968.

Thelen, H. A. *Classroom Grouping for Teachability.* New York: John Wiley & Sons, 1967.

West, J., and C. Sievers. "Experiment in Cross Grouping," *Journal of Educational Research* 54 (October 1960): 70–72.

Wick, J. W. In *An Evaluative Study of the Schools of School District 4,* p. 21. Barrington, Ill.: Field Services Committee, Northwestern University, 1968.

Wick, J. W., and R. E. Yager. "Some Aspects of the Student's Attitude in Science Courses," *School Science and Mathematics* 66 (March 1966): 269–273.

Wilcox, J. *A Search for Multiple Effects of Grouping upon the Growth and Behavior of Junior High School Pupils.* Unpublished doctoral dissertation, Cornell University, 1961.

EVALUATION AND IN-SERVICE PROGRAMS

Reasons for In-Service Education

Example of a Planned In-Service Program
Preparing the statement of goals
Stating outcomes behaviorally

Evaluation of the In-Service Program
Need for prior information
In-service and continuous assessment
Four areas to be evaluated

Education is a dynamic process. Some of us believe that the current level of change—the explosion of knowledge, the advances in technology, the increasing industrialization, the mobility of the populace, and the earlier maturity and sophistication of students—surpasses any other time in history. With the modern communication systems available to all, children today learn what is happening in remote corners of the world faster than it was possible in the past to find out the events in a nearby town.

Is change faster than it has ever been? Will even these heights be surpassed in the future? Even though they do not agree on the answers, most people will agree that change is occurring. The inevitability of change should be part of the school administration's decision-making process, and should be planned for.

One implication of constant change is that without continuous study, the teacher's knowledge and methods soon become out of date. It is not economically feasible to send all teachers back to college periodically; but it is not impossible to bring this new information (and review) into the school itself. Major curriculum reforms have taken place since many teachers finished their formal training, and knowledge in many subject matter areas has multiplied. Content once reserved for the higher grades may be moving to the lower levels.

Not only have there been curriculum and subject matter changes, but there have also been some relatively recent administrative reorganizations of the teaching staff. Many teachers have not learned how, and under what circumstances, team teaching is most effective, or about how to use teaching machines and programmed learning in their own programs. It is easy to inhabit a sort of educational island, remote from modern educational innovations. This isolation must be ended, for many researchers are convinced that good teaching has a high correlation with student achievement. In-service programs are designed to bring about ultimate changes in student behavior through changes in teacher behavior.

The evaluation of in-service programs, when it has been done at all in the past, has tended to be superficial. A frequent cause for this superficiality has been the lateness of the evaluator's entry on the decision-making scene. Evaluation, as we have stressed before, differs from research in the sense that the evaluator needs to be continually involved with the on-going program, whereas the researcher will generally remain away from this role. The evaluator needs to be a part of the group which specifies the general purposes of the program, designs techniques for implementing these, translates the general purposes into behavioral statements, and ultimately measures the level of attainment of these objectives. Each of these segments is discussed more fully in the sections which follow.

REASONS FOR IN-SERVICE EDUCATION

A very broad definition of in-service education would include *all of those activities engaged in by the professional staff during their service which are designed to contribute to their improvement on the job.* An in-service program can be a workshop prior to the opening of the school in the fall; it can take the form of meetings on specific topics during the school year; or an in-service program can consist of instruction in the workshop form, using university personnel.[1]

The evaluator must know *why* the district has initiated in-service activities. In the past, in-service activities have been initiated for one of these five general reasons:

1. Because continuous improvement of the district's professional staff is the goal, and the goal is important. Teachers, administrators, and special personnel should be constantly studying in order to keep up in their fields and to fill gaps in their education. Continuous in-service education is needed to keep the professional abreast of new knowledge, and to release his creative instructional abilities.

2. Because new teachers need continuing training as they begin their work. Most people currently make an artificial division between pre-service and in-service teachers. The pre-service teacher is the undergraduate, uncertified student; the in-service teacher is the graduate, certified professional. Does the act of obtaining proper certification make a former student an instant professional? The authors think not, and suggest that there should be a series of experiences planned for the newer members of the staff, designed to lead to

---
[1] For some other examples of workshop forms, see Haas (1957).

teaching competency. In fact, if an artificial dichotomy must exist, our suggestion would be to make a distinction between tenured and pre-tenured teachers, rather than between the in-service and pre-service stages.

The school district does not have to call in outside experts to deal with in-service training for new teachers. The experts are at hand—they are the experienced teachers in the district, the ones who have "been there." These personnel are in a position to make important contributions to the continuing development of the newer faculty, contributions that are only properly utilized if a framework for this process is established in the district. This, by the way, is one important way the district can reward its truly excellent teachers—by establishing them as part-time in-service directors. The position could be both economically and professionally rewarding.

3. Because of possible deficiencies in the backgrounds of staff members. A social studies teacher trained out of state may need some work on that state's history. The math teacher may need to teach some science, for which he has no background.

4. Because of job obsolescence. With change, job obsolescence often occurs, and the associated creation of new positions and new responsibilities. While some jobs are being eliminated, others are being created, and skills once sufficient are no longer adequate. The district must keep running full speed just to stay in the same place.

5. Because in-service programs have an important function in acquainting faculty members with each other. The staff has come, with varying viewpoints, from many different colleges and universities. Each year many teachers are carryovers from the year before, but some are new. If the administration "greases" the informal communication lines so that new teachers can help each other, the entire educational process will be improved.

EXAMPLE OF A PLANNED IN-SERVICE PROGRAM
The introduction to this chapter stressed the need for the early involvement of the program evaluator in the planning stage. The program evaluator does not have to be a person

from outside the district, nor must this be his only task within the program. At this point, we want to illustrate the process whereby the one charged with evaluation helps in the statement of the program, so that evaluation becomes more than superficial.

It is difficult to discuss program evaluation without focusing on one specific program. Since this is a measurement-oriented book, and since one often-needed topic for in-service programs is that of assessing student achievement, a small in-service program on that topic will be presented in some detail, to show techniques for program evaluation. The success of the program will depend to a great extent upon the clarity with which the planners state the program's purposes.

The topic of assessing student achievement is very broad. Topics such as educational objectives, stating behavioral objectives, purposes of achievement testing, different kinds of achievement testing items, scoring scales, reliability and validity considerations, and basic statistical procedures could be included. Unless the school district intends to excuse the entire staff for a quarter or a semester, all of these topics obviously cannot be included in a single in-service program.

Suppose it is assumed that the administrator of a specific district has taken to heart the exhortations of chapter 2 of this book; and has convinced himself that the manner in which students learn materials is, in fact, closely associated with the manner in which they are evaluated. He realizes that this implies that poorly conceived evaluation techniques will doom many of the larger objectives of the district to failure. To avoid this outcome, the in-service programs during the year will deal with educational measurement.

Before this specific program is defined, there are a series of issues related to creating an in-service program which need to be aired. These issues are only loosely related to the measurement theme of this book. Again, however, the program evaluator needs to know the procedures used to establish the program.

1. In the first place, the emotional climate which prevails in the in-service program is as important as the goals sought, and will be an important determinant of goal attainment. Emotional climate often relates to the degree of involvement of the participant. A program cannot be judged solely on its

goals; its value is also based on the degree of involvement, cooperation, and assistance of the participants, as well as the degree to which desired changes come about in their knowledge and behavior.

An important factor in participant-involvement is the degree to which the participants influence the planning stages. The purpose of this involvement in planning should not, however, be merely an attempt to placate teachers. If the general topic of the programs is to be educational measurement, the teachers probably have a better idea than the administration of the most critical specific questions which should be included in the program. The administrator may have a better perspective of the *general* needs of the teachers in the district, and it is appropriate for him to set the general topics. Within these general topics, however, the administration should encourage a high degree of teacher participation in the rest of the planning.

2. Individual differences exist among teachers, just as among students. An in-service program does not necessarily need to involve every teacher in the district. Not all teachers would want or need to participate in a program directed toward a new mathematics curriculum. An in-service program might be mandatory for the more recently hired teachers (say within the past three years) and optional to all others. Or there might be two programs operating simultaneously, with teachers given the option of choosing which to attend.

For the specific example of this section, the school administrator should prepare, or have prepared, a document which summarizes the field of educational measurement, including all of the subtopics which were mentioned earlier. Then a small committee consisting of teachers who represent different buildings, instructional areas, and instructional levels would discuss what the in-service program should accomplish.

3. It is important to remember, however, that where boundaries exist between what the teachers can suggest and what is reserved as administrative prerogative, these boundaries must be made very clear, or the very purpose of teacher involvement in planning will be negated. If the administration has decided that there will be an in-service program this year, and that the topic will be educational measurement, there is a clear implication that the teacher committee can-

not decide on a different topic or on eliminating the in-service activities completely. If the administration really does not care whether an in-service program occurs, or if the topic is really flexible, then the teacher committee should have this information. In any event, the guidelines must be clear and explicit to avoid the discontent resulting from a discrepancy between expectation and reality.

4. Although the potential participants must be involved, they cannot be expected to carry out all phases of planning an in-service program without some outside expertise. A neophyte pilot cannot plan his flight instruction, since he does not have a particularly clear picture of all aspects of flying or the difficulty of learning navigation, administrative procedures, or instrument manipulation. If the members of the planning committee have an incomplete understanding of educational measurement, they cannot be expected to make all the final decisions about time allocation, materials to procure, and instructional devices to be used.

PREPARING THE STATEMENT OF GOALS

The administration in the example set the topic of assessing student achievement. This topic is probably too broad for the normal sequencing of in-service meetings. If the teachers have been involved in planning, they will probably have steered the program more toward achievement measuring techniques and achievement score interpretation, with the result that the topic is narrowed to techniques for measuring achievement.

This title still gives no more than a vague idea about the content of the program. The planning is just starting. If the program is to be successful, far more detail must go into the statement of program goals. At this point, a statement about the program should be drafted, to include these sections:

1. Description of the program including statements of broad objectives.

2. For each broad objective, a series of specific statements of behavioral objectives (if possible), as well as the strategies which will be used to reach these objectives.

3. For each behavioral objective, a statement of the techniques which will be used to evaluate the degree of objective attainment.

Too many program directors stop with the first part of this document. It is the responsibility of the program evaluator to insure the completion of parts 2 and 3 as well. This is why the evaluator must get involved in even the earliest planning sessions.

This three-part statement will be quite lengthy for most programs. We shall not attempt to complete such a statement for our example, but it would be appropriate to at least begin the task. After all, the terms "clear," "explicit," "detailed," and "complete" will be more meaningful in the context of an example. We shall take a broad objective, translate it into behavioral language, suggest strategies which should lead to the attainment of the objective, and outline the evaluation technique to be used to determine whether the strategies have been successful.

> **Objective no. 1:** *The participants will become familiar with the major types of achievement tests, as well as with the situations for which each type is most appropriate.*

This is a broad objective. It is not behavioral. You can test its "behavioralness" by asking two questions: Given this objective, would any two program directors necessarily plan similar content for the program? Given this objective, would any two program evaluators necessarily design similar evaluation programs? The answer to both questions is negative. What does "become familiar with" mean? Would there be agreement on the "major types" of achievement tests? Would all writers and evaluators agree on the "situations for which each type is most appropriate"? How shall the objective be evaluated—with an oral exam, a multiple choice test, or observations in the classroom?

If the objective had been stated in behavioral terms, all program directors or program evaluators would have a pretty clear picture of what the participants would be *doing* when they fulfilled the objective. Such statements have action verbs. They describe observable acts by the participants. Suppose we begin translating this broad objective into behavioral terms:

> *A. The participant should be able to recall at least seven different achievement test formats.*

B. Given an achievement test format, the participant should be able to recognize the major use for that format.

C. Application: Given a short paragraph describing a situation where an evaluation is necessary, the participant should be able to supply the most appropriate achievement test format for that situation.

The decision regarding method of evaluation should not be arrived at capriciously. Some evaluators get stuck on one recall format, and would use, for example, supply-type items to the exclusion of multiple choice, matching, or true-false questions. Other evaluators ignore supply-type items completely, and base all items on a recognition format. A large proportion of standardized achievement tests are totally based on recognition, the most common form of which is multiple choice.

It is improper to become locked into a format without considering the interaction between format and objective. The objective comes first, and the format must follow. The objective must be stated without the constraint of a previously determined format.

It is not uncommon to hear some modern-day reformer comment with disdain: "That is just a recall item," implying that recall items are currently in bad repute. Complete dependence upon recall items will not encourage some higher levels of learning, but it is nevertheless necessary to have certain working information available—a citizen probably needs to know the multiplication tables, his telephone number, the time work begins, names of certain people, just to mention a few recall items. When a student does a laboratory experiment, he is more efficient if he can recall the names of the pieces of apparatus he is using, so that constant rechecks in the glossary are unnecessary. There are countless situations in which recall is most convenient. In stating objective A, the committee felt that in planning tests, teachers would not refer back to notes for the different item formats. It is more likely that the proper format will be used if the participant is able to recall its possibilities.

Another comment is appropriate regarding objective A. Note that the objective is stated in terms of minimum performance. Most sixth-grade students can solve simple multiplication problems; but few could solve five hundred such problems without a single error. Such an objective would be unreasonable, given the propensity of the human animal to make occasional errors on routine tasks. Objective A states that the expectation is that seven achievement test formats would be recalled out of perhaps eight different forms presented.

Objective C illustrates another key aspect of writing behavioral objectives. It is often important to state the *conditions of performance*. An objective such as "the student should be able to compute the standard deviation of six numbers" is not complete enough. What are the conditions? Will they be allowed to use a book? Will the formula be provided? Will a table of square roots be available? The pertinent conditions should be stated. Objective C is an application item. The participants will be expected to use the information provided in the in-service program. The stimulus provided will be a short paragraph; it might also have been a video presentation, a short play, an oral presentation, or a combination of these. The choice of presentation can often affect the responses, and should therefore be made explicit.

> **Strategy for objective attainment:** *The participants will first assemble in groups of seven or eight. A group leader will be designated in advance. Independently, each group will construct a list of achievement test formats, along with the major use for each format. The designated leader will have available a list constructed by an evaluation specialist, but this list will only be used after the group has made its own listing. This initial meeting will conclude after forty-five minutes, at which time the entire group of participants will reassemble. At this time, a composite list will be constructed from the individual group lists, and the group leader will lead a question-and-answer session.*

The strategy may seem very inefficient. To save time, why not just provide each participant with the original list, prepared by the specialist? Clearly, though, it is one thing to be handed such a list, prepared by others; it is another thing to participate in the preparation of the list. The second act demands a much higher level of involvement—which is one of the conditions for a successful in-service program. A second objective, as stated previously, is increased socialization among the staff. This strategy of instruction will oil the communication lines, especially if the groups are assembled at random.

The planners should state all necessary broad objectives, followed by appropriate behavioral objectives (if possible) and the strategies of instruction. This design phase should precede the first meeting of the in-service program, and should be done by a group which includes substantial representation of likely participants who work in close cooperation with the program evaluator. The advantage of having someone with evaluation expertise in the planning group should be apparent.

STATING OUTCOMES BEHAVIORALLY

This topic has come up before, in chapters 1 and 2, but it is such a pervasive one that some comments are appropriate at this time. Many administrators will argue, legitimately, that their overriding goals for staff development are so wide that behavioral outcomes using verbs such as "recall" or "explain" cannot possibly deal with their implications. And this may well be so.

As a matter of fact, it is probably true that the more abstract an objective is, the more difficult it is to state it in behavioral terms. The most important objectives of the school —"to develop good citizenship" or "to prepare students for the fullest possible individual fulfillment," for instance—are virtually impossible to state behaviorally. These notions are certainly true; and they give one type of educator grounds for saying: "Since I can't state these important objectives behaviorally, there is no use trying to state any objectives behaviorally."

On the other hand, there is this abstractionist's opposite— probably even more annoying—who is responsible for statements like: "If you can't state it in behavioral terms you don't really know what you're talking about," and "If the objective cannot be stated in behavioral terms you should not attempt to teach it."

Both are wrong, and as in so many other situations, a happy medium is best. In the in-service program we have outlined, there are probably some objectives of the planning committee which will be difficult to state in behavioral terms. Yet if they are objectives, there is no need to be ashamed of them.

For example, the planners might like to have the participants *appreciate* the relationships of objectives, strategies, and evaluation. "Appreciation" is slightly different from "explaining" or "recalling." When the teacher appreciates a thing, he might discuss it favorably with colleagues or with students, or might pay closer attention to an article on testing seen in the Sunday supplement or a professional journal. There are some intangible correlates of increased appreciation. Again, purists might say these descriptive comments are simply behavioral statements of what appreciation really means. But no listing of possibilities of appreciation can possibly capture the implications of the word.

The abstractionist may not be quite as annoying (for he really does not threaten us too much; if one sets out to "make a better world" in a half-day workshop, who is to say what failure is?). But he is probably more likely to doom in-service efforts to failure than is his opposite. In the vernacular of the young, the abstractionist is copping out. It is difficult to state goals in behavioral terms, and it can be very threatening. Far better to say: "We intend to instill in our teachers a complete understanding and appreciation of educational measurement concepts for the good of our students." The local weekly paper will eat it up and the taxpayers will get a warm feeling way down deep. But if that beautiful statement is translated into a couple of boring two-hour lectures, participants must wonder about the creditability of this administration.

The point is that one really cannot expect to bring about vast changes in fundamental philosophical viewpoints, or drastic changes in teacher behavior patterns, in a few in-service workshops, but worthwhile changes can certainly occur. Many of these will *not* defy behaviorally oriented statements.

EVALUATION OF THE IN-SERVICE PROGRAM

Evaluation is the central concern of this chapter, yet we have been dealing so far with planning an in-service program and stating proposed goals clearly. It should be clear how these elements relate to program evaluation. *If the purposes for having the programs are carefully stated, and especially if they can be stated in behavioral terms, the evaluation needed will be obvious.*

Behavioral objectives use words like "recall," "explain," "differentiate," "outline," "list," and "state." If they had been less clear words such as "understand" or "know," the participants would not have known exactly what the planners had in mind. Neither would the planners; and the program evaluator would be especially puzzled.

The program outline for an educational measurement in-service program could, in theory, have some additional implications. The administrator surely did not want the teachers to merely *learn* about the concepts of measuring change, proper use of evaluation types, and so forth; he was really more interested in having them *use* this knowledge in their classrooms. He might say: "You teachers better use this new knowledge in your classrooms because I'm going to be checking up on you," in which case (assuming the teachers had some respect for his authority) many would do it—but this is a rather heavy-handed approach.

It seems to the authors that it is important to actually measure the degree to which the behaviorally stated goals have been reached by the end of the in-service program. If the teachers have reached the knowledge levels that were prescribed and still do not use these additional tools for the improvement of the evaluation process, it is not out of lack of understanding or knowledge, but due to a rational decision to ignore these devices. The teacher, as a professional, is accountable to his students, and the day-by-day classroom program is the teacher's responsibility, not the administrator's. The administrator has fulfilled his responsibility to provide in-service instruction in a needed area. He can only force the teacher to use this new information with great difficulty.

NEED FOR PRIOR INFORMATION

In order to detect change after the program, it is necessary to have data available for a period prior to the in-service training. This pre-program information should be based on the same behaviorally stated questions that the planning committee has written for the program.

As with continuous assessment, the number of people tested should not be larger than necessary for the task. There is really no sense testing all the teachers who will participate in an in-service program, especially if this number is substantial. A sample of fifteen teachers (if it is a random sample, chosen by lots) will provide a relatively accurate estimate of the knowledge level of the group. If the program's behavioral outcomes are directed toward groups, so that the evaluation needed is obvious, it really is very easy and non-threatening to gather the information from a small group of teachers. It can provide important information about the effectiveness of the program.

IN-SERVICE AND CONTINUOUS ASSESSMENT

Of course, if the district has inaugurated a continuous assessment program in all the important data areas of the school program, much of the pre-test information would already be available. Under such a scheme, it might not even be necessary to have special evaluation for an in-service program; these data would be coming in on a regular and planned basis, and not only would prior knowledge be available, but information about the impact of the program and how lasting its effects were would be automatically accruing.

Continuous assessment could also be looked upon as a device to determine the particular areas in which the staff is in need of in-service training. With the example used in this chapter, it was assumed that the school administrator decided, on the basis of subjective evidence, that educational measurement training was needed. If he were studying small groups from his professional staff at periodic intervals, the administrator would be able to obtain more solid information about the teachers' knowledge of topics like educational measurement, programmed instruction, and the audiovisual program in the district, to mention a few.

FOUR AREAS TO BE EVALUATED

This chapter's example did not encompass all the diverse objectives decision-makers have in mind when an in-service program is conceived. There are other objectives; and some of these are more difficult to evaluate (since they are somewhat more difficult to state in behavioral language). In general, in-service program goals will fall under one of these headings:

Changes in knowledge and/or skills of the participants. These, of course, lend themselves quite nicely to behaviorally oriented statements and evaluations. Most in-service programs are not directed solely toward these goals; however, the great majority of them have *some* objectives that deal with increased knowledge and skill and that can be stated behaviorally.

Changes in attitudes and values affecting behavior. Perhaps the word "changes" is not always appropriate, since one goal of an in-service program might be to solidify existing (presumably desirable) attitudes. These are much more difficult to state behaviorally; but this is not always impossible.

Without getting too technical about it, a *behavior* is the response to some stimulus. In the laboratory, the stimulus can be controlled, and can be a simple thing. But a stimulus in the real world is complex. For example, the stimulus situation might be "a classroom setting where, at this very moment, a good evaluation would be very beneficial to many of the students." There are two extremes of response possibilities. The teacher responds to the situation by showing awareness of the evaluation need, and by selecting the most appropriate of the possible evaluation techniques; or the teacher may not respond in this desired manner .

Researchers (and in this case the school administrator) are most interested in the response which will occur in this *real* situation. But this will be very difficult to obtain data on, for a number of reasons, namely:

A. For one thing, the reseacher would have to stay in the teacher's classroom until the opportunity presented itself. The "complex stimulus situation" here cannot be a planned thing, but will just happen at its own proper time. If the researcher feels he must have data on more than one such event before his results can be valid, and if in addition there are a substantial number of teachers involved in the study, the time commitment may be prohibitive.

B. In addition, assuming that the researcher and/or the school administrator *did* take the time to wait for these events to occur so that the responses could be tabulated, it would be very difficult to avoid interacting with the situation. Many observers will say that after a certain amount of time in a classroom, "The students forget I am even observing." How many hours must an observer be in a classroom before the students really forget he is there? Does it ever *really* happen completely? Does the teacher respond to the students in the same way when the observer is present? Some may argue that an observer can be unobtrusive; we are not so sure. It seems highly possible that the teacher will make the "socially desirable response" when the observer is present: and the "typical response" when the observer is gone.

C. Teachers are professionals. A classroom teacher knows the students and the climate of that classroom far better than the administrator or researcher does. If the classroom teacher simply does not *know* about the proper selection and use of appropriate evaluation techniques, that is one thing. The administrator should make it possible for the teacher to have this needed information. If the teacher chooses not to use them, that is another matter. This choice is based on better information on that classroom than the administrator has. The point is that if placing an observer in the room is construed as a threat to the teacher's classroom decision-making authority, the administrator might do well to consider this action very carefully.

So let us assume that, for one reason or another, it is very difficult for the researcher to place himself in a position to observe the real life stimulus and response.

The researcher now attempts to devise a similar, but artificial situation which is easier to observe. Instead of waiting for the situation to occur in the classroom, the teacher is asked "What would you do under these conditions . . . ?" and the situation needing evaluation is described orally or in print. The response is also artificial. The teacher's *real* response to the stimulus is not seen; only the response the teacher *says* he would make. There are many reasons teacher's actual behavior may differ from this response:

A. The artificial stimulus setting may not be appropriate to the complex situation the researcher is attempting to measure. Possibly the words and pictures, or whatever is used in the artificial stimulus, simply cannot make even an approximation of the real classroom situation, and the results will be suspect.

B. It may also be very difficult to approximate the entire domain of possible real response situations. The real desired behavior of (1) noting the need for an evaluation, (2) choosing the proper one, and (3) using it correctly is complex and takes time and effort. Very little time and effort is required to answer a question on an artificial questionnaire. The respondent might be prefacing all answers with "I know in this situation it would be *desirable* to . . ."; but that is not the same as actually *doing* the desirable act. By the way, this prefacing may not be done out loud; and the respondent might not even know he is doing it.

C. There is another reason for a low relationship between a person's *attitude* and *behavior* (that is, he does not do what he says or implies he would do in a given situation). This involves ignorance. Ask a man if he will support a bond issue, without any other information, and he may answer "yes." When he learns more details of the issue, however, he may change his mind. In the situation discussed in this chapter, the teacher might say he will use the proper evaluation techniques, and know what these procedures are. But he may not know how much work this really is, and may change his mind when he finds out. By and large, the more the respondent knows about and has thought about the topic of the question, the closer will be the relationship between his attitudes and his behaviors.

D. There is, obviously, the issue of "social acceptability" of a response. It is not always acceptable to say one would fight vigorously the introduction of a certain ethnic or racial group into the neighborhood, or that one would have an extramarital affair if the opportunity presented itself, even if these were exactly what the person would actually do. Thus if the artificial situation demands a possibly "value laden" response, there may be a difference between attitude and behavior.

E. Finally, people do change—sometimes quickly. On payday a man might support the bond issue; on the 25th of the month, when the bank account is sick, he might not support it. He might support it at 10:00 a.m., but not at 3:30 p.m., when the day is beginning to wear a little. He might support it in a discussion with his boss; he might not support it in a discussion with the boys at the local tavern. On some issues people are less changeable than others, of course; but there can be differences in attitude and behavior due to this "probabilistic" characteristic of the animal.

None of the above should be construed as a complete negation of any attempt to predict behavior through the use of artificial situations. These types of measurements are important, and when measurement in the real situation is impossible, partial measurement is better than none at all.

There is at least one other important way that researchers "approximate" a person's behavior response in the face of a stimulus (when this actual stimulus-response is difficult to observe). Instead of trying to *mirror* the situation in some sort of artificial manner, he attempts to find *correlates* of this behavior. Would a pilot act irrationally if two of his four engines suddenly quit? Who knows—and the airline is not going to take the chance of staging such an event just to see what happens. However, suppose it is observed that people who are given to irrational acts also answer affirmatively to statements such as: "Some days I feel as though no one cares for me," and "Most laws are made for secret reasons"; whereas people who tend to act rationally will answer in the negative. Now the airline might administer such a test to potential pilots, and simply eliminate all those whose answer patterns mirror those of the irrational group.

This technique is widely used, and can provide useful information. There are some obvious drawbacks, however. How was the irrational group for the test situation defined? Are they defined by political conservatives as anyone who is a political liberal? There does not seem to be much correlation between being a political liberal and going to pieces in the cockpit of an airplane. There is a problem in defining the term—which is one reason this kind of approximation of a real situation sometimes breaks down. In addition, this type of survey has been shown to be fakeable. If a man wanted to show that he was "rational" (or "masculine," or "democratic," or some such term), it is apparently possible for him to see the implications of most questions, and answer them accordingly.

It is important to seek out changes in attitudes and values, for they do imply certain behaviors. The authors believe that it is also important for the school decision-maker to know the limitations of these measures, so that these limitations can be taken into the decision-making process.

Changes in personal relationships. This involves the relationship between the individual and the group, as well as individual motives and aspirations. This particular aspect can generally be a part of all in-service programs, even those which are primarily directed toward changes in knowledge and skills. In-service programs generally involve some kind of group interaction, and it is reasonable to assume that when the individuals on the staff know each other better, a more harmonious teaching climate will exist.

Changes in student behavior. This involves the evaluation of programs specifically directed toward changing the behavior of the students. That is, the program is directed toward the teachers; the effects on the students are supposed to occur through the effects of the program on the teachers. It is probably true that all in-service programs have as a final goal some sort of salutary effect on the students. Once again, however, the impact may be relatively small on the teachers (for instance, a one-day workshop on improving race relations). This small impact must then filter through the teachers, so the effects on the students may not be substantial. Add to this the difficulty of measuring such a concept in the first place, and the problem is somewhat like measuring a diamond with boxing gloves on. However, such indirect effects of a program can be measured over a period of time. This was discussed in chapter 2 in the example of student participation in extracurricular events.

Why should teachers be better at evaluation? So that they can improve the entire instructional process. This implies that better evaluators will have more learning going on in their classrooms than will poorer evaluators. Will we be able to detect the differences? Possibly . . . but the difficulties are legion. Change is difficult to measure when both pre-measurement and post-measurement are subject to error; evaluation expertise is only a small part of total teacher competence; the teacher may have little opportunity to make his expertise count in the instructional program; and so forth.

It would be ideal to measure the effects of a program on the students themselves, and not infer success from measurements made on the teachers. But this is generally pretty difficult. The administrator usually has to *assume* that improvement in a teacher's evaluation skills will lead to an improvement in his instructional skills, and finally to higher levels of learning in the pupils. Generally, the change in the teacher *can* be measured.

REFERENCES

Anderson, Robert H. "The Influence of an In-Service Program upon Teacher Test Behavior and Classroom Practices," *Journal of Educational Research* 44 (Nov. 1950): 205–215.

Clark, Maurice P., and Donald W. Nylin. "In-Service Education/ Tapping the Teacher Reserve," *Illinois Education* 50 (March 1962): 290–291.

Dagne, Frank A., and Carol Bales. "An Innovative TV In-Service Program," *Illinois Education* 57 (March 1969): 274–277.

Haas, C. Glen. "In-Service Education Today," in Nelson B. Henry (ed.), *In-Service Education for Teachers, Supervisors, and Administrators*. Chicago: University of Chicago Press, 1957.

Herrick, Virgil E. "The Evaluation of Change in Programs of In-Service Education," in Nelson B. Henry (ed.), *In-Service Education for Teachers, Supervisors, and Administrators*. Chicago: University of Chicago Press, 1957.

Jardine, Alex. "Current Practices for In-Service Education," *Nation's Schools* 46 (July 1950): 36.

Kinnick, B. Jo. "The Teachers and the In-Service Education Program," in Nelson B. Henry (ed.), *In-Service Education for Teachers, Supervisors, and Administrators*. Chicago: University of Chicago Press, 1957.

Maves, Harold J. "Insight Through In-Service," *Today's Education* 58 (April 1969): 42.

Parker, J. Cecil, and William P. Golden, Jr. "In-Service Education of Elementary and Secondary School Teachers," *Review of Educational Research* 22 (June 1952): 193–200.

Telfer, Richard G. "Staff Involvement: Key to Curriculum Improvement," *Clearing House* 43 (May 1969): 539–542.

Thorndike, Robert L. "Reviews: Pygmalion in the Classroom," *American Educational Research Journal* 5 (Nov. 1968): 708–711.

STAFF ATTITUDE AND MORALE

The Concept of Morale

Measuring Staff Morale
The interview
The questionnaire

Research About Morale in Schools
Work environment and morale
Teacher characteristics and morale
Decision-making, expectations, and morale
Curriculum development and morale
Student-teacher relationships and morale
Salary and morale
Performance and morale

The Attitude Survey
Coughlan's school survey: An example
Categories of survey findings
Deficiencies in the survey technique
Effective use of the survey

Continuous Assessment of Staff Morale

The school administrator's decisions affect a myriad of personalities. Other administrators may approve of a particular decision but the special professionals (school psychologist, guidance personnel, etc.) may not agree. The teachers may be pleased, but the maintenance crew displeased. How important is it that decisions be viewed favorably? What factors affect morale, anyway? How can we conceptualize morale; how can we measure it? How can *measurements* of staff morale and staff attitude be used to improve staff relations?

Much has been written about staff morale in industrial as well as educational settings. There is much variety, however, in the terminology used in these reports and in the way the construct "morale" is conceptualized.

THE CONCEPT OF MORALE

In a certain sense, the school administrator can be looked upon as an employer. The concept of employee morale, attitudes, and job satisfaction has been a subject of much inquiry. These are nebulous topics, and the individual researchers begin their investigations with a variety of philosophical orientations. Although each is slightly different, it is possible to categorize the approaches under four headings.

The work group. First, there is a group of researchers who have focused their attention on the *work group*. In terms of the school, one such work group is the teachers. If the work group of researchers[1] can be extrapolated from industry to education, we can conclude that it is more important for teachers to feel that they are a special and unique work group than for them to have improved working conditions. These studies have also suggested that a person's evaluation of his job status is related to good morale, as is his feeling that the organization's representatives (the superintendent, principal, etc.) look upon his group with respect and favor. All of these morale increasers focus on the group. In general, these investigations suggest that the morale of a

---

[1] See the work of Elton Mayo (1933) and Roethlisberger and Dickson (1941), which centered on the Hawthorne Plant of Western Electric (the famous Hawthorne Effect).

We are indebted to Professor Robert J. Coughlan of Northwestern University who wrote or outlined most of this chapter.

group of teachers will be enhanced if the group is characterized as being socially cohesive and cooperative.

Acceptance of the organization's goals. A second group of researchers has emphasized the link between an individual's morale and the extent of his identification with and acceptance of the organization's goals. This group of theoreticians tells us that if the teacher knows the organization's goals and accepts these goals as his own, good morale is more likely to occur. This notion of identification goes further than the "good group rapport" focus of the first approach.

"Identification with and acceptance of the organization's goals" is pretty tough to pin down; and recent writers have extracted three variables from the general statement.[2] We shall attempt to illustrate these in a school situation. If a teacher feels that his personal and social needs can be satisfied by his job, this teacher is exhibiting "belongingness." But his particular job must be more than a job in which he expects to achieve success; his job must be *rational*. That is, the teacher must also see his own job as being logically appropriate to the achievement of the organization's goals. A school secretary might accept the goals of the school as congruent with her own, but could have low morale if she believes her job is not important to the achievement of these goals.

Even when a teacher feels he belongs (can obtain satisfaction in the job), and in addition is convinced *his* job is important to the achievement of the organization's goals, he may still manifest poor morale if the organization's goals are not an integral part of his own needs and values. A black teacher, for example, might feel confident of having success in his job and obtaining satisfaction, and in addition be convinced that he is an important member of the team. However, if for some reason the implicit goals of the school conflict with his own value system, he is likely to manifest low morale. For example, he might perceive the school as perpetuating a white, middle-class culture. We say he cannot *identify* with the organization's overall goals.

The organization as the unit of analysis. A third approach

---

[2] The "three-variable" approach is based on the work of Getzels, Lipham, and Campbell (1968).

stresses the organization once more, and in fact takes the organization as the unit of analysis. These researchers, if asked to survey the morale in a school district, would go around asking teachers questions such as "What do you think of the principal of this school—his competence, communication skills, and personal practices?" They would look at the prestige the teacher gets from his job, as well as his satisfaction with pay and working conditions. With the organization as the unit of analysis, research has suggested that both the formal and *informal* organizational structures must be heeded. A memo is a representation of the formal organization; an exchange of ideas over coffee is a part of the informal organization.[3]

Individual job adjustment. A fourth approach to the study of morale has been the springboard for much recent research. Instead of focusing on the group or the organizational structure, this group of researchers has considered the link between level of morale and the individual's adjustment to the job.

The number of basic needs that teachers seem to have depends on which authority one is quoting. Maslow (1954) suggests five basic needs which are hierarchical—that is, the second need requires that the first be fulfilled, the third requires fulfillment of one and two, and so forth.[4] One way a school administrator can get at discrepancies between needs and reality in his staff is suggested by industrial investigations stimulated by the Maslow theory. The superintendent can define a concept such as "opportunity to participate in curriculum decisions." The staff answers three questions about the concept: "How much is there now?" followed by "How much should there be?" and finally "How important is this to me?" The answers are valued on a seven-point scale, beginning with "very much" and ending with "very little." If there is a large difference between what the respondent *perceives* as his opportunity to participate in curriculum

---

[3] The studies of Burns (1951–1952), Baehr and Renck (1968), and Coughlan (1968) are representative of the approach to morale study based on the organization as the unit of analysis.

[4] The suggested categories are (beginning with the most basic) physiological, safety, belonging and love, ego (self- and other-esteem), and self-actualization. Porter and Lawler's research (1968) is based on this theory and has been done in industrial settings.

decisions and his *desires* to participate, we can conjecture that this respondent is not satisfied in this area.[5]

A second way the school administrator can conceptualize the extent of a staff member's adjustment to his job is best illustrated with the diagram in Figure 12. The formulation[6] makes two interesting distinctions. It says that if the primary goal of the school administrator is to *avoid dissatisfaction* in his staff, he might consider concentrating on the work context—the teacher's worldly needs, and the need for good and pleasant working conditions. If the school administrator wishes to have staff members who are satisfied with their jobs, he might concentrate on what might be termed the "professional fulfillment" motivators. It is worthwhile to

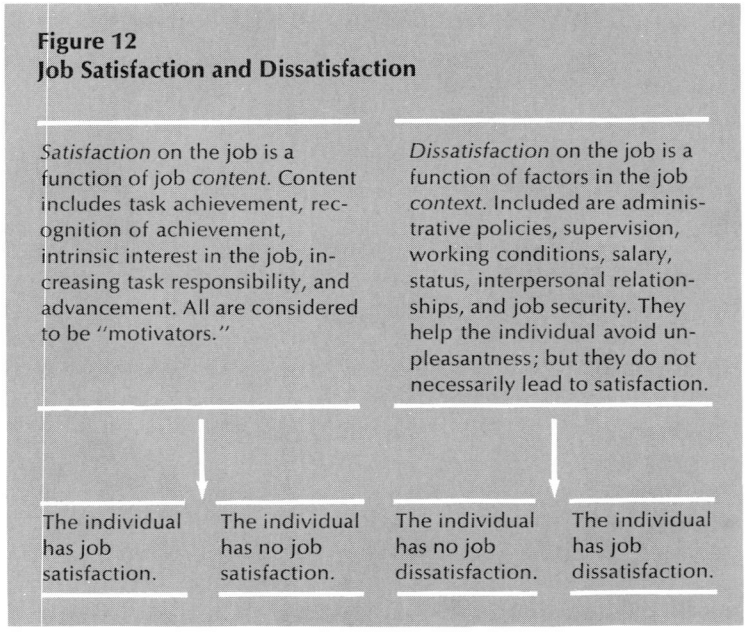

**Figure 12
Job Satisfaction and Dissatisfaction**

Satisfaction on the job is a function of job *content*. Content includes task achievement, recognition of achievement, intrinsic interest in the job, increasing task responsibility, and advancement. All are considered to be "motivators."	*Dissatisfaction* on the job is a function of factors in the job *context*. Included are administrative policies, supervision, working conditions, salary, status, interpersonal relationships, and job security. They help the individual avoid unpleasantness; but they do not necessarily lead to satisfaction.
The individual has job satisfaction. / The individual has no job satisfaction.	The individual has no job dissatisfaction. / The individual has job dissatisfaction.

---

[5] The discussion seems to be based on a respondent. It is generally not wise to use small groups of respondents, for anonymity must be maintained if the answers are to be considered unbiased. This point is discussed in greater detail presently.

[6] Due to Herzberg et al. (1959). More than twenty-five studies have been conducted with the explicit purpose of testing the validity and generality of this theory, which is called the "motivation-hygiene" theory.

consider the possibility that one group of events or practices can lead to satisfaction, but the absence of these factors does not necessarily lead to dissatisfaction; while a second group of events or practices can lead to dissatisfaction, but the absence of these factors does not necessarily lead to satisfaction. The school administrator must remember that: *When dissatisfaction is absent in the district, it does not necessarily follow that satisfaction is present.* The entire staff may be in middle ground. They are not satisfied; but then they are not dissatisfied, either.

Definition of morale. The terms *work attitude, job satisfaction,* and *morale* have been only implicitly defined in this discussion, and before leaving this section it would be well to define morale.[7] Our definition follows Guion (1958): *Morale is the extent to which an individual's needs are satisfied and the extent to which the individual perceives that satisfaction as stemming from his total job situation.* The definition implies that (a) morale is not a single dimension, but consists of many components; (b) morale is an individual attribute, although the organization does play a significant role; (c) morale is a function of the specific job situation, and not a generalized trait in the individual; and (d) morale can be defined in terms of human needs and the environmental sources of satisfaction of these needs.

MEASURING STAFF MORALE

In the next section of this chapter we will discuss some of the more important findings of research done on employee and teacher morale. First, however, it would be useful to outline the methods commonly used in such research. There are two basic instruments used to measure staff morale: the interview and the questionnaire.

THE INTERVIEW

Although widely used in measuring morale, interviews are expensive and time-consuming. For these reasons findings are seldom based on interviews with an organization's total population; instead, a sample is taken.

---

[7] Other definitions, quite similar to ours, have been set forth by Insko (1967), Getzels and Guba (1957), Morse (1953), Blum (1956), and Guba (1958).

In a *structured* or directive interview, the interviewer works from a schedule or list of questions in an attempt to standardize the interview procedure. The results of this type of interview are somewhat quantitative in nature and are often based on a framework for interpreting the data.

The *unstructured* or nondirective interview also attempts to determine the person's sentiments about aspects of his job; in this approach, however, the interviewer makes a point of *not* directing the thoughts and responses of the individual. Instead, the interviewer's role is to create a permissive climate so that the person is able to give a free account of the organization and his perceptions of it. The techniques of nondirective interviewing are based on active listening, and questions are asked only to help the person express himself openly and freely.

In analyzing interview data, the investigator looks for similarities among favorable and unfavorable comments from the workers interviewed, and these findings are then converted into composite expressions of group attitudes. Attempts are made to evaluate the intensity and frequency of the ideas and feelings expressed. For example, how strongly did the interviewees feel about salary? How often was pay mentioned? If only a few people complained about compensation, the investigator may conclude that salary is not a major problem.

The interview method requires a trained and experienced interviewer. He must know how to interpret the responses; but it is most important to be able to create a climate in which people will talk candidly. Although this requires a skillful and perceptive person, it can yield valuable attitudinal results, especially in determining *why* the interviewees have the prevailing complex of perceptions that they have.

THE QUESTIONNAIRE

The survey questionnaire is in effect a standardized interview procedure with the questions in written form. It has the advantage of being uniform in content and method of administration, and avoids the possibility of negative interaction between the interviewer and his subject. It is more economical and efficient than an interview, and can be administered with greater speed and accuracy.

Developing a questionnaire. There are two ways to develop a questionnaire. The most common method does not have a carefully worked out rationale for developing items or for interpreting the data obtained. This technique involves the use of judges who decide what statements to use on the basis of their clarity and their presumed ability to assess the attitudes of the respondents. Items are included if they seem to conform with an *a priori* rationale. A scale for measuring opinions toward any organization, program, or administrative practice can be developed by this method. However, the reliability and validity of such an instrument are generally unknown, and findings obtained from its use should be regarded with caution.

Questions can also be developed through use of more professional methods of test construction such as evaluative statistical methods of item analysis, measures of discrimination and reliability, and factor analysis. This type of questionnaire, standardized in content and yielding findings that can be interpreted in terms of norms, offers great promise for increasing our understanding of school personnel problems and needs. Under proper methods of administration, it can measure staff perceptions of the work relationship with a high degree of consistency and objectivity. If the anonymity of the respondents is preserved, considerable confidence can be placed in the results.

REASEARCH ABOUT MORALE IN SCHOOLS

The literature on work attitudes, job satisfaction, and morale is so voluminous that no attempt will be made to review it in this volume. Excellent summaries of research on industrial morale have already been provided by Vroom (1965). However, a number of studies relating to education will be recounted here, for they are important to administrators who must make decisions about factors related to high and low morale. The findings have been grouped under the headings of work environment, teacher characteristics, decision-making and expectations, curriculum development, student-teacher relationships, salary, and performance.

WORK ENVIRONMENT AND MORALE

One technique used in investigations of the factors associated with high and low morale has the following steps: (a) assemble a list of attitude items; (b) administer them to a large group of teachers; (c) pick out the group of teachers who score highest (for example, the upper third) and the group scoring lowest (the lower third); and (d) find the items which discriminate between the two groups—that is, the items to which the two groups answer in the most dissimilar manner.

Two common techniques for studying morale as a function of work environment are the use of the *situations list* and the *check list*. To assemble a situations list, the investigator simply asks the teacher to write down any situation in his work environment which is causing him extreme satisfaction or extreme dissatisfaction. One problem with such free recall techniques is that the teacher may have certain complaints about the environment which do not come to mind at that particular moment. To avoid this problem, a check list can be used. Such a list would contain the most commonly mentioned topics.[8]

What can be learned from the results of these investigations? For one thing, the boundaries of the work environment can be defined in many different ways. If the work environment includes interpersonal relationships with other teachers and with administrators, then interpersonal relationships affect morale. Other factors associated with morale include adequacy of equipment, supplies, facilities, and salary. These results are in harmony with the results reported previously for industrial situations.

TEACHER CHARACTERISTICS AND MORALE

Many studies have been made of the relationship between a teacher's characteristics (primarily personality characteristics) and the level of that teacher's morale. Using questionnaires and interview procedures with a sample of 1,800 teachers in more than 200 school systems in 43 states, Chase (1951) found that, as a potential source of job satisfaction, freedom to plan one's own work was given the highest possible rating by more than three-fourths of all teachers. The desire for professional status was also important: in interviews, respondents repeatedly spoke of the satisfaction of

---

[8] An early user of the "discrimination" technique, mentioned first, was Hoppock (1935). His work was continued by McClusky and Strayer (1940), who used the free response procedure. The work of Shilland (1949) is an example of the check list method. Other work in the area of morale and work environment was done by Redefer (1959).

working with teachers who had a professional attitude and high work standards.

In a poll of University of Illinois graduates, Schultz (1952) reported that morale was related to sex and marital status, with more male than female teachers and more married than single teachers being very *dissatisfied* with their work. An inquiry form was provided for free response statements of why they liked or disliked their present position. The factor identified as being most crucial to satisfaction was administrative behavior, although salary, working conditions, and supplies were mentioned to a lesser degree.

Suehr (1962) administered a sentence completion test for measuring morale to a sample group after obtaining information about their background and characteristics. Some of the more interesting findings of the study include: Three times as many males as females composed the low morale group. The higher the teacher's intelligence, the greater the probability that his morale was low. Teachers with low morale were often the youngest children in their families, missed more days of school, felt that their personal appearance was above average, perceived themselves as more stubborn, had above-average self-confidence, had higher levels of aspiration, and were extroverted. Teachers with high morale felt that they were realizing their fullest potential in teaching, had fulfilled their parents' expectations, had taught longer, worried less, were from upper middle-class families, had parents who were both happy in their roles, felt that their childhood family life was very close, and were introverted. Teachers with rural origins were represented three times as often in the low-morale group.

What does this all mean to the decision-maker? Should he avoid hiring male teachers, since they will tend to have lower morale? Should he avoid hiring last-born, conceited, good-looking, stubborn, extroverted teachers, since they will tend to have lower morale? The results give only general tendencies—group tendencies—and do not say much about individual cases. To be sure, there will be dissatisfied teachers who are first-born introverts, and satisfied teachers with all the background characteristics listed for teachers with low morale.

The only real value the research results have for the administrator is that they give him a better understanding of the factors associated with job satisfaction and morale. What are the general characteristics of being last-born, for example, which tend to conflict with the general characteristics of the teaching situation? The research studies have determined that there is a correlation between morale and each of the traits mentioned above. But is this a *causal* relationship? Or is the relationship coincidental? The research reports provide a framework for decision-making. They do not suggest prescriptions or rules for individual cases.

DECISION-MAKING, EXPECTATIONS, AND MORALE

Intuition would tell us that teacher morale would be associated with the term *decision-making* from two points of reference:

1. The teacher's morale would be higher if he had a fairly clear conception of who is responsible for making decisions. Where does the buck stop? Who is responsible for class assignments? Who makes decisions about student disciplinary action? To whom does the teacher go to request additional audiovisual aids; who can *decide*—and be held accountable for—the decision?

2. The teacher's morale will also be aided if he believes he is capable of making, or at least influencing, the decisions which he believes legitimately belong within his sphere of responsibilities. For example, the teacher probably will not feel compelled to participate in a decision about the purchase of a popcorn machine; but the teacher will feel that the planning of his instructional program and the textbooks used are both within his domain of responsibilities.

A questionnaire study by Sharma (1955) indicated that the decision-making practices of the school are important determinants of teacher morale. He found that teachers have clear conceptions and definite expectations of which level of the school district should appropriately be involved in a wide variety of decisions. Satisfaction seems to be related to the extent to which decision-making practices meet the teacher's expectations. Satisfied teachers reported that they were able to influence decisions in those areas in which they desired to do so; dissatisfied teachers reported that they could not participate in decision-making areas that were important to them.

Bidwell (1956) devised a series of thirteen job situations which describe teacher-administrator interactions. By selecting among three alternatives, the respondent categorized administrative behavior as either democratic, autocratic, or laissez-faire. He found that teachers who perceive administrative behavior as being consistent with their expectations tend to be satisfied with their job situation, whereas those whose perceptions are inconsistent with their expectations tend to be dissatisfied, so job satisfaction seems to depend upon job expectations. This study would seem to refute the position of those who recommend democratic administration as productive of high morale for all job situations.

In Chase's study (1951), enthusiasm for the system was related to the degree to which the teachers participated in curriculum and policy-making. Again and again, teachers who were enthusiastic about the system in which they were working praised their freedom to experiment and to adapt programs to the needs of pupils; or cited as important to satisfaction the fact that they were regarded as competent to make their own decisions and to work out their own procedures.

CURRICULUM DEVELOPMENT AND MORALE

Coffman (1951) utilized the Teacher Reaction Inventory, developed at Columbia University, in an attempt to relate teacher morale to curriculum construction. He reached five conclusions:

1. Teacher morale is related to staff judgments of the success of curriculum development programs.

2. The most successful programs of curriculum development are carried on in school systems in which teachers enjoy their work and have good relationships with superiors and associates.

3. The principal is the key person in fostering high morale in programs of curriculum development.

4. Teachers' feelings about salary are relatively unimportant compared to curriculum developments.

5. A high degree of satisfaction with the curriculum is not conducive to instituting changes in programs of instruction.

STUDENT-TEACHER RELATIONSHIPS AND MORALE

It is a little difficult to conceive of a teacher with high morale who dislikes the age group of the children with whom he is working. No amount of pleasant colleague relations, good working conditions, high salary, or decision-making authority could really compensate for such a feeling. Of course, a teacher who likes the age group with which he is working has a greater tendency to be satisfied with his job.

This has been borne out in a 1968 NEA survey. Of the teachers surveyed, about three-fourths said they would "certainly" or "probably" choose teaching as a career again, and the most frequently cited source of gratification was working with pupils.

There are some very general research results which relate a liking for children to a number of characteristics. For example, there are differences among teachers classified by subject area; teachers in the primary grades seem to have more favorable attitudes toward pupils; special field majors seem to have the least favorable attitudes toward students; and favorable attitudes seem to be detected more often in schools where the pupil achievement levels are high. As with other research reports, we must view these relationships as only suggestive, and not prescriptive in individual decisions. We cannot say that teachers like children *because* they went into an early childhood education program; nor can we say that those who like children will enter an early childhood education program. The research has duly noted a relationship; but the researchers have not explained what the cause of the relationship is, and they have not pointed out what its practical significance is.

SALARY AND MORALE

As we have already said, a poor salary can lead to job dissatisfaction, but a good salary does not necessarily lead to job satisfaction. It may only avoid job dissatisfaction. Salary is important to morale. When teachers were asked to rank a series of job factors in order of their importance in improving teacher morale, salary was found to be of primary importance. It was followed by recognition of achievement, and good physical plant and equipment (Miller, 1959).

The relationship between morale and salary schedule has also been investigated. In a series of studies attempting to relate merit-rating salary schedules with those having no merit component, researchers have determined that the type of salary plan did not significantly affect teacher morale.[9]

PERFORMANCE AND MORALE

The issue of greatest significance to job satisfaction and morale is that of its relationship to job performance. Two scholarly reviews of the literature on work attitudes appear to demonstrate that the association between morale and productivity is much weaker than earlier investigators had assumed. These views, carried out by Brayfield and Crockett (1955) and Herzberg et al. (1957), found that the straightforward "high satisfaction leads to high performance" hypothesis was unsupported by the evidence.

Porter and Lawler (1968) point out that most of the early studies tend to be either conceptually naïve or greatly oversimplified in design. Both the Porter and Lawler (1968) and Vroom (1965) studies posit a similar but more complex relationship between satisfaction and productivity. They hypothesize that satisfaction comes about when certain needs are fulfilled; i.e., job satisfaction is generated when the individual receives rewards from his work situation. Some of these rewards are intrinsic to the person and his feeling of accomplishment. In such cases, the individual himself is the source of the reward. Other rewards are provided by the work environment, for instance a promotion or increase in pay. Porter and Lawler argue that the amount of reward may be unrelated to how well the person has performed. The issue then becomes: Does the organization actively and visibly provide rewards in proportion to the quality of job performance? Porter and Lawler maintain that if it does, and if the individual realizes this, then high satisfaction should be more closely related to high performance. On the other hand, failure to find an association between job satisfaction and productivity in an organization may simply mean that the employees are not being rewarded differentially for superior performance.

The fundamental policy implication of the Porter-Lawler hypothesis is that administrators should insure that their best teachers are the most satisfied teachers. The goal would be

---

[9] For a discussion of this issue and the questionnaire used in these investigations, see Chandler (1959), Mathis (1959), Richardson and Blocker (1963), and Koplyay and Mathis (1967).

not to maximize job satisfaction but to maximize the relationship between satisfaction and productivity. Porter and Lawler regard performance as a function of the interaction of the reward system and the individual's expectations for rewards for superior work. The more highly a reward is valued and the greater the expectation that superior work will lead to this reward, the greater will be the individual's effort to attain the reward through improved performance.

Summary. Early efforts in the study of morale were generally directed toward an investigation of group solidarity and the degree of internalization of organization goals. The hypothesis was that group "we-feeling" and identification with organization goals would have positive effects on work attitudes, job satisfaction, and morale.

It has become apparent, however, that morale involves something more than identification with the organization and group spirit. For a high level of morale to be maintained in a teacher group, other conditions must be present. Among the most important of these is some measure of achievement. In short, levels of morale and productivity both seem to be related to the needs and expectations of individuals in response to the total work environment.

THE ATTITUDE SURVEY

Experience has shown that attitude surveys can be an important addition to administrative procedures for improving the morale of school personnel. Attitude surveys provide a sound basis for determining the objectives, content, and emphasis of in-service programs for staff development. Burns (1952) suggests six ways in which the survey procedure can contribute to strengthening administrative effectiveness and staff morale:

(1) *As a diagnostic procedure.* The attitude survey technique enables the administration to get measured perceptions of a wide range of problems and issues in the school district. If anonymity is preserved, the quality and reliability of survey results suffer a minimum of contamination from staff concealment. Diagnoses can be focused on particular schools and departments, as well as on specific topic areas,

so that the procedure analyzes both problems and problem locations. The results tell what is troubling staff personnel and where problems are most pressing.

(2) *As an expression of administrative concern for staff welfare.* The attitude survey technique provides an opportunity for school personnel to express their ideas and sentiments to those who count. Everyone likes to be consulted, particularly when the purpose is to make the school and district a better place in which to work. The fact that the administration invites expressions of opinion generally creates feelings of release and respect for the administration on the part of those who are surveyed. Active involvement and the concrete demonstration of the administration's interest in the staff and the school contribute to healthy staff response.

(3) *As a two-way communication procedure.* The attitude survey technique focuses on the weakest aspect of communication in any scalar organization, i.e., the upward flow of suggestions, problem information, and feelings. The anonymous questionnaire is less subject to censorship than regular upward communication through status levels in the district. The cost is low enough so that it is practical to survey all the individuals in the system.

(4) *As a participative procedure.* Attitude surveys tend to be employed most frequently in districts characterized by more democratic and less authoritarian administrator-teacher relationships. It seems that such administrations recognize that the technique is a positive means for consulting their staffs on those aspects of the work that seem to be of greatest concern and importance to them.

(5) *As a procedure for fostering decentralization.* The aim of an attitude survey should be to solve problems through an analysis of the thinking and feelings of those closest to the problems themselves. Teachers and their supervisors, therefore, should be key figures in a follow-up program of survey feedback. They should participate in the interpretation of results and recommend action which can be taken within the schools or departments to deal with the problems identified in the survey. In these efforts, they should be assisted and supported by the central office administration. This means that each school staff should be given the training, materials, facilities, and necessary time for problem analysis

and action. This approach fosters a sense of individual initiative and group responsibility at the levels where district policies and programs are being implemented. Those who are engaged in survey feedback and problem-solving procedures acquire a positive point of view about their role in the district which persists long after the survey. This perspective can make an important contribution to the long-range development of personnel in the district.

(6) *As a means of developing organization teamwork.* The attitude survey technique can improve cooperation in the district in several ways: by integrating the objectives of the individual and teacher group with those of the larger organization; by building understanding and acceptance for action necessary to reach district objectives; by sharing responsibility for taking action and making it effective; and by developing common interests and consensus within the system.

COUGHLAN'S SCHOOL SURVEY: AN EXAMPLE

Attitude surveys frequently measure different aspects of the work environment. The one with which we are most familiar, Coughlan's School Survey (1970), measures the perceptions of respondents in four broad areas:

A. *General administration*—including administrative practices, professional work load, nonprofessional work load, materials and equipment, and buildings and facilities.

B. *Educational program*—including educational effectiveness, evaluation of students, and specialized services.

C. *Interpersonal relations*—including school-community, principal-teacher, and colleague relations.

D. *Career fulfillment*—including voice in educational program, performance and development, and financial incentives.

The survey questionnaire itself is a 120-item, self-reporting inventory. In general, it contains a series of statements, worded in the language that school personnel use, through which they can express their ideas and sentiments about their work. In previous investigations, the items were evaluated with respect to their discriminatory power, relevance, and clarity and then classified through two independent factor analyses into fourteen categories. These factors or categories of items are presumed to represent basic dimensions in the structure of morale for professional personnel in schools.

The material for all survey results comes from the responses to items on the questionnaire form. For each statement, the respondent checks either "Agree," "Disagree," or "?" if he was undecided. About half the items are worded positively and the other half negatively. Individual *item* scores are computed as the percentage of respondents of a group who replied favorably to each item. Summary scores are the averages of the item scores within each *category* and are also reported in percentages. Results for both categories and items are reported on percentage grids.

As noted earlier, a person's response to a work attitudes questionnaire seems to depend on two sets of interrelated factors: (1) his personal and social needs and expectations; and (2) the events, situations, and circumstances of his work.

Responses to the questionnaire and the attitudes expressed in these responses are viewed as symptoms: symptoms of the interaction between the teachers and their work environment; symptoms of the adequacy or inadequacy of their perception of and adjustment to the job; and symptoms of the success of the administration in building and maintaining satisfying work relationships. These symptoms cannot be understood apart from the context in which responses to the questionnaire were made.

In most instances, the attitudes expressed by the respondents represent a complex of feelings. Thus the total *pattern* of attitudes must be understood before the circumstances underlying particular attitudes can be discovered. In the work situation, moreover, an event which occurs on the job is not interpreted differently by each person in the group. Insofar as the teacher group has shared similar experiences and has developed norms or standards of behavior which are observed by fellow teachers, the interpretation of any given event will tend to be similar for most teachers in the group.

Some attitudes that teachers share about their work may be based on objective conditions which are apparent to everyone. Other attitudes reflect more subjective interests and expectations. For example, a teacher's attitude toward his salary is not simply an objective appraisal of pay. It is also based on subjective considerations: impressions of pay in other school districts, opinions about what constitutes equity in salary matters, and so on. The same is true of his attitudes toward professional work load, materials and equipment, principal-teacher relations, and other categories measured by the survey instrument. However, it must be kept in mind that the teacher believes his attitudes to be objective and factual. An individual's satisfaction with his pay or work load will be as great whether it results from objective considerations or from more subjective factors such as his personal impressions and expectations.

Two types of profiles are provided in the report of School Survey findings: *summary* and *detail*. Detail profiles present a more specific analysis of results; they show why the particular groups scored high or low on a particular category. Summary profiles provide measures of the general level of morale and the pattern of attitudes for each of the groups whose scores are profiled.

In interpreting School Survey results, emphasis is placed on analyzing the pattern of significantly high and low areas in a profile—what might be called the "pattern of attitudes." If each item in the survey is thought of as an index of sentiment, a combination of these items will reveal patterns reflecting the broader sentiments which lie behind the particularized responses to the items. By placing emphasis on the *pattern* of response, rather than on the absolute level of response, the much investigated but only partially resolved problem of rank-ordering attitudinal dimensions in terms of their importance to morale becomes secondary.

CATEGORIES OF SURVEY FINDINGS

In general, there are four types of School Survey analyses that are of considerable use to the school district and its staff administration. These are:

Overall system findings. The survey provides an indication of the general level of morale of personnel throughout the entire school system. The underlying pattern of attitudes can be broken down into four key areas and fourteen categories of items. These overall findings can provide a broad diagnosis of school district relationships, programs, policies, and procedures.

Intra- and inter-school findings and analyses. Survey findings pinpoint specific issues in various schools and departments within these schools. Through an analysis of these issues, meaningful suggestions can be obtained from each school staff about types of programs that would be helpful in solving or alleviating identified problems and meeting staff needs.

Comparative findings and analyses in terms of norms. The survey results, in terms of system-wide, departmental, or specialist group scores, can be compared with norms or other bench-mark data. This means that a school district can compare its scores on such categories as administrative practices, work load, educational effectiveness, school-community relations, and the like, with scores obtained from other similar school systems.

Comparative findings and analyses through time. Through longitudinal studies, the trend of overall system, school, and departmental attitudes can be charted and studied. This enables administrators to measure the effects of programs of improvement overtime.

DEFICIENCIES IN THE SURVEY TECHNIQUE

There are a number of possible weaknesses in attitude surveys that should be noted. Many surveys rely on a simple tabulation of overall results instead of trying to analyze relationships between items. The mere scoring and computing of percentages can often be misleading. Other surveys treat each item as the unit of analysis; they rely on item findings alone and regard these as an end in themselves. A much more reliable and productive approach is to look for relationships within and between categories of items.

Errors of inference in interpreting survey findings are also frequently made. There is a tendency to overgeneralize from the results in terms of global statements that fail to consider alternative explanations, qualifications, and the like. This tendency to oversimplify interpretations through deceptively easy explanations masks what in reality is often an exceedingly complex work situation.

Furthermore, there can be distortions in the questionnaire employed. What respondents say on a questionnaire is obviously limited by what the questionnaire permits them to say. For example, if the questionnaire overemphasizes certain aspects of the work environment, then the survey results will be distorted. The professional and personal biases of those who conduct the survey must also be considered—people with an ax to grind are sometimes allowed to have an excessive influence on the interpretation of findings.

The most prevalent weakness in attitude survey procedures is a failure to integrate findings meaningfully. Any questionnaire is fundamentally an artificial way of determining the basic attitudes of people. The questionnaire itself forces the respondent to react in a way that reveals only limited aspects of his ideas and feelings. The decision to conduct attitude surveys with a questionnaire is greatly influenced by the factors of cost and administrative convenience, so it is essential that valid interpretations be made of the data. This requires a thorough understanding of work attitudes, organization dynamics, and the values, reactions, and beliefs of school personnel in American society. Only in this way can the attitudes of a particular group of teachers be integrated into a significant pattern.

EFFECTIVE USE OF THE SURVEY

If beneficial results are to be realized from the attitude survey procedure, three administrative requirements should be met.

First, the purpose of the survey must be clearly stated and understood by all concerned. It should in some specific way improve the efficiency and effectiveness of the school system and make it a better one in which to work. It should be clearly understood that survey findings will not be used to embarrass or threaten people in positions of leadership or undermine individuals or schools that have particular problems. The clear purpose of the survey process must be *constructive* rather than punitive; otherwise, apprehension and defensiveness will interfere with the identification and solution of problems.

Secondly, it must be said that few school systems have a tradition of sharing information about problems. Moreover, communication is often one-way—downward to the teachers with little upward feedback. The problem-solving which does occur is often carried out in an authoritarian or paternalistic atmosphere.

The most essential requirement for conducting a successful survey is that of freely sharing and candidly assessing the results with all those who have been involved. This includes *all* the findings, both favorable and unfavorable. It also means presenting results in an understandable way, allowing for group discussion at the school level, and giving the school staff the resources and encouragement it needs to analyze what teachers are saying in their school, why they are saying it, and what can be done about it.

Conference discussion techniques seem most appropriate for sharing findings with the rest of the system. An open climate and an accepting atmosphere are essential in these discussions. Participants must feel free to come to grips with problems in their schools. If this is done effectively, the best ideas and experiences of those closest to problems can be constructively used. People will come to understand the causes of their problems and can plan for their solutions. Having been involved in the identification and analysis of problems, they will then more readily accept responsibility for undertaking action on their own as well as for making recommendations for corrective measures which lie beyond their own sphere of authority.

Finally, it should be emphasized that the central office must be willing to act upon recommendations from individuals and schools. If communication between levels of the school organization is to be maintained, top school administrators must take the appropriate action or explain why this cannot be done.

Summary. Experience with attitude surveys to date indicates several specific ways in which survey findings can be used by administrators in strengthening the morale of professional personnel in their schools. Survey findings indicate the general level of morale in the system, and they also single out satisfactions and dissatisfactions which are general in the system or are localized within a given school or department.

Through identifying and analyzing problems, the survey can help to determine the objectives, content, and emphasis for programs of improvement and staff development. It can help clarify *what* needs to be done to strengthen the system, *how* it is to be done, and *who* should do it.

The dissemination and discussion of survey findings promote free expression of ideas and experience. It encourages participation in the decision-making process. The survey procedure can increase and improve communication about problems and possible solutions throughout the entire school district. The procedure can, therefore, set up the climate and conditions for making long-needed changes in the school system.

CONTINUOUS ASSESSMENT OF STAFF MORALE

In chapter 3 the concept of continuous assessment was introduced. It was noted that: "The administration should determine which areas of the district's program need continuous assessment for proper decision-making; and continuous sampling programs should be initiated in these areas." The morale and job satisfaction of the staff must be included in this category.

Continuous in this sense might be defined as monthly. Recall that this need not involve every teacher. If the district employs 150 teachers, the group could be separated at random into 10 groups of 15 each; and one group could be used each month from September through June. A completed instrument like Coughlan's School Survey could be used.

Such a continuous procedure would allow the school's decision-makers to spot trends or changes in staff attitude. Too often administrators begin questioning teachers only after a traumatic and irrevocable event has occurred. Measurement should be used in the positive sense—to help the administrator *avoid* serious problems. Measurement done in calm times helps the administrator keep his perspective in more difficult moments.

REFERENCES

Baehr, Milany E., and Richard Renck. "The Definition and Measurement of Employee Morale," *Administrative Science Quarterly* 3 (1968): 157–184.

Bidwell, Charles E. "The Administrative Role and Satisfaction in Teaching," *Journal of Educational Sociology* 10 (1956): 1821–1822.

Blum, Milton L. *Industrial Psychology and Its Social Foundations.* New York: Harper and Brothers, 1956.

Brayfield, Arthur H., and Walter H. Crockett. "Employee Attitudes and Employee Performance," *Psychological Bulletin* 67 (1955): 13–53.

Burns, Robert K. "Attitude Surveys and the Diagnosis of Organization Needs," Personnel Series, no. 157. New York: The American Management Association, 1952.

———. "Employee Morale—Its Meaning and Measurement." Research Reprint Series. Chicago: Industrial Relations Center, The University of Chicago, 1951–1952.

Chandler, B. J. "Salary Policies and Teacher Morale," *Educational Administration and Supervision* 45 (1959): 107–110.

Chase, F. S. "Factors for Satisfaction in Teaching," *Phi Delta Kappan* 33 (1951): 127–132.

Coffman, W. E. "Teacher Morale and Curriculum Development: A Statistical Analysis of Responses to a Reaction Inventory," *Journal of Experimental Education* 19 (1951): 305–332.

Coughlan, Robert J. "Dimensions of Teacher Morale," *American Educational Research Journal* 7 (March 1970): 221–235.

———. *Organizational Systems and Teacher Groups*. Chicago: Industrial Relations Center, University of Chicago, 1968.

Getzels, J. W., and E. G. Guba. "Social Behavior and the Administrative Process," *School Review* 65 (1957): 423–441.

Getzels, J., J. Lipham, and R. Campbell. *Educational Administration as a School Process*. New York: Harper and Row, 1968.

Guba, Egon G. "Morale and Satisfaction: A Study of Past-Future Time Perspective," *Administrative Science Quarterly* 3 (1958): 195–209.

Guion, Robert M. "Some Definitions of Morale," *Personnel Psychology* 2 (1958): 59–61.

Herzberg, Frederick, et al. *Job Attitudes: Review of Research and Opinion*. Pittsburgh: Psychological Service of Pittsburgh, 1957.

Herzberg, F., B. Mausner, and B. B. Snyderman. *The Motivation to Work*. New York: John Wiley and Sons, 1959.

Hoppock, R. *Job Satisfaction*. New York: Harper, 1935.

Insko, Chester A. *Theories of Attitude Change*. New York: Appleton-Century-Crofts, 1967.

Koplyay, J. B., and B. C. Mathis. "The Relationship Between Teacher Morale and Organizational Climate," paper presented at the annual meeting of the American Educational Research Association, February 16, 1967, in New York City. (Mimeographed.)

Maslow, A. H. *Motivation and Personality.* New York: Harper and Brothers, 1954.

Mathis, Claude. "The Relationship Between Salary Policies and Teacher Morale," *Journal of Educational Psychology* 50 (1959): 275–279.

Mayo, Elton. *The Human Problems of an Industrial Civilization.* New York: Harper, 1933.

McClusky, Howard, and Floyd J. Strayer. "Reactions of Teachers to the Teaching Situation: A Study of Job Satisfaction," *School Review* 48 (1940): 612–623.

Miller, Antoinette. "Teachers Say Better Salaries Boost Morale," *Texas Outlook* 43 (1959): 14–16.

Morse, N. C. *Satisfactions in the White-Collar Job.* Ann Arbor: University of Michigan, Survey Research Center, Institute for Social Research, 1953.

NEA Research Division. "Morale-building Changes," *NEA Journal* 57 (1968): 20.

Porter, L. W., and E. E. Lawler. "What Job Attitudes Tell About Motivation," *Harvard Business Review* 46 (1968): 118–126.

Redefer, Frederick L. "Factors That Affect Teacher Morale," *Nation's Schools* 63 (1959): 59–62.

Richardson, Richard C., and Clyde E. Blocker. "Twenty-five Years of Morale Research: A Critical Review," *Journal of Educational Sociology* 36 (1963): 200–210.

Roethlisberger, F. J., and William J. Dickson. *Management and the Worker.* Cambridge, Mass.: Harvard University Press, 1941.

Schultz, R. E. "Keeping Up Teacher Morale," *Nation's Schools* 50 (1952): 53–56.

Sharma, C. L. "Who Should Make What Decisions?" *Administrator's Notebook* 3 (1955): 1–4.

Shilland, P. D. "A Teacher Morale Survey," *Educational Forum* 13 (1949), 479–486.

Suehr, John H. "A Study of Morale in Education Utilizing Incomplete Sentences," *Journal of Educational Research* 56 (1962): 75–81.

Vroom, Victor. *Motivation in Management.* New York: American Foundation for Management Research, 1965.

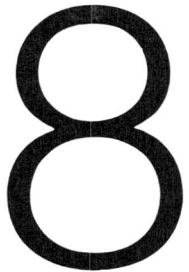

8 RECRUITING AND RETAINING TEACHERS

Research About Teacher Recruitment and Retention
Teacher characteristics and job descriptions
Clinical and actuarial methods of recruitment

Models for Decision-Making
Three steps to hiring teachers

Problems of Teacher Retention
Career patterns of men and women
Common causes for leaving
Inadequate preknowledge
District-specific causes
Personal causes

Gathering Data to Improve Recruitment and Retention

In this book, we have stressed the measurement aspects of important issues about which school personnel must make decisions. With many of the issues—such as test score reporting, outcome evaluation, and homogeneous grouping—the role of measurement is central. With other topics the role of measurement is less apparent. To be sure, the measurement-oriented journals have a decided lack of reports on the important issue of teacher recruitment and retention.

The authors feel that teacher recruitment and retention decisions are among the most important that the school administrators must make. Educational measurement specialists may not be saying much about the topic, but educational researchers have been trying to psych out teachers for a long time. This accumulation of studies has suggested characteristics of people who choose teaching and of teachers who choose to leave the profession. Our goal for this chapter is to review this research to discover what methods an administrator can use to recruit the best teachers and then keep them.

It is the authors' opinion that teacher recruitment is most effective when there are systematic procedures developed for selecting individuals. These procedures include quantitative measures whenever possible. Recruitment and retention policies do not conjure up pictures of neat and precise quantitative techniques. It is our viewpoint, however, that many of these "un-neat" decisions could be much improved through the use of some creative measurement programs.

RESEARCH ABOUT TEACHER RECRUITMENT AND RETENTION

Each year, approximately 10 percent of the total teaching population leave the fold. This figure of course varies considerably from district to district. Obviously, many of these teachers leave because they have reached retirement. Of those who leave for reasons other than retirement, the motivation of marriage and/or a family causes the early retirement of a large group of women. When men leave the field for reasons other than retirement, the motivation is likely to be economic. Of course there are other reasons for people to leave teaching—such as being fired or being incapable of dealing with students—but after you take out the retirements, the women leaving for family responsibilities, the men looking for greener economic pastures, the great majority have been accounted for.

TEACHER CHARACTERISTICS AND JOB DESCRIPTIONS

Mitzel (1960) reports that there has been, unfortunately, very little attention given to meaningful or measurable criteria for teacher effectiveness in research relating effectiveness to recruitment. Many researchers have attempted to find things like "the characteristics of *good* teachers." There exists in this question a criterion problem. What is "good"? It might be defined as "a teacher who stays," or "a teacher who constantly challenges the administration to provide maximum educational opportunities for each child," or "a teacher with a master's degree or better"—each definition would call for a different list of characteristics. The school administrator should ignore research results in which the researcher has failed to define his terms in a most explicit manner.

The authors believe recruitment will be improved if the purpose for recruitment is made very explicit. It is imperative that the position for which an individual is to be recruited is carefully defined. Bauthues (1968) has suggested that this statement of purpose is the first requirement in teacher recruitment.

Researchers in the past have suggested models through which the school administrator can be more explicit about recruitment—that is, in attempting to define the variables that a decision-maker needs to consider in the description of a position which is available. Mitzel (1957) suggests two general headings: environmental (school location, size, and organization; community economic factors) and pupil variables (attitudes, interests, and abilities).

Ryans (1960) also hypothesizes two variables which might have an effect on whether a teacher could be effective in, and stay in, a particular school system. In Ryans' model the general social environment—such as the conventions and values of social groups and curriculum objectives of a particular school system—comes first, followed by a concern with the unique features that one may find in a school setting—such as the particular subject matter, the particular types of pupils, or the particular types of activities that may be occurring. In many ways Ryans' suggestions closely match those of Mitzel.

It is evident that leaders in the field are convinced that in order for one to recruit well he must project a proper image of the factors that may affect teacher satisfaction or teacher work in the school system. Many of these were reviewed in chapter 8. Kleinman (1960) found in a study of situational factors regarding teacher satisfaction that the amount of a teacher's knowledge of situational factors prior to accepting a teaching position was positively related to the degree of the teacher's satisfaction with the particular school system involved. Thus prior information is required not only for teacher recruitment, but it seems to influence the teacher's decision about remaining in a particular setting as well.

The work of Mitzel (1957) and Ryans (1960) along with studies which have supported their frameworks (for example, Rosencranz and Biddle, 1964) have suggested that the school administrator provide a structure for recruiting teachers. Such a structure would be useful to both the school administrator and the applicant. One listing of factors relevant to both the administrator and the applicant has been provided by Palmer (1968) in Table 10.

Table 10
Situational Factors

Community	*School System*
Nature (including beliefs, traditions, business and industry, religions)	Administrative Expectations
	Decision-Making Process
	Local School Board (including its nature and expectations)
Size	
Expectations	
Support of Schools	
Aspirations	
Laws and Customs	

School	*Classroom*
Physical Characteristics	Physical Characteristics
Staff Characteristics	Pupil Characteristics
Instructional Program	Instructional Program
Principal's Role and Characteristics	Instructional Materials
Supportive Personnel's Role	Size
Size	

As can be seen in Table 10, the situational factors are concerned with community, the school system, the school, and the classroom. A job description which includes the details of these four variables would help the decision-maker determine the type of individual he needs, and would also be available to individuals interested in the position. If a very complete description were available, individuals who did not fit the job description would probably not apply for the position—with the result that teachers who do apply would probably stay longer.

Where does quantitative measurement fit in? The discussion now becomes district-specific. We can assume that wide variations exist for each of these situational factors across districts; and that a teacher who will accept a position where one set of factors exists will not accept a position where these are markedly different. Most districts have a history of recruitment experience, and this experience should be used to make future recruitment more effective. Measurement will not be "neat" here, but some very clear tabulations of reasons for leaving and reasons for staying should be kept. In addition, the measurements included in the job description should be clear and unambiguous. They must be stated so that the applicant understands their implications.

For example, it is not enough to say: "The district has a per-pupil expenditure rate of $700"; the school administrator must be sure that the applicant understands the significance of that factor. Is the figure commendable? What are the implications of that statement? Just as with test score reporting, it cannot be assumed that prospective teachers understand the implications of the data. If there is one counselor for every one thousand pupils, will the prospective teacher *know* that this figure is not satisfactory? We suggest that many will not. Many will accept the position thinking there is adequate counselor help, but when they learn to interpret this ratio correctly in terms of what it means to them on the job, this inadequacy will contribute to their decision to leave.

Many of the items listed in Table 10 may require such interpretation: for example, interpretations of size, expectations, support of schools, and physical and staff characteristics. Of at least equal importance would be some type of cost-of-living interpretations. Clearly an $8000 salary goes farther in one community than in another. Consider the chagrin of a man who accepts a position, only to find that the cost of living is so high there that he must locate his family elsewhere and commute to work. It is not difficult to imagine this man leaving the position before too long.

The implication is that the administration should accumulate district-specific job descriptions. With increased experience at the task, the most prominent retention-oriented factors will be isolated.

CLINICAL AND ACTUARIAL METHODS OF RECRUITMENT

Another way of conceptualizing recruitment, suggested by Bauthues (1968), places actuarial recruitment techniques at one end of a continuum, and clinical techniques at the other. The conceptualization seems satisfactory, as long as a value axis is not superimposed—that is, neither is better than the other.

The clinical position might be termed individualistic, for in it each human organism represents a unique structure—a unique pattern of behavior. The pattern consists of a dynamic combination of traits, abilities, motives, and values. This viewpoint implicitly suggests appropriate measurement schemes. To adequately describe anything unique or to predict an individual's behavior, the observational techniques must be very sensitive. To the clinician, *Measurement* suggests terms like *open-ended, non-directive, non-statistical,* and so forth.

If the clinical approach is adopted, it is impossible to collect all the necessary information in a paper-pencil manner, at least not in a manner that adequately describes the entire unique organism. The authors heartily agree that the individual and the position that the individual is applying for are each complex; taken jointly, it is surely impossible to statistically arrive at any complete description of position and individual which would lead to a complete and successful statistical mating of the two.

For the recruiter with a clinical orientation, the most common way of collecting information is in a personal interview with the potential teacher. Perhaps the great dependence on personal interviews is unfortunate. Hickey (1968) states that the interview has become to some individuals the rationale for the total selection, to the exclusion of more thoroughly tested and reliable procedures. What reason have we to believe that one characteristic of a good teacher is the ability to perform well in an interview? This is not meant to be a total criticism of all individuals who attempt to interview teachers, but there is very little evidence of the empirical reliability of teacher interviews in terms of either teacher recruitment or retention.

In contrast, the actuarial position is based on defining and measuring performance outcomes. The recruiter seeks empirical evidence which is indicative of the relationship between the dependent and the independent variables involved in the selection of teachers. Scott (1964) states that the actuarial position accepts the fact that behavior may consist of a pattern of interrelated variables but insists that behavioral dimensions are held in common among individuals although in varying degrees. The real advantage of the actuarial approach is that it requires a careful definition of terms and a very thorough search of all the subjective and objective factors in teacher recruitment and retention. This search should of course be district-specific.

The authors in no way intend to imply that in teacher recruitment one should use either the clinical or actuarial approach, but rather that neither should be used to the exclusion of the other. The actuarial approach should lead to a definition of as many relevant variables in the particular school district as are possible. The interview can then take on a structure based on these results, and better teacher recruitment will occur as a result of using the methods in combination.

MODELS FOR DECISION-MAKING

How does the administrator institute the most valid decision-making procedures when there is more than one candidate with the minimum qualifications for a position? There are a number of decision schemes.[1]

For example, the administrator could attempt to categorize each piece of information about a candidate under headings such as "physical characteristics" or "sympathy with student point of view." There might be a demographic category (age, sex, marital status), an experience category, and an educational backgrounds category. Not all categories would come from the actuarial data—some, for example, "apparent need for a structured instructional program," would come from the clinical approach.

When the information has been categorized, values could be assigned to each item, and a score obtained in each category for each applicant. These scores could be summed

---

[1] Much of this discussion is patterned after the suggestions of Toops (1945) and Bauthues (1968).

to obtain a final score for each candidate. Or instead of a simple sum, the categories might be weighted on the basis of past experience. That is, if "sympathy for the student point of view" is more important than "need for a structured instructional program," the scores in the first category might be multiplied by a factor of days before they are added into the final sum.[2]

A real problem can come out of such a scheme, however. It is possible for a person to score high in all categories but one, where he will score a zero; and this may be a category which will make or break the applicant. For example, suppose the applicant is outstanding in every way—except that he has a physical disability and cannot manipulate stairs. If the job is in a three-story building without an elevator and requires presence on both the first and third floors, the applicant would have an unpleasant time. The example is pretty specific; but more general cases can be cited. For example, some positions may simply be unsuitable for young single girls, or ambitious married men, or people not of a given religion. These, by the way, are examples of district-specific characteristics—the administration probably has enough data from past unsuccessful and successful hirings to know which of these apply.

Before the category method can be applied, there are specific characteristics which the applicant *must* have before he can be considered. If the district demands an M.A. degree, there is not much sense in cluttering up the files with information about people who do not have this degree. The administration might set up a *series of major requirements,* beginning with the most general. For example, all the applicants must be under 65 (2 eliminated); must have a B.A. degree (1 more eliminated) . . . and so forth, until the remaining candidates have met all minimum requirements.

The preceding method is based on a philosophy of "Let's take the best of those who apply." Another point of view would be "Let's define exactly what we want in the job, and wait until he comes along"—the *ideal profile* approach. There may be reasons (based on past experience) to require a married man with certain specific abilities, and so forth. The characteristics included in the profile would be considered

---

[2] From a statistical point of view, a multiple regression equation is suggested—assuming the district can agree on a criterion.

essential for success on the job, and no one would be hired who did not have these characteristics. In a district where far more applications are received than there are jobs to fill, the procedure might work quite well. Where the ratio of applicants to available jobs is lower, the "Let's define exactly what we want" might be changed to "Let's define the minimum characteristics we will accept." The district might prefer a teacher with an undergraduate physics major for its physics classes; but they would accept, as a minimum, a minor in physics.

Another slight alteration of this ideal-profile method once again involves a computation of a score. This time, each applicant is compared to the ideal profile, characteristic by characteristic; and a *difference score* is computed, based on the difference between the applicant's profile and the ideal profile for the job; and the applicant with the lowest deviation score presumably gets the job.

There is a final selection technique possible, which is somewhat different from the rest. With this technique, the administration looks for the *most outstanding characteristic* in each candidate; and hiring is based on the strength of this characteristic. For example, a man might be a truly outstanding director for theatrical productions. The district knows little about his teaching ability, scholarly background, and so forth, but hires him because this one characteristic is so outstanding. A faculty filled in such a manner might be a very interesting group; but one wonders about the resulting overall teaching strength. Perhaps it would be detrimental to have the entire staff hired from this viewpoint; but a few such people might have a salutary impact on the rest.

THREE STEPS TO HIRING TEACHERS

The first and most important procedure in teacher recruitment is that of defining the particular position. That is, explain explicitly and unambiguously the professional and community factors that may affect the particular job.

Secondly, individuals involved in teacher recruitment should collect both clinical and actuarial information about the applicants. To a large degree, the clinical methods should depend upon those standards and needs that have previously been defined and measured for the particular school system or unit.

Finally, once all of this information has been collected, the decision-maker must summarize it in a manner suitable to the selection procedures of his school system. We have suggested some alternative decision schemes.

If these three steps are followed, teacher recruitment will be better organized and more effective in helping potential teachers find jobs that best fit their teaching abilities and personal needs. It is the opinion of the authors that good recruitment will result in better teacher retention.

PROBLEMS OF TEACHER RETENTION

The authors have noted a tendency for many educators to begin discussions about teacher recruitment/retention patterns with a "clean slate," as if nothing at all were known for sure about this topic. This is inaccurate. The research to date has revealed certain career patterns in teachers which are well known by all who would listen.

CAREER PATTERNS OF MEN AND WOMEN

Label the following statements "in general," for they will describe prevailing group trends. The career patterns of men and women in teaching must be thought of separately, for some distinctly different pressures (factors) are involved for each.[3]

Women settle on a teaching career earlier than do men. They finish college and immediately accept a position, which they stay in for a few years—perhaps three or four. Somewhere along the line she probably marries and eventually leaves the position to raise a family. When the children are gone or the responsibilities lessened, she may return. If she does, she will probably stay in that teaching position until retirement.

Male teachers decide upon the teaching profession later than do females. For this reason, and because of the possibility of military service, men tend to be older when they accept their first position. The man just entering the teaching field will stay in the profession longer than will the just-entering female. However, young men will eventually leave

---

[3] Many of the concepts introduced in this discussion are suggested by Charters (1967).

the profession (probably when they are in their thirties) for other occupations, both in and out of the educational field. These men will not return to the classroom.

The descriptions above obviously do not apply to all. Some women decide on teaching at age 35; some men as early as junior high school. Not all men leave the profession, and not all women get married or leave the profession when they have children. The descriptions above, however, are probably applicable to more than a majority of teachers. These are the obvious things—the things "everyone knows." There is no sense pretending that they are revelations, and doctoral dissertations need not "discover" them any longer.

With these factors as a background, it is easier to discuss some district-specific topics. What can be said about the *deviations* from the pattern in a particular district? Given that these factors explain as many as 60 percent of the career decisions, what are the local factors which may be responsible for the 40 percent which is not explained?

COMMON CAUSES FOR LEAVING

During the last twenty years there have been a series of studies to determine the reasons a teacher decides to leave a position after only one year on the job, and to find out why some teacher education graduates never accept a job. A review of this literature reveals nineteen factors which are most commonly linked with teacher retention problems (see Nelson and Thompson, 1963, for example). Unfortunately, the lists do not contain percentage figures, which would be revealing.

The summary of reasons associated with leaving separate quite naturally into three major divisions. This breakdown follows:

I. Inadequate preknowledge; problems that are avoidable if the recruitment practices suggested earlier in this chapter are used.
    a. salary dispute
    b. teaching load unsatisfactory
    c. pressure groups intolerable
    d. inadequate knowledge in teaching areas
    e. unfair teacher evaluation techniques
    f. inadequate facilities
    g. too much routine clerical duty

II. District-specific causes; problems that are avoidable at the local level.
   a. too many assignments beyond regular classes
   b. inadequate supervision
   c. poor assignments
   d. assignment of too many difficult discipline problems
   e. lack of opportunity to develop new ideas
   f. problem with a poor school board
   g. unsatisfactory faculty relationships

III. Personal causes; problems which center on the individual and not the district.
   a. poor mental hygiene
   b. inability to handle classes
   c. competition with industry
   d. bad health
   e. marriage

INADEQUATE PREKNOWLEDGE

The first major category includes those expressed reasons for leaving which might have been avoided had recruitment procedures been more adequate. That is, if a person is going to leave after one year over a salary dispute, one has to wonder if he really was informed about things like salary schedules, typical raises, etc., before he took the job. As was noted earlier, a salary dispute can involve more than just the salary figure. A man who *thinks* he is receiving a satisfactory salary may be rudely awakened if he arrives in the community and finds an unexpectedly high cost of living, or a particularly high cost for housing. The local district administrators probably know that these things are true, and it is poor practice to make the new teacher find out for himself.

In addition to knowing what his salary will be for the first and subsequent years and having some idea about the purchasing power of this salary in the community at hand, the new teacher should have a very clear picture of what his teaching load will be. First-year teachers are generally loaded down with more classes than experienced teachers (Douglass et al., 1961); and the beginning teacher spends more time in classroom preparation than do experienced teachers (Koos, 1922). The class load for the new teacher should not come as a surprise to him, for this can lead to dissatisfaction —but simply informing him may not be enough. Again, the new teacher must be given a perspective. If the recruiter tells him, "Your class load will be five classes per day," the neophyte may see no reason to object. However, if he arrives in the district to find that all the experienced teachers are assigned only four classes per day, there is a distinct possibility that some resentment may develop.

Every district has its pressure groups. To be sure, any two parents with their child might be termed a pressure group. Some communities have district-specific groups, however, and these pressure groups are surely well known to the local administration. There is no reason to expect the prospective teacher to know about them, however, until he is on the job. Once again, if it appears that in the past some teachers left the district due to the presence of certain pressure groups, then it behooves the administration to carefully explain the situation to every teaching candidate, so that cases where this conflict might be a contributing factor can be avoided *before hiring*. These pressure groups, which might take the form of strong religious groups, militant ethnic groups, or groups with strong political leanings at either extreme can be a major contributing factor to faculty unrest.

The other four causes of leaving due to inadequate preknowledge include inadequate knowledge of teaching areas, unfair teacher evaluation techniques, inadequate facilities, and too much routine clerical duty. The same comments apply to all: the recruiter should tell the candidate exactly what to expect in his job. When the candidate cannot be expected to have experience against which to compare these statements to make valid value judgments about them, the recruiter has the responsibility of filling in this background—that is, if the recruiter *really* wants to reduce the amount of teacher turnover in the district.

As has been suggested, measurement plays two roles in this procedure. First, some rough tabulations should be kept of past reasons for leaving in the district. After the obvious ones are accounted for, the district-specific ones should be particularly noted. These factors should be discussed forthrightly, in an effort to screen out the candidates who would be negatively affected by them. Statistics can be used to fill in background areas for prospective teachers—to make them aware of the implications of certain statements about the district. For example, the recruiter might include in his discussion tabulations of salary and typical salary increases in adjacent districts. Even if this relationship puts the local district in an unpleasant bargaining position, it should be known to the candidate in advance, so that those who place high importance on this sort of thing will not accept the job. The point is, an individual might accept a job he really does not want, due to inadequate information; but when this occurs, he probably will leave the job after a short time and be less than satisfied while there. The local district probably wants to avoid both eventualities.

DISTRICT-SPECIFIC CAUSES

The second major category of expressed reasons for leaving a job are district-specific, but probably could not have been avoided in the recruitment process. These are mostly procedures in the local district which are detrimental to certain teachers, especially the new one, and which, by and large, are avoidable. Regardless of whether these procedures are instituted by design or by chance, the administrator should be alert for the appearance of one or more of these factors on the tabulation of reasons for leaving he should be keeping.

A heavy teaching load may be discouraging, but will cause less disillusionment if the individual knows about it in advance and has accepted this aspect of the position. What is discouraging is an overload of other activities—committees, supervisory assignments, etc.—which can add up to a discouraged new faculty member (see Alexander and Saylor, 1959). These extra activities can also cut into the time the new teacher needs to try out new ideas learned in his recently completed educational training. Only the newest teachers will have been exposed to the most recent developments; and the press of other activities should not be allowed to interfere with these teachers' introduction of these new developments into the existing school program.

Other factors belong in this category. If the teacher feels a need for guidance from the more experienced faculty members, for example, and cannot seem to obtain it, discouragement can occur. Too often a new teacher comes into the classroom to an accumulation of difficult discipline problems dumped on him by the more experienced faculty. A nonsupportive or contradictory or interfering school board can be a problem, as can unhappy personal relations with other teachers. Hopefully, not all of these elements exist in *any* district; but the school administrator should be alert for them.

PERSONAL CAUSES

The third general category, dealing with personal reasons for leaving a position, includes the two obvious reasons—marriage and family for women, competition of other positions for men. In addition, however, are things like poor mental hygiene, inability to handle the students, and bad health.

Possibly the incidence of job-leaving due to poor mental hygiene could be reduced through improved interview techniques. Good mental hygiene is defined as "an emotional condition characterized by thought and behavior patterns which are satisfying to the individual and in reasonable harmony with the society in which he lives" (Douglass and Mills, 1948). The recruiter might avoid some problems along this line by including in the interview questions which would establish those who are not "in reasonable harmony" with the society in which they live.

GATHERING DATA TO IMPROVE RECRUITMENT AND RETENTION

When a teacher decides to leave his position because of dissatisfaction, it would be unusual if a single factor was totally responsible. An individual, for example, can stand sluggish traffic, or bad weather, or an intransigent student, or an insensitive colleague, or a late check. It is only when they all happen on the same day that he becomes subject to irrational acts. The teacher, similarly, can probably shrug off a few of the discouraging aspects which spring up on the job. When they accumulate, however, the discouragement and disillusionment might be irrevocable.

It is probably the rare individual who was happy with his job yesterday, but today something happens and he writes a letter of resignation. Most of us are not that precipitous. Teachers probably do not go instantly from being satisfied with a job to complete dissatisfaction and eventual departure.

In chapter 7 the topic of staff attitude was discussed. The authors suggested that continuous sampling techniques be used to get at some of the attitude *trends* in the faculty. These suggestions are particularly appropriate if a district has problems with retaining teachers. It is not enough to ask a teacher who has already made up his mind why he is resigning. The teacher probably could not answer honestly even if he wanted to, for he is probably incapable of retracing each step which culminated in his final decision. But if the administrator had periodically sampled the expressed feelings of his teacher, the process would be easier to trace. The administrator might be interested in his teachers' comments about salary, pressure groups, adequacy of supervision, and all the other factors listed in the first two categories of the list of causes for leaving. We suggest that if data on these topics were collected under a continuous assessment design, decision-making about recruitment and retention of teachers would improve.

The implication is that the school administrator should not only dwell on the negative—determining errors in recruitment practices and finding out why teachers leave, but might also "accentuate the positive" (to quote a very old song). Instead of looking only at why teachers leave, some investigations might be made to find out about those who remain.

The actuary prepares tables which tell him, for example, what proportion of today's thirty-year-old teachers will still be in the field twenty-five years from now. The school administrator might get some interesting information by plotting a series of *survival curves* (see Charters, 1967). A survival curve is plotted by looking back into the district some reasonable amount of time—say ten years; and accumulating survival data for each person hired. It is best to plot separate curves for males and females; and if enough data are available, other subgroups might be isolated—such as females taking their first job, or males hired after experience on another faculty. Figure 13 shows a hypothetical graph of three such survival curves. The data for this figure are hypothetical. They conform, however, to common teacher staying patterns. The horizontal axis designates years after initial hiring. For this district, approximately 85 percent of the females hired for their first position will still be in the school one year later. Five years after first hiring, about 53 percent of the original group of males, as compared to 25 percent of the original group of females, will still be in the classroom.

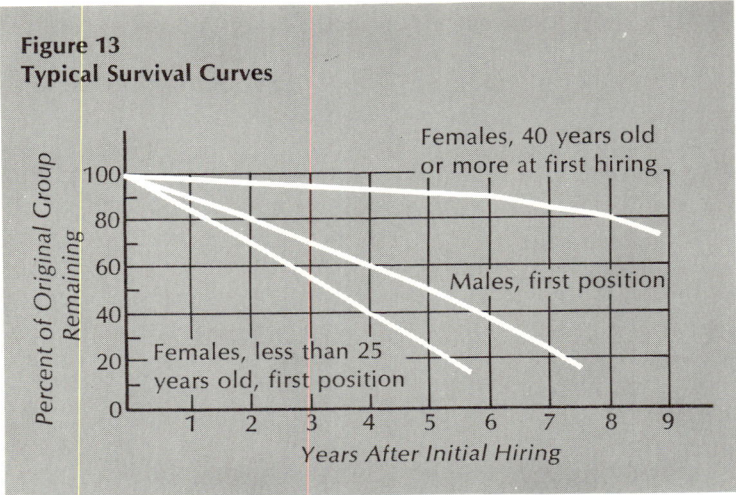

**Figure 13
Typical Survival Curves**

Three curves have been shown on this figure. The three conform to general expectations for teachers. That is, after about five years, the young females will mostly have retired, at least temporarily, from the classroom. The young males hired will also drift away from the classroom, but at a slower rate; and of the females hired after their family responsibilities are pretty much past, the survival rate will be relatively high.

These are not the only groups which might be defined for graphing. A district which is relatively large and includes a number of separate school buildings might accumulate the information from each different building and prepare a separate curve for each building; or for each subsection of the district. The survival rates for primary, elementary, junior high, and high school teachers might be compared; or any number of other district-specific groups.

These survival curves can be very instructive. For one thing, they do accentuate the positive—that is, they give information about those who remain, instead of stressing those who leave. In addition, it should be of considerable interest to a district to find out whether their curves are contrary to the common patterns. For example, perhaps the young males in the district remain through their thirties; maybe they do not last as long as the young females. Perhaps the young females tend to remain in the classroom right through their child-bearing years. Perhaps the teachers from one building in the district do have a remarkable survival rate. Why? What are the factors which might be thought of as causal? Information like this is valuable to the decision-maker.

In addition, survival curves make long-range planning an easier matter. When enough information has been accumulated, the curves will be relatively stable unless some truly monumental changes occur in the district. With these curves available, the administration can better predict the number of teachers required for the next year and in subsequent years, and the recruitment policies and procedures can be planned for years in advance.

REFERENCES

Alexander, William M., and J. G. Saylor. *Modern Secondary Education.* New York: Rinehart and Co., 1959.

Bauthues, Donald. *The Format and Processing of Information in the Selection Process.* Paper presented to a symposium of the American Educational Research Association Annual Convention, February, 1968. (Mimeographed.)

Charters, W. W., Jr. "Some 'Obvious' Facts About the Teaching Career," *Educational Administration Quarterly* 3 (Spring 1967): 183–193.

Douglass, Harl R., R. K. Bent, and C. W. Boardman. *Democratic Supervision in Secondary Schools,* 2d ed. Boston: Houghton Mifflin, 1961.

Douglass, Harl R., and H. H. Mills. *Teaching in High School.* New York: Ronald Press, 1948.

Hickey, Michael. *Personality and Behavioral Characteristics Pertinent to the Selection of Teachers.* Paper presented to a symposium of the American Educational Research Association Annual Convention, February, 1968. (Mimeographed.)

Kleinman, Lou. "A New Dimension in Teacher Selection," *Journal of Educational Sociology* 34 (September 1960): 24–33.

Knox, W. B. "A Study of the Relationship of Certain Environmental Factors to Teaching Success," *Journal of Experimental Education* 24 (1956): 95–141.

Koos, Frank H. "The Load of the High School Teacher," *American School Board Journal* 65 (August 1922): 47–49, 133–134.

Koos, Leonard V., J. M. Hughes, P. W. Hutson, and W. C. Reavis. *Administering the Secondary School.* New York: American Book Co., 1940.

Mitzel, Harold E. *A Behavioral Approach to the Assessment of Teacher Effectiveness.* New York: Office of Research and Evaluation, College of the City of New York, 1957.

———. "Teacher Effectiveness," pp. 1481–1485 in *Encyclopedia of Educational Research,* 3rd ed. New York: Macmillan, 1960.

Nelson, Robert H., and Michael L. Thompson. "Why Teachers Quit: Factors Influencing Teachers to Leave Their Classrooms After the First Year," *The Clearing House* 37 (April 1963): 467–473.

Palmer, Dale. "Situational Factors to be Considered in the Selection Process," paper presented to a symposium of the American Educational Research Association Annual Convention, February, 1968. (Mimeographed.)

Rozencranz, Howard A., and Bruce J. Biddle. "The Role Approach to Teacher Competence," in Bruce J. Biddle and William J. Ellena, eds., *Contemporary Research on Teacher Effectiveness.* New York: Holt, Rinehart & Winston, 1964.

Ryans, David G. *Characteristics of Teachers.* Washington, D.C.: American Council on Education, 1960.

Scott, William E., Jr. "The Actuarial-Clinical Controversy in Managerial Selection," *Business Horizons* 7 (Winter 1964): 89–99.

Toops, Herbert A. "Philosophy and Practice of Personnel Selection," *Educational and Psychological Measurement* 5 (Summer 1945): 95–130.

9 EVALUATING TEACHER EFFECTIVENESS

Considerations in Measuring Teacher Effectiveness
Interaction of teacher characteristics and school environment

Personality Measures
Types of personality measures
Reliability and validity considerations

Evaluation by Expert Observation
Drawbacks to assessments by experts
Rating scales
Students as raters
Methods of observation

Measurement by Pupil Performance
Pupil performance and teacher expectancy

Measurement by Pupil Behavior in the Community

Decision-Making Model

One of the most pressing problems facing any profession today is that of the evaluation of the work of members of the profession. Education, like many other professions, has difficulty establishing the criteria of good performance. The criteria often employed seem rather gross and indirect measures of the real behaviors being sought.

The problems of establishing levels of teacher effectiveness are not diminishing, for the majority of observers will agree that the largest single factor in establishing the classroom environment is the teacher himself. So often in the past a good teacher has been equated to "the perfesser"— a scholarly sort of person, well versed in the subject matter specialties. The authors will agree that while knowledge in the subject matter is certainly a necessary condition for effective teaching, it will not insure success. The teacher of today can be termed a "social engineer." That is, the teacher is constantly trying to manipulate the environment in the classroom so that a roomful of individuals having very diverse characteristics can all be reached. In addition to teaching content in the courses, the teachers are trying to help pupils meet the ever-changing social relationships that they must be involved with, and help each individual grow and understand not only himself, but others as well.

The effectiveness of a teacher in a classroom is certainly a multi-dimensional construct. Direct evaluation of such a complex construct may be difficult, but there are indirect ways of attacking the problem. Unfortunately, in the past researchers have dealt only with small segments of the problem, and have not investigated the *general* concept of teacher effectiveness (Barr and Jones, 1958). These studies will not answer questions of general effectiveness. The school administration must be willing to commit time and resources to the task of defining criteria for teacher effectiveness.

CONSIDERATIONS IN MEASURING TEACHER EFFECTIVENESS

Basic to all the approaches to be discussed is the assumption that teacher differences make a difference in the pupils' performance. This assumption has been verified by Webb and Bowers (1957). In recent years, many studies have indicated correlations between teacher characteristics and different measures of students. These studies are usually descriptive in nature; of course, to *describe* is one thing, to *prescribe* is another. As has been stated before, a correlation does not necessarily imply a cause and effect relationship.

INTERACTION OF TEACHER CHARACTERISTICS AND
SCHOOL ENVIRONMENT

Age, sex, amount of schooling, type of schooling, income of father, student teaching grades, college grade point average —all of these have been considered in studies of teacher effectiveness. The correlation between these variables and teaching effectiveness is generally very low or nonexistent. The problem in all of these measures is that of interaction, and if it were overcome, perhaps these relationships would be stronger.

A teacher is not "effective" in a vacuum; effectiveness really relates to the interaction of the teacher and his students in the classroom. Studies which attempt to relate teacher characteristics to teaching effectiveness imply that the classroom environment is a constant—the same everywhere. The question "What are the dimensions of an effective teacher?" cannot be answered without asking, "In what situation?" Each of the following is a public school teacher: The only third-grade teacher in a rural Iowa community of five hundred; a social studies teacher in a suburban high school serving students whose parents are affluent; a second-grade teacher serving an all-black, inner city population; a physics teacher in a middle-class high school; a teacher whose student population is predominantly Jewish; a junior high school teacher of physical education; and a kindergarten teacher. They have certain things in common, to be sure, but each environment described is unique in very important ways. Does anyone really believe that the same characteristics are associated with effective teaching in all of these diverse situations? It would be very hazardous to generalize; still, many studies have seemed to imply that the interaction between characteristics and school environment is inconsequential.

Instead of looking for the correlates of effective teaching, researchers need to start looking for the correlates of effective physics teaching, or of effective kindergarten teaching, or of effective elementary school teaching in the inner city, and so forth. The interaction of teacher characteristics and school environment should not be ignored.

PERSONALITY MEASURES

A teacher of chemistry really should know this field, and a teacher of kindergarten should have some specific training for this task. But another important determinant of an effective teacher is his personality. For example, teaching is opportunistic. That is, unplanned events occur which can be treated as either a disruption or an unexpected opportunity to further the educational program. There are presumably certain personality traits associated with this ability to seize the moment. Many other examples could be given; and the accumulation of these will explain why many researchers have used personality measures to seek correlates of effective teaching.

Of course, a number of questions come to mind. Which traits have researchers focused on? How have they measured these traits? Many facets of a teacher's personality can be measured, using a variety of techniques, but the specific meaning of the results is illusive. If a person sets out to determine the effectiveness of a teacher through the use of a personality inventory, he must first define those personality characteristics which will be termed acceptable to the construct of teacher effectiveness.

Many personality constructs are over-defined. That is, they mean more in general than they do specifically; different terms mean about the same thing. What does it mean to have a good self-concept? When asked if they have a general understanding of that term, most students will nod their heads in the affirmative. But if you press them further with very specific questions which force them to apply this general understanding (e.g., Is a person with a good self-concept also dogmatic? Does he tend to set goals a little too high, very high, or just right? How does he react to new environments? Who would make a better teacher in the inner city—one with high self-concept, or low? Who would make a better actor?), it will quickly be seen that different people interpret the construct "good self-concept" in very different ways. Some will say it takes a high self-concept to be comfortable in new environments; others will say one with a high self-concept has become that way because he has learned to cope with his own environment. The point is this: Any researcher who concludes something like "teachers with a high self-concept are more effective" has the responsibility of defining very carefully what he means by that construct;

otherwise, consumers will interpret the statement many different ways.

We have discussed the interaction between teacher characteristics and the environment. When personality correlates of teacher effectiveness are studied, another kind of interaction effect can lead to misinterpretations. It may not be one or two specific personality traits that make a teacher effective, but rather the interaction of many traits. A high degree of "flexibility" might be associated with effective teaching. But a teacher low in "flexibility" might compensate through arduous preparations; and a teacher high in "flexibility" may be a failure due to overwhelming body odors. If a teacher has three parts "liberal-mindedness," how much "communality," "flexibility," and "sociability" will be needed to balance out to an effective teacher? How much "sociability" is required to balance low ratings in "liberal-mindedness"? A teacher's effectiveness is not a function of single measures, but depends upon the interaction of many factors.

TYPES OF PERSONALITY MEASURES

A summary of the history of personality measures or an overview of the field would be out of place here. Both of these needs are fulfilled by Sarason's work (1966); and the reader is also directed to the work of Horst (1968). *Personality measures,* as the term is used here, include item collections which go under other names. Some of these other names are *interest inventories* (e.g., the Strong Vocational Interest Blank, 1943), *temperament tests, preference tests* (e.g., the Kuder Preference Record, 1939, and the Edwards Personal Preference Schedule, 1953), *adjustment inventories* (e.g., the Bell Adjustment Inventory, 1938), *attitude measures* (especially toward specific topics), and *descriptive ratings.* Herein, the term *personality measures* includes all of these. The general term is distinct from *achievement measures* which are directed toward the cognitive domain. The distinction among the terms listed is in the use made of the results, rather than the manner of presentation.

Personality measures are generally presented in a paper-and-pencil format. There are a number of different response modes possible. In many instruments, a statement is made (the stimulus); and the subject responds "yes/no," "yes/?/no," "agree/don't know/disagree," or on some sort of numerical scale. Others ask the respondent to choose which of two to four statements he is most in agreement with. These forced-choice formats can be somewhat threatening; one usually does not like to choose between two statements which are both repugnant. (Which would you rather do—starve to death or die of thirst?)

RELIABILITY AND VALIDITY CONSIDERATIONS

The term *reliability* implies adjectives like "stable" and "precise." A test is *reliable* if it measures the same result over and over again. A test is *valid* if it measures what we want it to measure. Obviously, a test cannot be valid if it is unreliable. Validity is the final goal—a test which purports to measure mathematical ability but *really* is measuring reading skill is useless, but reliability is a necessary condition for validity. A test can be completely reliable and totally invalid—which means it is measuring precisely the wrong answers each time it is used.

There are a number of ways to measure reliability, but personality measures fit a test-retest format best. This very simple method simply involves administering a set of items to the same group at two separate times. If the test is reliable, the same people will tend to give the same answers. The person who obtained the highest score the first time will tend to do so the second time, the person with the second highest score the first time will do so the second, and so forth.

Validity, as we said, is the goal; but as the reliability goes down, the measurement errors increase, and the possibility of validity decreases. It is legitimate to ask that any measure used in education have an acceptable validity, which implies a relatively high reliability. Achievement tests, especially those batteries which are on the national market, can be expected to have reliabilities in excess of 0.85. Many have reliabilities in excess of 0.90. The reliability of some personality measures tends to be quite low. Reliabilities as low as 0.35 and 0.40 have been reported. Validities are limited by reliabilities, so that these low reliabilities cause us to seriously question the use of such measures to determine teacher effectiveness. This is especially true if the purpose is to measure the effectiveness of a *specific* teacher; less so if the measure is to be interpreted in the group sense.

Another consideration is that the validity of a construct itself can be low because the constructs are very situation-specific. Consider a construct such as "extroversion-introversion." This seems to be a more clearly definable construct than one like "self-concept." However, individual introversion levels in a group of people will depend on the group situation. These writers have colleagues who are forthright and outspoken in any sort of an intellectual setting, but are complete wallflowers at a football game or cocktail party. This means, once again, that the terms *extroversion* and *introversion* are overdefined. A person's real measure on such constructs is a function of each specific situation. This may well explain the low reliabilities usually seen in measures of personality constructs. When we examine a group the second time, their perception of their situation may have changed, and they therefore respond differently.

The authors are not enthusiastic about the use of personality measures to determine teacher effectiveness. We suggest that approximately the same levels of reliability and validity be required of these measures as from achievement tests, especially if the results are to be applied to an individual.

EVALUATION BY EXPERT OBSERVATION

One of the most frequently used measures of teacher effectiveness is the judgment of "experts" who have observed the teacher in action. The use of expert judgment is administratively probably one of the easiest methods available; however, it is based on the assumption that it is possible for school principals, administrators, and supervisors or other educational experts to recognize good teaching when they see it, and to make comparative judgments about teachers. It is interesting to note that as early as 1937, Sandiford was suggesting that the judgment of experts was the *only* valid criterion for judging teacher effectiveness. This is a rather strong statement, but in the face of other available techniques, it may still be quite appropriate today. It removes much artificiality from the measures, since it requires that the expert observe the teacher in the actual classroom setting.

DRAWBACKS TO ASSESSMENT BY EXPERTS

The primary objection to this kind of assessment is that it is quite subjective. The "expert" brings along a whole set of personal biases about what an effective teacher does in the classroom. The expert must be very flexible, recognizing that there are different ways to conduct a class or present a lesson. On the other hand, we must demand that the expert's judgments be stable, which is the same as demanding that measures should be reliable. This means that we expect the same expert to give identical ratings to the same lesson when he hears it in January as he did three months earlier. It also means that different experts would rank a group of teachers in a nearly identical manner. If expert judgments are used to rate the effectiveness of teachers, it is very important that the school administrator pay careful attention to these measures of reliability. The experts must be placed in the classroom for long enough periods of time so that their judgments are reliable, even if this involves an extensive time commitment.

RATING SCALES

One technique for reducing the time required by expert judges in the classroom is to use rating scales. With a rating scale, the observer does not need to spend so much time recording his observations in the classroom, and he can spend more time observing the behavior of students and teachers. The rater responds to predetermined categories on the rating schedule. Note, however, that this does not necessarily decrease the amount of subjectivity in the ratings.

The very presence of these predetermined categories can be detrimental. If the rater is not particularly familiar with the concepts on the scale, or if the concepts are not behaviorally defined, it is likely that rater responses will be quite divergent. Borgsmiller (1969) has questioned the reliability of ratings when the rater is unsure of the relevance of the scale item to the concept being evaluated. That is, the rating scale itself may be influencing the ratings. If rating scales are used in a district, it is very important that the school administrator insure that all the raters have the same interpretations of the items on the scale; and that these interpretations conform with those of the school administration.

STUDENTS AS RATERS

One of the most logical techniques for evaluating teacher effectiveness is through the use of pupil ratings. Pupils probably know more about the individual teacher than experts who judge for a short period of time, and can add to information gained through the use of rating scales. The use of such an approach to assessing teacher effectiveness has some patently obvious drawbacks, but if used properly, could add another dimension to the overall picture.

Unfortunately, students have a tendency to rate teachers on factors other than effectiveness. This is hard to overcome, since it is also difficult for the school administration to inform the pupils about the specific concepts to be rated. The most serious problem, however, and one which should be carefully considered in interpreting student ratings, is the tendency for students to have a rather short-term picture of things, and an inadequate knowledge of the ultimate goals of the teacher. The student may not know until much later how much a particular teacher helped. The student may even have been helped tremendously by a teacher—without realizing it! One way to get around this problem, of course, is to wait until some later time to ask the students for their ratings. But students forget; and the students may then give the generally accepted rating rather than their own personal observation.

METHODS OF OBSERVATION

The methods of observation should also be given attention. The amount of time spent and the timing of the observations are important. For the observations to be meaningful, it is important that the experts observe and evaluate the individual teachers several times during the school year. These should not all be at the same time of the day or the same day of the week. The experts are trying to assess general teaching effectiveness, and this rating should not be limited to a particular unit or instructional area.

Should the observations be a surprise to the teacher, or should he know? If we tell him that he is to be observed, should he also be informed of the exact date and time for the observations?

If the observation period is scheduled in advance so that the teacher has time to prepare for the observer, it is made under *optimum* rather than *average* conditions. Such a procedure makes for a more cordial, less threatening situation. It might be well to find out how well a teacher *can do,* and this could then be the administrator's goal for this teacher.

On the other hand, the teacher might be informed that observations are going to be made over the course of a year and be told what the purposes of these observations are, but not given the exact times. Then the observer is more likely to see the *average* classroom behavior of the teacher. However, the very presence of the observer may affect some teachers in unpredictable ways so that their teaching behavior is still not typical.

Finally, the observer could arrive on the scene completely unannounced. The authors question the wisdom of such techniques, for the negative reaction this might occasion from the teacher probably cancels out any benefit which could have been obtained from the observation efforts. The observer who arrives unannounced has no real advantage over the observer who was announced. We believe teachers should know about the observation efforts.

MEASUREMENT BY PUPIL PERFORMANCE

When a teacher inaugurates an instructional program, he intends that pupils in the room will change in some predetermined direction. For instance, they will know more, and will behave differently, and their attitudes may change. One way to measure the effectiveness of a teacher is to determine what changes have taken place in that teacher's pupils. This approach to the investigation of teacher effectiveness has been quite thoroughly developed, and frequently used.

Mitzel and Gross (1956) have raised some very relevant questions about the notion of judging teacher effectiveness through measuring pupil performance. Most fundamental of these questions are: "What kinds of changes are expected?" and "What kinds of changes are acceptable?" Must all the students change by the same amount, or are there certain entering characteristics of students which determine how much change is acceptable? To say that a teacher of a mentally retarded class is only effective if he brings about as much change as a teacher in a regular classroom hardly seems fair. If pupil performance is to be used as a measure of teacher effectiveness, then the classroom environment must be taken into consideration. The complex characteristics of the pupils, as well as the entering status of each, will limit the possibility of success for some teachers.

As was mentioned earlier, the teacher's behavior will have much influence on the environment in the classroom; but the teacher's control over the total school environment is minimal. That total environment may be detrimental to the learning process, affecting all teachers generally, or affecting only specific teachers with particular characteristics. The national origin, race, sex, age, religious persuasion, or hair style of a particular teacher may interact negatively with certain prevailing characteristics in the school's community. The environmental limitations in such a teacher's classroom will be specific, perhaps unshared by the teacher next door. If the pupils in the room do not perform up to expectation, it may therefore be due to factors beyond the teacher's control—indeed, possibly even unknown to the teacher.

PUPIL PERFORMANCE AND TEACHER EXPECTANCY

Several studies have indicated that the student's relationship with the teacher can influence his academic performance (see Davidson and Lang, 1960; Flanders, 1965; Flanders and Havumaki, 1960; Hill and Sarason, 1966; Lippitt and Gold, 1959; Ludwig and Maehr, 1967; Mayer, Kranzler, and Matthes, 1967; Rosenthal and Jacobson, 1966; Spaulding, 1964; and Staines, 1958). The concept of a self-fulfilling prophecy is raised; that is, the student does poorly or well because that is how the teacher *expects* him to perform. The authors agree that the notion is very appealing, and could, in fact, be true. The study by Rosenthal and Jacobson (1966) purports to prove this concept. Although the study has received widespread attention, it has been seriously questioned on methodological grounds, to the point that the results are in very serious doubt (see Mayer and Beggs, 1969; Thorndike, 1968).

So it can be seen that the use of pupil output as a measure of teacher effectiveness, though very appealing, has its limitations. What are the input characteristics of the students? How do these characteristics interact with the learning process and with the characteristics of the teacher? What is the effect of the total school environment? Is pupil performance a function of teacher expectancy? To these criticisms must be added the question of long-term versus short-term results. Will output measures emphasize short-term gains to the exclusion of the more important long-term benefits of a particular teacher? Those who would criticize this approach to determining teacher effectiveness have much ammunition at their disposal.

The authors agree that the student characteristics associated with learning probabilities are not well defined; that school environment is important; that input characteristics do differ; and that long-term benefits are more important than are short-term gains. The school administrator should be aware of these; and should take them into consideration when making decisions.

Still we believe that the measurement of student changes should be the single most important determiner of teacher effectiveness evaluation. If the long-term goals are difficult to measure, does it logically follow that we should therefore exclude measurement of short-term goals? Certainly not! Most goals of a third-grade teacher in a particular classroom of a particular school district could be defined very specifically in behavioral terms, and could be measured without ambiguity. The nearest many districts have come to doing this is to use standardized achievement batteries. But these are too general for the specific district. Performance on the tests is very much a function of the organization and pacing of the district.

There are certain things that the fourth-grade mathematics teacher expects the third-grade teacher to have accomplished. These skills are specific, as are skills in reading, language arts, and handwriting. These specific things are measurable; *change* in student performance can be measured. Expected amounts of change are prescribable, given certain input characteristics. One scheme for doing this is outlined in chapter 3.

A teacher is a professional, and a professional should be expected to be held accountable. When the author goes to the dentist with a toothache, he expects immediate ameliorative action. If this action is not forthcoming, that dentist had better be prepared to explain why.

The public expects changes to occur in the classroom. They have every right to have these expectations. This does not mean that all students will undergo the same changes, or even equal amounts of change. The entire class cannot be expected to finish a year all at the same competency level. But changes can be expected in each. If the lawyer does not win a lawsuit, there may be mitigating circumstances—perhaps the original statements were false. If the teacher does not bring about the expected change in some pupil, there may also be mitigating circumstances which should be taken into consideration. But most expected change can be prescribed, and subsequent achievement can be measured. We believe this is the most fundamentally honest way to measure teacher effectiveness.

If this technique is used, the measurements must be very broadly based. If a single test or a series of short measures is used, there will be the distinct possibility that the individual teachers will teach for the test and ignore broader goals. To be accurately indicative of knowledge in the broader domain, a test must be a random sample. If the students are instructed about those particular items (which is "teaching for the test") to the exclusion of instruction in the broader domain, then this measure of teacher effectiveness is essentially useless.

However, there is a way to circumvent this problem. It is easier to describe than to do. If the scope of behavioral objectives which are *tested for* is very broad, then teaching for the test will be the same as teaching to reach all the objectives. This implies more than a half-page of general objectives for each instructional program. It implies an exhaustive listing of the specific and important goals in the classroom. The list for third-grade arithmetic, for example, might be five pages long. The list would contain the specific behaviors expected, perhaps including variable levels of attainment. The school's professional staff would have to agree that these were the important short-term goals for third-grade arithmetic; and the teacher would be aware of these goals. We can see no reason why the teacher should not be held accountable for their attainment.

In chapter 4, the techniques for reporting pupil progress to various groups were surveyed. The advice at this point stressed the need for choosing a measurement scale to fit the purpose at hand. If student change or growth is to be used as a measure of teacher effectiveness, then the scale used should directly reflect growth. It was noted earlier that grade equivalent scales, despite their drawback of being often misinterpreted, do directly reflect change or growth in the pupils. In chapter 4 we explained how grade equivalent scales are made, and how the local district can make its own grade equivalent scales for local goals and organization.

Beggs (1966) investigated the question of the best timing during the school year for the assessment of the performance of individual students. He concluded that testing during the first month of the school year might not be too wise, for this is the time during which students are relearning material from the previous years, and regrouping for learning. His investigations also suggest that testing should be avoided during the last month or so of the academic year, for he noted a decline in the accuracy of responses to tests from April to May. If tests are to be given to detect change, the authors suggest that this be done in late September or early October, and again in early May. This suggestion is for schools which prefer to test only twice. If an exhaustive list of specific behavioral outcomes were prepared for each grade, however, testing and evaluation would necessarily be continuous.

MEASUREMENT BY PUPIL BEHAVIOR IN THE COMMUNITY

Another approach to the measurement of teacher effectiveness deals with the behavior of pupils in the community. Clearly the primary goal of the schools is not to produce students who are successful in a school environment, but rather students who are successful in the community environment. Assessments of the student's behavior in the community deal with some of the long-term changes alluded to earlier, and these are very hard to measure. These kinds of characteristics are broadly based, and when they show up in a student it is difficult to attribute them to a single teacher; and conversely, when they do not show up, it is difficult to name a single individual as the reason. With this approach, the authors believe teacher effectiveness must be viewed collectively, and perhaps expanded to include school effectiveness, with the teachers joined by the administration and professional staff as the objects of inquiry.

A very obvious problem exists with these investigations, of course: information is most easily accumulated while the students are in school. However, such limitations could give a biased picture of the student's behavior. Observations are needed about the student when he is not in school. These measures are clumsy to obtain, of course, but could provide the school with some real insight into the kinds of teachers and methods of instruction which have made an impact on the school's students.

DECISION-MAKING MODEL

Before a school administration can seek out district-specific characteristics of effective teachers, it must define its effective teachers. We believe that a decision-making model dealing with teacher effectiveness should contain two important elements. These are:

1. First, the effective teacher has to be defined. While it would be nice to do this in terms of the ultimate goals of the school for the pupils' behavior in society at large, the difficulties in this approach make it somewhat impractical. We believe the focus should be on the attainment of classroom objectives.

2. The school administration should conceive and organize its methods of assessing teacher effectiveness to include the teachers as active and willing participants. Most teachers *want* to be effective, and the administration's attempts to assess their weaknesses, intended to make them more effective, do not need to be seen as threatening.

The actual measures—measures of teacher characteristics, measures done by expert observers—come into the picture only after the definition of an effective teacher has been made. Why do some teachers tend to achieve the goals set for the performance of their pupils? Why do some teachers seem to do so well with students whose entering characteristics included high initial performance? Why are certain teachers successful in arithmetic, but not reading? And most important, what is success in teaching? We suggest that success be defined in terms of goal attainment by pupils.

But remember that this goal attainment must be carefully and specifically defined, so that teacher and administrator are both "singing out of the same hymnbook." Close attention must be paid to the curriculum guide, textbooks, and supplementary material. Previous and future instructional programs are important. Individual performance differences cannot be ignored. The task of defining the teaching goals specifically to everyone's satisfaction can probably never be done completely; but it can be done to a close approximation. Our suggestion to define effectiveness in terms of student change *does not equate* to a test-retest program using a standardized achievement test battery. These are not specific enough for a given district; teachers would tend to teach for the test. These tests do not sample the larger domain of expected outcomes intensely enough.

The teaching-learning process is very complex. Many factors are associated with a student's success in achieving goals; most agree that the teacher is one of the most important of these factors. Many teachers and administrators will object strongly to our strong insistence upon measuring teacher effectiveness through evaluation of pupil changes. We believe that many of these objections reflect past misuses of these techniques, when pupils were measured by tests not closely linked to the curriculum, and the goals of the administration and teacher were not carefully defined. We believe that teachers want to be effective; want help in becoming more effective; and will not object to assessments of their effectiveness *if* criteria of acceptable performance are clearly defined and well understood by all involved.

REFERENCES

Barr, A. S., and R. E. Jones. "The Measurement and Prediction of Teacher Efficiency," *Review of Educational Research* 28 (June 1958): 256–265.

Beggs, Donald L. "Uniformity of Growth in the Basic Skills Throughout the School Year and During the Summer." Unpublished Ph.D. dissertation, University of Iowa, 1966.

Borg, Walter R. "Personality and Interest Measures as Related to Criteria of Instructor Effectiveness," *Journal of Educational Research* 50 (May 1957): 701–709.

Borgsmiller, Patricia A. "Salience of Concepts and Commitment to Extreme Judgments in the Response Patterns of Teachers." Dissertation prospectus presented to the Graduate School, Southern Illinois University, 1969.

Davidson, H. H., and G. Lang. "Children's Perception of Their Teachers' Feelings Toward Them Related to Self-Perception, School Achievement, and Behavior," *Journal of Experimental Education* 29 (1960): 107–118.

Evans, Kathleen M. "Methods of Assessing Teaching Ability," *British Journal of Educational Psychology* 21, pt. 2 (June 1951): 89–95.

Flanders, Ned A. "Teacher Influence, Pupil Attitudes, and Achievement," Cooperative Research Monograph No. 12. Washington, D.C.: U.S. Department of Health, Education, and Welfare, 1965.

Flanders, N., and S. Havumaki. "The Effect of Teacher-Pupil Contacts Involving Praise on the Sociometric Choices of Students," *Journal of Educational Psychology* 51 (April 1960): 65–68.

Heilman, J. D., and W. D. Armentrout. "The Rating of College Teachers on Ten Traits by Their Students," *Journal of Educational Psychology* 27 (1936): 197–216.

Hill, Kennedy T., and Seymour B. Sarason. "The Relation of Test Activity and Defensiveness to Test and School Performance over the Elementary School Years: A Further Longitudinal Study," *Monographs of the Society for Research in Child Development* 31 (1966): 1–76.

Horst, Paul. *Personality: Measurement of Dimensions*. San Francisco: Jossey-Bass, 1968.

Lindquist, E. F., and A. N. Hieronymus. "Manual for Administrators, Supervisors, and Counselors," p. 13, *Iowa Tests of Basic Skills*. Boston: Houghton Mifflin, 1964.

Lippitt, R., and M. Gold. "Classroom Social Structure as a Mental Health Problem," *Journal of Social Issues* 15 (1959): 40–49.

Ludwig, David J., and Martin J. Maehr. "Changes in Self-Concept and Stated Behavioral References," *Child Development* 38 (1967): 453–469.

Mayer, G. R., and D. L. Beggs. "Interpreting Ability Test Results to Elementary School Teachers." Paper presented at a meeting of The American Personnel and Guidance Association, Las Vegas, April 1969.

Mayer, G. Roy, Gerald D. Kranzler, and William A. Matthes. "The Elementary School Counselor and Teacher-Pupil Relations," *Elementary School Guidance and Counseling* 2 (October 1967): 3–14.

Mitzel, H. E., and C. F. Gross. *Critical Review of the Development of Pupil Growth Criteria in Studies of Teacher Effectiveness*, Research Series, No. 31. New York: Board of Higher Education, 1956.

Rosenthal, Robert, and Lenore Jacobson. "Teachers' Expectancies: Determinants of Pupils' I.Q. Gains," *Psychological Report* 19 (1966): 115–118.

Rugg, H. "Is the Rating of Human Character Possible?" *Journal of Educational Psychology* 13 (1922): 30–42.

Sandiford, P., et al. *Forecasting Teaching Ability*, Bulletin No. 8. Toronto: Department of Educational Research, University of Toronto, 1937.

Sarason, I. G. *Personality: An Objective Approach*. New York: John Wiley, 1966.

Spaulding, R. L. "Achievement, Creativity, and Self-Concept Correlates of Teacher-Pupil Transactions in Elementary Schools," pp. 110–117 in Celia Stendler (ed.), *Readings in Child Behavior and Development*. New York: Harcourt, Brace & World, 1964.

Staines, J. W. "The Self-Picture as a Factor in the Classroom," *British Journal of Educational Psychology* 28 (June 1958): 97–111.

Thorndike, Robert L. Review of *Pygalion in the Classroom*, in *American Educational Research Journal* 5 (4): 708–711.

Thorpe, Louis P., et al. "Test Coordinator's Manual for Forms C and D," p. 7, *SRA Achievement Series*. Chicago: Science Research Associates, 1964.

Webb, W. B., and N. D. Bowers. "The Utilization of Student Learning as a Criterion of Instructor Effectiveness," *Journal of Educational Research* 51 (September 1957): 17–23.

ASSESSING COMMUNITY ATTITUDES: THE SCHOOL BOND ISSUE

Hiram Public School: An Example

Expressed Attitudes and Actual Behavior

Some Sampling Decisions

The Questionnaire
Developing the questionnaire
Tryout of the questionnaire

Sample Size and Accuracy of Prediction
Is the return large enough?

Statistical Procedure and Decision-Making

Measuring Other Community Attitudes

Continuous Assessment of Community Attitudes

School bond issues have become an American tradition. Current expenditures, including recurring items such as teacher salaries and educational materials, are usually budgeted at least a year in advance. These are supported through local tax levies (although the recent trend has been toward increased state and national aid for local school districts). The tax levies are increased or decreased slightly as reflections of increases and decreases in the yearly budget.

But when the time comes for a major and nonrecurring expenditure of the type required when current facilities need major repairs or when new buildings are needed, the administration must ask the community to approve special funds—and the inseparable companion of such funds, special tax levies. Although some towns have unblemished records of bond issue approvals, communities more commonly have both approvals and disapprovals recorded in their recent history. Bond issue elections cost money, and they involve a great investment of time and effort by the school administration. An administration would be able to make much more informed decisions if reliable measurements of community attitude were available *before* the introduction of a bond issue.

HIRAM PUBLIC SCHOOL: AN EXAMPLE

To make this chapter more explicit, suppose we consider the following hypothetical situation:

When a large new industry chooses to locate in a certain town, the decision is a cause for general jubilation among the citizens of the chosen location. But the school superintendent knows that the large numbers of new workers will bring an influx of new students, and that means crowded classrooms. In order to accommodate the increase in the number of students, the superintendent of the Hiram Public School District felt that a new school building would be required, since substantial increases in enrollment were highly probable. When the superintendent submitted his proposal for a new school building to his school board, they agreed that there was a definite need for the building. They further decided that a bond issue would have to be approved by the community in order to secure special funds for the building. However, the members of the school board expressed concern about voter approval. The superintendent was commissioned by the board to gather information about the attitude of the community toward a school bond issue. The board members felt that a failure would have unpleasant repercussions. The consensus was that the bond issue should only be presented to the community if the superintendent's survey indicated that it would pass with an acceptable level of confidence.

It must certainly be true that some districts bring bond issues before the voters even when they know there is a high probability of failure. For example, the board might wish to bring to the surface latent anti-school feelings of which the general population is unaware. In the absence of such conditions, however, it is likely that the board's reasoning in our hypothetical Hiram Public School District is more realistic—they do not want to bring the issue before the voters if they suspect it will fail. If a preliminary study indicates that an issue has only 1 chance in 20 of passing, or even 1 in 5, most boards would conclude that an educational campaign is a prerequisite to the actual bond issue.

EXPRESSED ATTITUDES AND ACTUAL BEHAVIOR

When a researcher decides to assess community attitudes, it is necessary to make certain judgments regarding the relationship between the *expressed attitudes* of the respondents and the *actual behavior* which they manifest.[1] In situations where there is an observed discrepancy, the following possibilities become apparent:

1. There is the possibility of purposeful deceit on the part of the respondent.

2. There is also the possibility that when deceit occurs it is not purposeful, but is the result of erroneous self-judgment. A man might indicate on a questionnaire that he is devoid of ethnic prejudice; but when his moment of truth arrives, this first response is proven untrue.

---

[1] An interesting experiment regarding student attitude toward cheating and actual cheating behavior is reported in "Professed Attitudes and Actual Behavior" by Stephen M. Corey, *Journal of Educational Psychology* 28: 271–280, in which he reported that the relationship between behavior and attitude was negligible.

3. Attitudes change. A survey taken in January might indicate that approval is a real possibility, and be an accurate prediction of a vote taken in January. But certain intervening events—be they local or national—can make the prediction inaccurate for February. As an example of such changes, one need look no further than the fluctuations in the public's attitude toward the President, as it is periodically measured by national surveys. These surveys are generally reliable, so that the large changes are more likely a manifestation of real change than a manifestation of sampling error.

Simply stated, the question at hand is: *Will the community approve a school bond issue to build a new school building?* This question is reasonably free of emotional overtones, which diminishes the possibility of (1) or (2). Attitude changes, however, could and do occur immediately prior to a school bond election. The superintendent can only hope that during the time between survey and vote, any increase in negative feelings can be offset by public relations in behalf of the issue.

SOME SAMPLING DECISIONS

The primary question of approval leads to three auxiliary questions:

1. The technique, or media, question: By what methods can the appropriate information be obtained? A mail survey is a possibility, but so is a telephone survey or door-to-door sampling. The superintendent might use a totally unscientific approach—by sampling only from the acquaintances with whom he attends parties, sports events, or bars.

2. The sampling question: How can one best select a sample from the community in terms of ease of data collection and sample size? Should all members of the community be included in the sample, or is a smaller group satisfactory?[2] If a sample is to be used, how should that number of people be selected? For instance, if the sample size is to be two hundred, should the first two hundred citizens to visit the school

---

[2] Sample size is discussed in some detail in chapter 3.

be chosen? Probably not—since visiting the school indicates a special interest in its activities; and because the sample would not be random, and the data might be contaminated. Should two hundred people in a high-rise apartment building in the district be chosen? Again, probably not, since they might not represent the attitudes of people living in the district's other housing environments.

3. The decision-making process: What statistical analysis of survey results should be done to provide the superintendent with an answer for his board, based on the results of the survey?

For the problem posed in the Hiram Public School example, suppose we assume that a mailed questionnaire will be used for gathering data from a random sample of all eligible voters. In addition, it is decided that the hypothesis of the study will be that the number of voters in favor of the bond issue is higher than the percentage required to pass it.

THE QUESTIONNAIRE

The most direct method of obtaining the desired information is through the use of a questionnaire. One review of criteria for constructing questionnaires is presented by Scates and Yeomans (1950):

1. The questionnaire must be short so as to not take too much time.

2. The questionnaire should not arouse a negative response—it must appeal to the respondent so that he will complete it.

3. The questions should be worded in a direct and straightforward fashion.

4. The questionnaire should elicit responses that are unambiguous and definite.

5. The responses should not be embarrassing to the individual.

6. The responses to the questionnaire as a whole must answer the basic question for which the questionnaire was designed.

These considerations are important to the superintendent. In addition, he might feel that his campaign in favor of the bond issue would be strengthened if the following information was also obtained:

1. What is the opinion of those people who have children in school?

2. Is the community attitude toward the new industry favorable?

3. Is the community aware of the impending influx of new elementary school–age children?

4. Is the community aware that more classroom space will be needed in the near future and that this is because there will be so many new children?

DEVELOPING THE QUESTIONNAIRE

With the basic questions in mind, the construction of the questionnaire can begin. The summary from Oppenheim (1966) and Selltiz et al. (1959) might be most helpful in planning the content, wording, and form of response. In terms of question content, this summary suggests that:

1. The question must be useful.

2. The respondents must be able to answer the questions.

3. The question should be concrete and specific.

4. The question should be augmented by other questions if it does not stand alone.

Other suggestions for writing questions include:

1. The question should be clearly and simply stated; avoid ambiguity.

2. The wording of the question should not indicate the bias of the author.

3. The question should not be stated in such a manner that may be objectionable to the respondent.

4. The form of the response to the question should be definite, uniform and adequate for the purpose.

The superintendent's complete questionnaire is shown in Figure 14, which also indicates the directions for answering the questions. Good (1963) points out that in writing directions for a questionnaire, there is the challenge of avoiding both the extreme of incompleteness and the opposite extreme of so much complexity and detail that the respondent is discouraged from answering the questions.

The questionnaire's primary purpose is reflected by the last two questions. Question 4 indicates an attitude; while question 5 asks the respondent to indicate what he would do if a bond issue is presented. One might expect that the answers to questions 4 and 5 in each case would be identical. However, there is the possibility that a positive attitude ex-

Figure 14
Facsimile Questionnaire

```
                    The Hiram Public School Survey

Directions: Please respond to each of the five (5) questions
            by marking (X) for the appropriate response (Yes
            or No).
      Note: Your identity will not be known to the researcher.
            Return the questionnaire in the enclosed envelope
            within five (5) days.

        Response                       Question

1. Yes ( )  No ( )    1. Do you have children in the
                         elementary grade schools this
                         year?

2. Yes ( )  No ( )    2. A large new industry will soon
                         locate in our community. Do you
                         believe this industry will be
                         beneficial to our community?

3. Yes ( )  No ( )    3. Many of the workers at the new
                         industry will have school-age
                         children. Do you believe the
                         presence of these children will
                         overload the present elementary
                         school classrooms?

4. Yes ( )  No ( )    4. Assuming that the school superintendent
                         and the school board decide that the
                         school will be overcrowded, do you
                         think that the school board should
                         purchase more space for the elementary
                         classrooms?

5. Yes ( )  No ( )    5. Would you support a school bond
                         issue for a new elementary school
                         building?
```

pressed on question 4 might not be strong enough to motivate the respondent to a "Yes" on question 5. Such a situation would necessitate a public relations campaign on the part of the administration. The direction of these efforts with the public will also be aided by the results of questions 1 through 3.

TRYOUT OF THE QUESTIONNAIRE

Before any instrument of this type is printed and distributed in its final form, it should be tried out on a small sample of typical respondents. The pre-testing or tryout period would consist of asking a small number (perhaps between ten and fifty) of people to respond to the questions and to comment on them. The actual responses given by these individuals are not of major importance; the tryout sample is obtained primarily to see whether the items conform to the specifications listed earlier. For example, are the items ambiguous? Can the respondent understand the meaning of the question? Are negative attitudes generated? The respondents should be asked to interpret the questions to the researcher, and misunderstandings of their meaning may indicate that rephrasing of the questions is required.

Although this initial tryout may seem trivial, it is fundamental to the construction of an adequate questionnaire. The researcher who writes the questionnaire is often too close to his material to be aware of subtle misinterpretations that the respondents will make. The tryout period should *never* be skipped. The researcher must have some evidence that the respondents are answering the questions he *meant* to ask.

SAMPLE SIZE AND ACCURACY OF PREDICTION

The population in question for the Hiram Public School study includes all eligible voters. The size of this population precludes actually contacting all eligible voters, so it is necessary to use a sample. Since the precision of the estimate depends upon the sample size, the superintendent must decide: (a) how precise the estimate must be; and (b) what probability of error is acceptable.

With these preliminary decisions made, he can better decide on the sample size requirements. The size of the required sample will increase as the superintendent demands increased precision and decreased probability of error. With this in mind, suppose the following demands are made by the superintendent:

(a) The estimate must be within 4 percent of the real value. That is, if the real value is 50 percent, the estimate must be somewhere between 46 percent and 54 percent.

(b) The probability that the estimate is not in the desired range—that is, the probability of error—is set at 15 percent. Stated from the positive point of view, this means that the superintendent wants to be approximately 85 percent confident that the population value will be within ±0.04 of the sample value.

Three factors are involved in choosing the correct sample size for the stated conditions. These are:

1. The desired interval.

2. The confidence level required (that is, how confident must the researcher be that the population value is in the specified interval?).

3. The actual proportion of the population that supports the bond issue.

Figures 15, 16, and 17 have been compiled to aid in the proper sizing of samples under varying specifications. Figure 15 deals with an interval of ±0.02 around the sample proportion. Figures 16 and 17 deal with intervals of ±0.04 and ±0.06, respectively. Each table allows the researcher to choose among three confidence levels—namely, 75 percent, 85 percent, and 95 percent. The horizontal axis indicates the sample size, and the vertical axis gives the proportion in the sample responding favorably (over a range of 0.25 to 0.75). Two examples of how these tables may be used follow.

Example 1. Consider the problem at hand. The specifications are for an interval of ±0.04 from the sample value, with an 85 percent level of confidence that the population value is in this interval. Figure 16 is the ±0.04 table. If the superintendent has no notion about the actual proportion of the population favoring the issue, he probably should guess that the value is 0.50. Find 0.50 on the vertical axis of Figure 16, and trace the line across to the curve marked "85% Confidence." The sample size required is just under 325.

This sample size is based on an estimate of the actual population value. What if the actual proportion of favorable voters in the *sample* turned out to be 0.65? Reading along the line which begins at 0.65 on the vertical axis, we see that a sample size of approximately 290 would be adequate for 85 percent confidence that the population value is within ± 0.04 of the sample value—that is, that the population value is between 0.61 and 0.69 (since the sample value was 0.65). Assuming that the sample of 325 had been used, the level of confidence that the population value is between 0.61 and 0.69 would be somewhat higher than 85 percent (since the level of confidence increases with sample size). Would it be 95 percent? Beginning on the vertical axis at 0.65 and tracing across to the 95 percent curve, we see that a sample size of about 540 would be needed for a 95 percent level of confidence that the population value is between 0.61 and 0.69.

Example 2. Suppose a district has taken a random sample of 200 and has obtained favorable responses from 0.60 of them. What kind of confidence statements can be made? Figure 15 shows that a sample size in excess of 800 would be required for a 75 percent confidence statement that the population value is within ± 0.02 of 0.60. That is, the district is less than 75 percent confident that the population proportion favoring the issue is between 0.58 and 0.62.

It can be seen in Figure 16 that with a sample of 200 and a favorable response proportion of 0.60, the district can have a confidence level of slightly over 75 percent that the proportion of the population that is favorable is between 0.56 and 0.64. Finally, on Figure 17, tracing across the graph along the 0.60 line, it can be seen that the district can be between 85 percent and 95 percent confident that the population value is between 0.54 and 0.66 (± 0.06 from the observed value).

Educators who have been conditioned to the traditional "oh five" level of significance may cringe at these relatively low levels of confidence. From the graphs it should be clear that increased levels of confidence and ever smaller intervals both contribute to increasing the sample size. In chapter 3 we discussed the issue of sizing samples to reflect the ac-

Figure 15
Population Proportion To Be Within ±0.02 of Sample Proportion

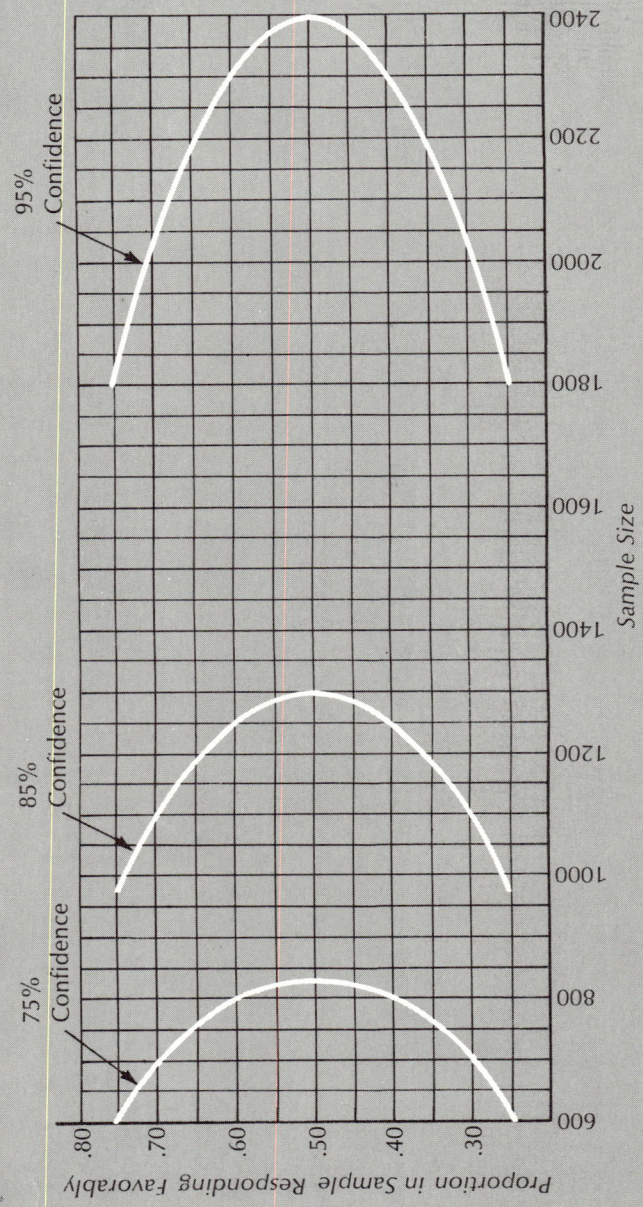

Figure 16
Population Proportion To Be Within ±0.04 of Sample Proportion

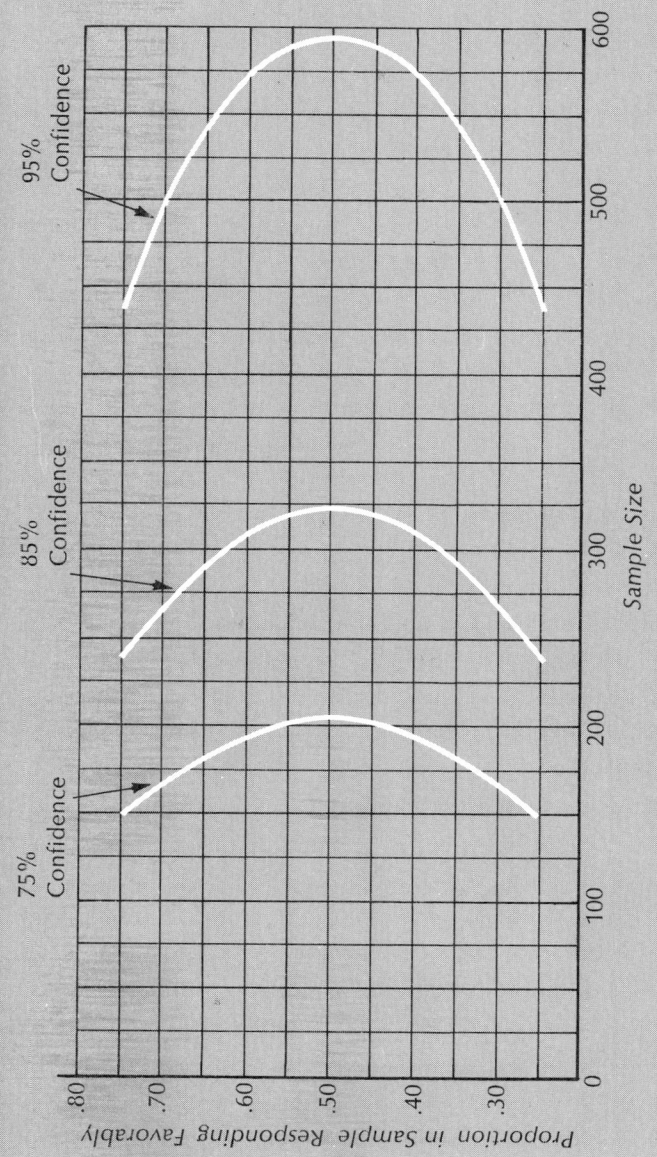

**Figure 17
Population Proportion To Be Within ±0.06 of Sample Proportion**

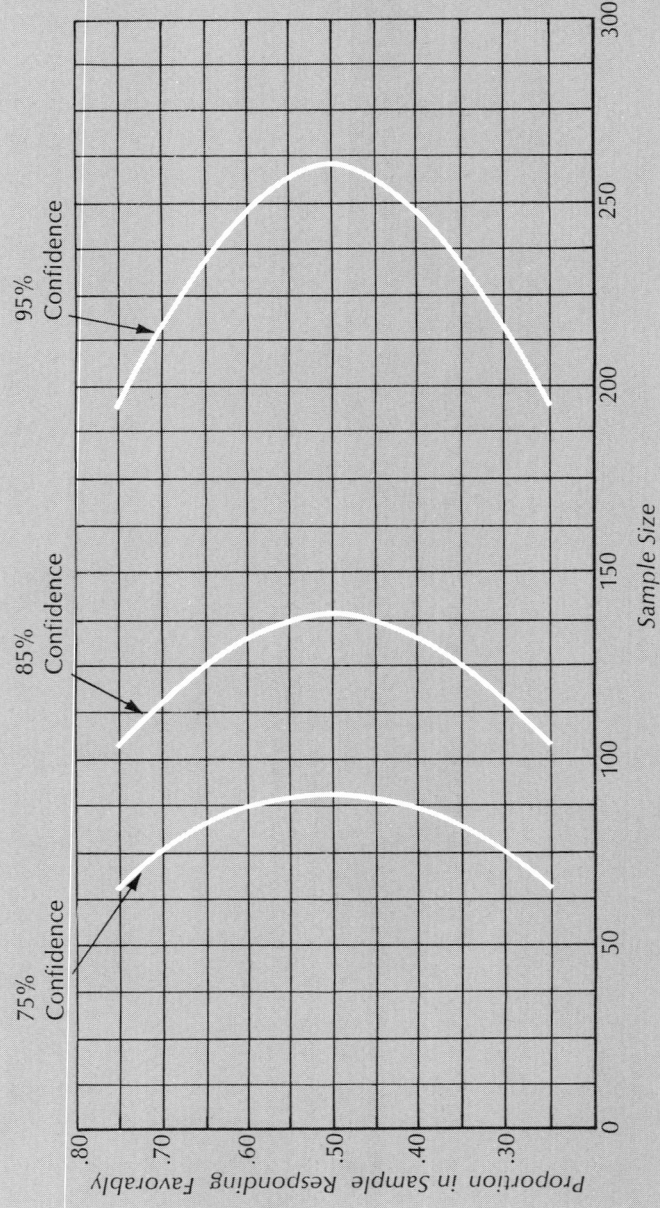

curacy needed. Does the superintendent need to know that 84.23 percent of his student body would like to burn the school down? No—a statement that he is 85 percent confident that this figure is between 80 percent and 90 percent would be enough to bring about some changes. One of the authors plays poker. He would like to bet only when he is assured of winning the pot. However, this would mean waiting for the flushes, full houses, and straight flushes which seem to avoid him with annoying regularity. Waiting for these before betting would mean he would rarely bet; and what sense playing at all if you never bet? We do not mean to equate the decision about offering a bond issue with playing poker; but are trying to point out that determining the sample size should be a rational decision based not on what is perfectly safe, but on what the district actually needs.

One final comment before getting back to the superintendent and his bond issue. This entire discussion began with the question about the proper sample size for a given set of specifications (85 percent confidence, an interval of ± 0.04). The size determined (about 325) was based on an *estimate* of the population value. When the sample is in, *it* is a better estimate of the population value than the original one. The confidence statements, after the sample is in, should be based on the proportion of the sample responding favorably, and not on the original estimate.

To be eligible to vote, a citizen generally must register; and if the superintendent is fortunate, he will be able to secure a list of the population of potential voters (i.e., registered voters) on the school bond issue. In order to select his sample in a random manner, the superintendent assigns a number to each potential voter, and using a table of random numbers (see Blommers and Lindquist, 1960) selects a sample of 325 individuals. Using this procedure, the superintendent can assume that he does have a random sample from the population.

IS THE RETURN LARGE ENOUGH?

Although the sample is random the superintendent should be aware of the factors which could affect the quality of the research findings. Deming (1944) and Hyman (1955) have listed some of the factors to be:

(a) Imperfections in the design of the questionnaire.

(b) Changes that take place in the universe before tabulations are available.

(c) Bias arising from nonresponse (including omissions).

(d) Bias arising from late reports.

(e) Bias arising from an unrepresentative selection of respondents.

(f) Other sampling errors and biases.

After the sample has been designated, the superintendent mails the questionnaire to the individuals in the sample. If no questionnaires are returned because of wrong address, the superintendent assumes that all 325 individuals in the sample had received the questionnaire.

At the end of the five days that were designated, only two hundred questionnaires had been returned. The superintendent mails reminders to all individuals in the sample. After ten days, the superintendent has received 290 questionnaires. That is, approximately 89 percent of the sample responded. Of those responding, 203 were favorably disposed to the bond issue and 87 opposed it, so that the proportion favorable was 0.70.

How large must the returning percentage be to be adequate? Can the superintendent go on with the analysis at this point, or should he send still another reminder? Only rarely does a mail questionnaire result in a 100 percent return. Is the general attitude toward the bond issue the same in the population of nonreturnees as it is in the returnees? This question is the same as asking "Is the group which returned their samples a biased group?"

A biased return can occur for a number of reasons. When returning a questionnaire requires a considerable amount of time and effort, for example, the returnees will be from the polar positions on the issue. That is, those with an ax to grind and those strongly in favor will take the trouble to respond; but the potential respondents in the middle range on the issue will simply not take the time or effort to respond. A mail questionnaire to determine the percentage of nonreaders in a city would surely have a biased return, since the nonreaders presumably could not read their mail, so would not respond.

The question of an adequate return for questionnaires has always been a real problem for the educational researcher. Good (1966) suggests that the goal for questionnaire return should be 90 to 100 percent of the questionnaires distributed. Shannon (1948) found the mean percentage of questionnaire returns to be 81 percent. Snedecor (1948) provides an example of a problem of incomplete returns which arose during World War II. In an effort to determine the need for farm laborers, a selected list of farmers were asked to complete a questionnaire dealing with this problem. The results of the survey indicated that the "average" farm needed three or four farm laborers. In reviewing the questionnaires returned, it was obvious that the vast majority of the returns came from large farm operators who had the time to complete the document. The much more extensive group of small operators, who needed no help, did not respond.

In efforts to avoid the problem of biased results due to incomplete returns, many researchers have specific procedures for follow-up of questionnaires not returned. One or two reminder postcards, spaced two or three weeks apart, can be used. Beggs and Hieronymus (1968) followed their initial questionnaire with a second mailing of the entire questionnaire two weeks after the initial mailing date. This procedure was found to be quite effective, and only one out of seventy individuals did not respond.

If the results of the follow-up procedures are not favorable, so that the return percentage is still low, the researcher should seriously reconsider the questionnaire itself. In general, those questionnaires that are properly constructed should receive a satisfactory return rate.

A decision is necessary at this point. Is the return large enough to go forward? The superintendent might try assuming the worst—that *all* nonreturnees were unfavorably disposed to the bond issue—to see how this alters the sample proportion. To compute the new proportion, consider the following relationship:

$$\text{C.S.P.} = (PR)(RF) + (1.0 - PR)(1.0 - NA)$$

where:

C.S.P. = corrected sample proportion (favorable)
PR = proportion returning
RF = proportion of returnees favorable
NA = proportion of nonreturnees against.

For the hypothetical problem under consideration, the proportion returning was 0.89 (PR = 0.89), the returnees favorable was 0.70 (RF = 0.70), and we will begin by *assuming the worst*—that all nonreturnees are against the proposition (NA = 1.00). Then the corrected sample proportion would be

C.S.P. = (0.89)(0.70) + (1.0 − .89)(1.0 − 1.0)
C.S.P. = 0.623

The worst thing that could happen would be a reduction in the sample proportion in favor from 0.70 to 0.623, which would occur if all 35 nonreturnees were, in fact, against the issue. Such an occurrence seems unlikely, and the superintendent might be interested in finding out the corrected sample proportion favorable if 75 percent of the nonreturnees opposed the issue. The calculations stay the same as above, except that NA changes from 1.00 to 0.75.

C.S.P. = (0.89)(0.70) + (1.0 − 0.89)(1.0 − 0.75)
C.S.P. = 0.6505

If the decision does not change, even under the worst possible assumption, then the returning proportion is large enough. In cases where the decision would change under differing assumptions of the proportion of nonreturnees favorable, the nonreturnee group should be considered very carefully. In many (perhaps most) instances, where the researcher's most diligent efforts have failed to uncover suggestions of bias in the nonreturnees, it is probably safe to *assume* that the extreme levels of bias are absent. If the superintendent reconsiders his questionnaire, rechecks his mailing procedures, listens carefully for community reaction to the questionnaire, and so forth—and still sees no reason why the nonreturnees would be extremely biased against the issue, it would be reasonable for him to assume that not *all* 35 nonreturnees opposed the issue.

Generalizing to other sampling situations, it is true that assumptions are easy to make, and very inexpensive. The superintendent *could* check his assumption. He might send interviewers into the city to call on the 325 people in the sample (since the returns were anonymous, he does not know which 35 did not return their forms). The interviewers could keep working until the superintendent was convinced that the nonreturnees were (or were not) a biased group. Such a procedure will be expensive, however. He might be accused of doing a $10,000 analysis on $500 worth of data.

On the other hand, a 99¢ analysis of a half-million dollar project is equally incorrect. If the decision at hand is very critical, and the assumption regarding the nonreturnees would change the decision, then the assumption should be checked, regardless of the cost of so doing.

STATISTICAL PROCEDURE AND DECISION-MAKING

Assume that the 70 percent of returnees favorable to the issue is a true reflection of the proportion in the entire sample. Assume further that, according to law, 60 percent of individuals voting in a bond issue must approve the issue before it is considered as passed. This 60 percent figure varies of course—in some states a simple majority of those voting is satisfactory.

The superintendent could base his decision on statements taken from Figures 16 and 17. From Figure 16, it can be seen that he is more than 85 percent confident that the population value is within ±0.04 of the sample value—that is, between 0.66 and 0.74. From Figure 17, we read that he can be *more than* 95 percent confident that the population figure is between 0.64 and 0.76 (that is, within ±0.06 of the sample value). The proportion needed to pass the issue is 0.60, so that he is more than 95 percent confident that the population value is not 0.60 (since 0.60 is not between 0.64 and 0.76). If "more than 95 percent confident" is enough for this superintendent, he should recommend to the school board that the bond issue be presented.

The three figures are somewhat limited in scope, however. They only give three confidence levels and three interval sizes. We will here review the technique for formally testing a statistical hypothesis so that it can be applied to any similar situation. The steps in the hypothesis test can be closely patterned after the explanation in Blommers and Lindquist (1960).

Step 1: State the statistical hypothesis. For the superintendent, the real issue is concerned with the question: Does at least 60 percent of the population approve of the issue? The superintendent states his statistical hypothesis as follows:

$$H_o: \phi < .6$$
$$H_1: \phi \geq .6$$

The superintendent is hopeful that he will reject H_o and be left with H_1 as acceptable.

Step 2: Specify the level of significance to be used. This decision must be made by the superintendent, based on his knowledge of the ramifications of certain types of possible errors. The decision should not be left to the statistician. For this reason, it might be well to consider, in nonmathematical terms, the alternatives open to the superintendent.

In reality, either less than 60% of the population favors the issue; or else 60% or more of the population favors the issue. No other alternative is possible.

If less than 60% of the population favor the issue, (a) then the hypothesis (H_o) as stated is correct, and (b) the superintendent probably will not want to even offer the issue to the public (except, perhaps, after an extensive and successful public relations campaign in favor of the issue).

Now if the hypothesis is true and a sample is taken, an error could occur, due to an idiosyncracy of some kind in the sample. If the hypothesis is true, rejection of it would be an error—called, in statistical circles, a Type I error. What would be the ramifications of a Type I error here? Less than 60% of the population would favor the issue; but the superintendent would be led to believe (by the sample) that more than 60% were in favor, and thus allow the issue to go before the public; where it would be voted down, barring an intervening change of heart by the population.

On the other hand, what if 60% or more of the population really favors the issue? Here (a) the hypothesis as stated is *false,* and (b) the superintendent would like to bring the bond issue before the voters—*fast.* Now if the hypothesis is false, and a sample is taken, once more an error could occur due to some idiosyncracy in the sample. This time the error would occur if we *failed to reject* the false hypothesis—an example of what is called a Type II error. What are the ramifications of a Type II error here? Actually, more than 60% of the population favor the issue; but the superintendent would be led to believe (by the sample) that less than 60% are in favor. He would probably thus decide to not even attempt an issue which would pass, if attempted.

Only one of the two types of error is possible in any single situation; but the superintendent and the board do not know which it is. They must decide, on the basis of the evidence on hand, which error would be more serious. Their selection of a significance level will reflect their decision.

If they select a very small significance level, say .01 or

.001, it will reflect their concern over a Type I error—their feeling that it would be worse to have the issue voted down than to err on the side of failing to present an issue which would pass if presented. A larger significance level, say .05 or .10 or even .20, would reflect their greater concern over *not* presenting an issue that *would pass,* as opposed to having an issue voted down.

Suppose we assume that the board decides on a significance level of .10, which seems like the most reasonable alternative in this case—unless a negative vote on this issue would cause deep-seated problems in the district. Then we continue with the procedure:

Step 3: Specify the critical region to be used. With a sample size of 325, it is possible to use a normal curve approximation. Thus any table of z-scores can be consulted, to obtain the critical region R: $z \geq 1.28$.

Step 4: Compute the value of the statistic. When the sample is large, it is possible to use the z-score approximation for this situation, based on the formula:

$$z = \frac{\text{(observed proportion of sample in favor)} - \text{(hypothesized prop. in favor)}}{\sqrt{\frac{\text{(hyp. prop. in favor)}(1 - \text{hyp. prop. in favor)}}{\text{number in sample}}}}$$

If this computed value is greater than (or equal to) 1.28, the hypothesis should be rejected in favor of the alternative. Suppose the sample indicates that 70% are favorable. The value of the statistic will be

$$z = \frac{.70 - .60}{\sqrt{\frac{(.60)(1 - .60)}{325}}} = \frac{.10}{.027} = 3.68$$

Step 5: Make a decision. The superintendent compared the obtained z with the critical region and noted that 3.68 is greater than 1.28, so the obtained z is in the region. Thus he rejected the H_o ($\phi < .6$) and accepted the H_1 ($\phi > .6$).

With this information available the superintendent was able to go back to the school board and state that he was of the opinion that the school bond issue would pass. While this was the basic research question asked by the school board, it is well to consider the use of the additional information which was obtained from the questionnaire.

For example, the superintendent might have found that a very large proportion of the parents who had children in school indicated that they would approve the bond issue, while only about half of the remaining individuals in the sample indicated a favorable attitude. There are two ways of interpreting this information from a very practical point of view. Since the parent group is most favorable, the superintendent might consider concentrating his efforts primarily on getting out the vote of this group. On the other hand, he might want to concentrate his real public relations campaign on the nonparent group, in an attempt to sway a significant proportion of them over to the positive side of the ledger.

The questionnaire also included an item designed to assess the attitude of the respondents toward the new industry. If the prevailing attitude toward the new industry was favorable, it would behoove the superintendent to link the need for a new school with the presence of the new industry. If, on the other hand, the respondents indicated an unfavorable attitude toward the new industry, the superintendent might be wise to center his campaign on the need for new facilities due to the natural evolution of the community.

Although the questionnaire was quite short, it provided an excellent set of data for the superintendent and the school board. It is important to note that the questionnaire was based on the major research question and that care was taken to follow proven techniques of questionnaire construction. The statistical technique involved was trivial. The most important phase of this research was defining the issues and developing the questionnaire.

MEASURING OTHER COMMUNITY ATTITUDES

The maintenance of a satisfactory school-community relationship by the school administration is generally considered to be more an art than a science. A cynical superintendent might contend that a satisfactory relationship exists if community rebellion is absent. The ability to accurately gauge community attitudes might be one of the defining characteristics of the successful administrator; and this ability *is* an art.

The trend in the past few years has been toward larger enrollment in the individual school district. Associated quite naturally with larger enrollments are larger communities to deal with—larger at least in the sense of numbers of voters. Those people who make up the school administration are most likely a pretty homogeneous group. Their individual spheres of influence and contact undoubtedly overlap to a great extent, and tend to miss many important elements in the community, with the result that the administration's picture of the community will generally be unrealistic due to lack of information. Probably this gap in information increases with the size of the school district. One might argue that when the school administration does not have a true picture of community attitudes, more scientific sampling techniques are called for.

Some public and private agencies have been highly successful in correctly assessing and predicting group attitudes. The almost mystical ability of television pollsters to accurately predict election outcomes based on very small samples is one example. These predictions involve carefully constructed sampling techniques which involve only a very small proportion of the country's population. For other highly refined sampling techniques, one need look no further than the Consumer Price Index (CPI) and Gross National Product (GNP), both of which yield results of an accuracy no longer doubted by the general public. These measurements involve the backing of agencies with far greater resources than those of the average school district, but then the magnitude of their questions is perhaps also on a proportionately grander scale.

A fact often not known by school administrators is that the accuracy of a sample is a function of sample size—but not of the proportion of the community included. That is, a sample of 500 is equally as accurate in a town of 10,000 as it is in a town of 100,000—*if it is a representative sample in both cases.* Insuring a representative sample is an ability which the professional pollsters have honed to a fine edge. School districts have well-defined boundaries; and statistical information about the population patterns in the district are generally not difficult to obtain, if the administration does a little scratching around. This scratching might be done at the census bureau, which tabulates its returns every ten years in a block-by-block manner. In many communities commercial firms publish a city directory which lists the location of homes and the names of the families living at each location.

Even in the absence of such a listing, the problems of obtaining a relatively accurate picture of voters throughout the district are not insurmountable. It would not be too difficult to estimate, on a detailed map, the number of voters in each square block area. In areas where one-family dwellings are placed on large lots, the estimate would be based on this information. Where high-rise apartments exist, the square block estimate would be based on the approximate number of rental units in that square block area, times the average number of eligible voters per unit.

CONTINUOUS ASSESSMENT OF COMMUNITY ATTITUDES

Information obtained from the census bureau, city directory, or map of voter density patterns could be used to regularly select random samples of voters for continuous assessment. As outlined in chapter 3, concept no. 5 of continuous assessment directed the researcher to define the important issues and regularly obtain data concerning them to aid in decision-making. What issues, related to school-community attitudes, are important? The community's attitude toward a school bond issue is just a part of a larger question—the total picture of fiscal behavior of the school authorities. Continuous information regarding community attitude toward financing would provide not only estimates of the absolute levels of support at a given time, but would pinpoint trends in community support. Trend data could be very useful to the school authorities as a means of heading off impending problems.

It is also important to know whether the community understands the purposes of school programs, especially new ones, and what the community's attitude toward these programs is. These are only a few examples of school-community issues about which continuous data would be beneficial.

A school administrator serves at the pleasure of his school board. The school board serves at the pleasure of the community. The community is often slow-moving and unwieldy, but its will eventually prevails. A school administrator with a well-defined educational philosophy cannot be expected to follow the will of the community when his philosophy conflicts with the community's will. But his job would be much easier (and, to be practical, more secure) if he could at least define in what ways such a conflict exists. Foreknowledge of this sort allows him the chance to sell his viewpoint to the community—the community's attitude may be based on insufficient information or misinformation.

Many school districts now have budgets in excess of a million dollars. By investing a very small fraction of this budget in a program of continuous information-gathering from the community, decision-making should be more efficient. The investment would more than pay for itself.

REFERENCES

Beggs, Donald L., and A. N. Hieronymus. "Uniformity of Growth in the Basic Skills Throughout the School Year and During the Summer," *Journal of Educational Measurement* 5 (Summer 1968): 91–98.

Blommers, Paul, and E. F. Lindquist. *Elementary Statistical Methods in Psychology and Education.* Boston: Houghton Mifflin, 1960.

Deming, W. E. "On Errors in Surveys," *American Sociological Review* 9 (August 1944): 359–369.

Good, Carter V. *Essentials of Educational Research.* New York: Appleton-Century-Crofts, 1966.

———. *Introduction to Educational Research,* 2nd ed. New York: Appleton-Century-Crofts, 1963.

Hyman, Herbert H. *Survey Design and Analysis.* Glencoe, Ill.: The Free Press, 1955.

Oppenheim, A. N. *Questionnaire Design and Attitude Measurement.* New York: Basic Books, 1966.

Scates, Douglas E., and Alice V. Yeomans. *The Effect of Questionnaire Form on Course Requests of Employed Adults.* Washington: American Council on Education, 1950.

Selltiz, Claire, et al. *Research Methods in Social Relations,* rev'd ed. New York: Henry Holt, 1959.

Shannon, J. R. "Percentages of Returns of Questionnaires in Reputable Educational Research," *Journal of Educational Research* 42 (October 1948): 138–141.

Snedecor, George W. "On the Design of Sampling Investigations," *American Statistian* 2 (December 1943): 6–9.

EDUCATIONAL MEASUREMENT AND DESEGREGATION

History of Litigation: Why the Delays?
Six statements of cause

Hobson v. Hansen: The Track System

Summary

A question: Which institution is our best hope for realizing individual fulfillment, while at the same time building national strength and universal welfare? The most likely answer: The schools. Some might argue that our faith in the schools is built on a dream and not on reality; but recent public attitudes suggest that the schools are assuming a more dynamic leadership role in reaching these goals. Each goal is very general, however, and is the function of a large number of actual decision points. Related actions taken by school authorities should be kept under constant surveillance to make sure they are appropriate to the larger quest. Many diverse pressure groups can focus their fury on the professional educator, forcing shortsighted decisions to meet problems of the moment. The school is an agency to implement the historical dream of the people. When an accumulation of short-term decisions direct the school's course away from the dream, the public will (and must) seek redress. In a nation which prides itself in the rule of law, we can only hope that redress can be brought about in the courts or balloting places, rather than by coercion or violence. In recent times, many groups have felt the need to go to the streets to demand changes in current educational practices which they believe are not in the public interest. Are these people too impatient? Or are the currently available remedies insufficient? The truth is illusive; but the result—violence in place of orderly change—is disappointing.

Members of the school's public have challenged the school in the courts on topics other than the desegregation issue. Bond issues and bonding capacity, salary issues, land acquisition, busing procedures, and curriculum decisions are under close public scrutiny. Educational and psychological research has also come into conflict with the public. The Spring 1967 issue of *Journal of Educational Measurement* (Vol. 4, No. 1) surveys this issue in a supplement entitled "Invasion of Privacy in Research and Testing." These and other illustrations of areas of conflict between school and public are all worthy of study. We have chosen, however, to direct attention to the role of educational measurements in the litigation dealing with the desegregation of the schools. This litigation brings into sharp focus some fundamental questions regarding the use, interpretation, and limitations of current educational measurements.

Perhaps today, more than ever before, professional educators must guard against short-term decisions, based on existing pressures, which have detrimental long-term implications. So great is the school's responsibility for the future course of events that one shudders to think of what uninformed or unprincipled choices might bring. Once there was time for the public to redress errors in the courts, but sometimes events move too suddenly today. Today's problems are based on yesterday's decisions: tomorrow's educators will live with the mistakes we make today.

Our goals, then, for this chapter are in the spirit of minimizing today's mistakes. We will present a status report on certain court litigations in which the public is seeking redress from school practices which are highly dependent upon educational measurement.

One of the most frustrating and persistent problems facing today's school administrator and his staff is that of assignment or placement of pupils. The legislature of the state of Illinois, for example, has the inherent responsibility of administering its system of public education, but it, like most other states, has delegated this responsibility to its local boards of education. These boards, in turn, place the assignment decisions on the shoulders of the chief school administrators and their supporting professional staffs. The local district decides which school the child shall attend; which grade or class he shall be assigned to in that school; and which group or track he shall be assigned to in that grade. Educational measurement can play a not inconsequential role in each of these decisions. Each of these assignment decisions—to the school, to the class, and to the group—has been the subject of some court procedure. It is through this litigation that educational measurements have come into conflict with the public's will.

HISTORY OF LITIGATION: WHY THE DELAYS?

The Supreme Court of the United States, in the historic *Brown* v. *Board of Education* (1954), ruled that school systems should begin desegregation procedures "with all deliberate speed." A considerable amount of time has passed since that decision was handed down by the Court. In many districts, the extreme "deliberateness" of the process has been a cause for much consternation to desegregation advocates. A survey of litigation from the time of the *Brown* case will show that the Court has not forgotten its original decision. School officials at all levels should be interested in a review of this considerable litigation.

SIX STATEMENTS OF CAUSE

In this book we have attempted to focus on the role of educational measurement in the decision-making processes of the schools. Educational measurement has played a significant role in the litigation regarding desegregation, as shall be seen. It is necessary for us to go somewhat far afield, and to include a survey of all the litigation, so that the role of educational measurement can be seen in the proper perspective. The cases in which tests play a part will be difficult to understand without knowledge of previous litigation. Our technique will be to make a statement which summarizes certain segments of the litigation, or which shows trends in the thinking of the various courts which have rendered decisions in this area. These statements shall be followed by excerpts from some of the cases.

> **Cause no. 1:** *One reason for the delays—the courts have ruled that the plaintiffs must exhaust all currently existing administrative channels available for obtaining redress for their complaints before the Court will even hear their case.*

In a North Carolina case, the plaintiffs sought redress in the courts in a case in which the plaintiffs believed racial discrimination was present. The lower court ruled that the case could not be heard because the plaintiff had not yet exhausted all existing administrative remedies. The plaintiffs appealed and in the case of *Carson v. Warlick* (1956), the U.S. Court of Appeals, Fourth Circuit, upheld the action and said:

Somebody must enroll the pupils in the schools. They cannot enroll themselves; and we can think of no one better qualified to undertake the task than the officials of the schools and the school boards having the schools in charge. It is to be presumed that these will obey the law, observe the standards prescribed by the legislature, and avoid the discrimination on account of race which the Constitution forbids. Not until they have been applied to and have failed to give relief should the courts be asked to interfere in school administration.

Again in 1958, in *Shuttlesworth* v. *Birmingham Board of Education of Jefferson County, Alabama,* the United States District Court, Fifth Circuit, affirmed the principle set forth in *Carson* v. *Warlick,* that the Alabama School Placement Law provided the legal machinery for the admission of qualified pupils to the schools without regard to their race or color. It said:

The School Placement Law furnishes the legal machinery for an orderly administration of the public schools in a constitutional manner by the admission of qualified pupils upon a basis of individual merit without regard to their race or color. We must presume that it will be so administered. If not, in some future proceeding it is possible that it may be declared unconstitutional in its application. The responsibility rests primarily upon the local school boards, but ultimately upon all of the people of the State.

> **Cause no. 2:** *The courts have not presumed to assume the role of school superintendent in the many districts. The court does not actively set down a set of rules for each district. The court expects each district to make its own rules, and assumes that these are constitutional. If certain citizens do not think the rules as prescribed by the local district are constitutional, they can seek redress in the courts.*

In the *Brown* case, the Supreme Court had specified for the schools what they could not do. The Court told the schools that they could not have *de jure* (legally sanctioned) segregated schools. It was not the responsibility of the courts, however, to actually design the desegregation plans for the districts. The courts had no intention of replacing local school boards and superintendents; their responsibility was in the area of making sure that the plans devised by the local districts did follow the guidelines of the *Brown* case. The attitude of the court (U.S. District Court, Fourth Circuit) in this matter is expressed in the case of *Groves* v. *Board of Education of St. Mary's County, Md.,*

Undoubtedly the District Judge should not take the formulation of a plan for the integration of the schools out of the hands of the school authorities but, on the other hand, he may not disregard his own responsibility to determine not only whether a plan is offered in good faith but whether it is reasonable in all its aspects; and this includes the duty to determine whether an exception to the plan in a given case should be made.

This attitude was reaffirmed in *Calhoun* v. *Latimer* (U.S. Court of Appeals, Fourth Circuit, 1963):

> Whether to effect a plan, to speed it up, or to otherwise modify it is in the first instance for the school board. This is likewise true as to problems arising in connection with the administration of a plan. The courts are ill equipped to run the schools. Litigants must not ignore school officials, and school officials must not abdicate their function to the courts.

However, this did not necessarily mean that the local board could sit back and wait for certain citizens to begin litigation before taking action to desegregate the schools. In the case of *Monroe* v. *Board of Commissioners of the City of Jackson, Tennessee* (U.S. District Court, Sixth Circuit, 1964), the court said that no such demand on the part of citizens was necessary.

> **Cause no. 3:** *One aspect of the challenge to the rules set down by local districts, the "face validity" question —Are the rules discriminatory "on their face"?*

In the *Carson* and *Shuttlesworth* cases, mentioned earlier, the plaintiffs based their suits on the assumption that the entrance criteria had been established to perpetuate a segregated school system. However, the court judged each "on its face"; and established that the statutes were based on criteria that were reasonable, and not based on race.

A somewhat different challenge, under this same heading, is illustrated by *Thompson* v. *County School Board of Arlington County* (U.S. District Court, Fourth Circuit, 1956). After the *Brown* case made racial segregation illegal, Arlington County designed a screening process for pupils who applied for a transfer from one school to another. The screening was based on five criteria: attendance area, overcrowding, academic accomplishment, psychological problems, and adaptability. The plaintiffs in the *Thompson* case felt that since these rules were devised after the *Brown* case, they presumably were devised to restrict the transfer of blacks to the all-white schools. The court thought differently, and said:

> True, previously no such tests were known; they came into being in the latter part of August, 1958 in connection with the instant school assignments. But this does not prove discrimination.

These tests were not used previously because there was no necessity. The removal of the rules and custom of segregation was an abrupt change. It was a social epoch, beginning a new era. Accommodation to its demands meant new methods as well as facilities. The assignment of pupils took on an added obligation. At some time and place, assignment regulations had to be adopted. Therefore, the instant criteria are not discriminatory as born of a social change. Otherwise, after the erasure of race as a factor in pupil placement, no assignment plan could ever be validly adopted.

This court did not accept the face validity of all rules set down by the districts. In the *Thompson* case ruling (1956) the court held that since Virginia's Placement Act required the applicants to accept the school which the placement board found most appropriate, the law was tantamount to requiring the applicants to accept racially segregated schools. The *Brown* case had placed this school board in an uncomfortable dilemma, for they were faced with the loss of state monies if pupils of different races attended separate schools—that is, if they obeyed the mandate from the highest court in the land.

Another example is *Dove* v. *Parham* in which the U.S. Court of Appeals, Eighth Circuit, determined that the authorities were using entrance requirements to further segregation. There seems to be no question that school officials have the legal right to adopt certain tests to determine to what grade a pupil should be assigned or what school he may attend. It is when these laws are used to maintain separate schools for the races that legal controversies arise. In *Dove* v. *Parham,* the court noted that the board of education of the Dollarway School District of Jefferson County, Arkansas, intended to subject pupils seeking transfers to such devices as the California Mental Maturity Test, the Iowa Silent Reading Test, the Otis Quick Scoring Test of Mental Ability, the California Language Tests, the Bell Adjustment Inventory, and other tests which were, according to the court, at least in the elementary area, "new adornments upon the entrance doors to school houses and classrooms." The court chastised this school district for using the Arkansas Pupil Placement Law to continue to maintain a system of segregated schools.

The courts made no secret of their intention of judging both "face validity" and technique of application, with an eye toward schemes which would thwart the thrust of the opinion expressed in the *Brown* case. In the case of *Jones v. School Board of City of Alexandria, Virginia,* the court (U.S. Court of Appeals, Fourth Circuit, 1960) interpreted the board of education's plan for desegregating its schools based on residence and academic preparedness:

The two criteria of residence and academic preparedness, applied to pupils seeking enrollment and transfers, could be properly used as a plan to bring about racial desegregation in accordance with the Supreme Court's directive. The record in this case is insufficient in demonstrating that the criteria were not so applied. On the other hand, these criteria could be used in such a way as to be a vehicle for frustrating the constitutional requirement laid down by the Supreme Court. If this is later shown to be the case, then the action of the School Board would not escape the condemnation of the courts. If the criteria should be applied only to Negroes seeking transfer or enrollment in particular schools and not to white children, then the use of the criteria could not be sustained. Or, if the criteria are, in the future, applied only to applications for transfer and not to applications for initial enrollment by children not previously attending the city's school system, then such action would also be subject to attack on constitutional grounds, for by reason of the existing segregation pattern it will be Negro children, primarily, who seek transfers.

In this case, the court reviewed individually the board of education's reasons and criteria for rejection of the seventeen pupils involved and reversed eight of the board's pupil decisions.

Here we see the courts scrutinizing the actions of school authorities to make sure that school officials have developed arrangements for elimination of segregation and have taken appropriate steps to put their program of pupil assignment into operation so that it will apply equally to all children.

> **Cause no. 4:** *A second aspect of the challenge of local district rules is that rules which are nondiscriminatory "on their face" may be administered by local authorities in such a manner as to be discriminatory. The rules themselves may not be discriminatory; it is the manner in which they are carried out which is open to challenge.*

The case of *Thompson v. County School Board of Arlington County* was mentioned earlier. This district was under the surveillance of the court for an extended period. It is important to remember that the courts had accepted the transfer criteria in the Arlington County Schools "on their face," for the courts had to assume that the board would not use the rules to perpetuate segregated schools. In a 1958 ruling involving Arlington County, the court ruled that the evidence established that four of the thirty Negro pupils' applications for transfers, which had been denied by the board, should have been approved. Here the court was ruling on the application of the law, and not on its "face validity."

Thus it can be seen that the courts have not questioned the educational measurements. They have only questioned cases where the rules seem to be applied in what amounts to a discriminatory manner. In the case of *Pettit v. Board of Education of Harford County* (U.S. District Court, Fourth Circuit, 1960), a black student applied for a transfer to a different school. His current school had only a commercial curriculum and a general curriculum, while the school to which he sought to transfer had these two, plus an academic curriculum. Since he intended to continue his education after high school, he felt that he needed the advantages of the academic curriculum.

The court had previously approved the Harford board of education's plan for admission to the district's high schools. The plan provided that the admissions would be approved or disapproved on the basis of the probability of success and adjustment of each individual pupil, based on the school committee's use of the best professional measures of both achievement and adjustment. However, in the *Petitt* case, the court held that the student's request for transfer had been refused even though his IQ was adequate for the academic curriculum, and that he was entitled to the chance of making good at the school which he desired to attend. In ordering the admission of this pupil, the court admonished the school authorities that "at no time shall he be assigned to a course of study, graded, promoted or demoted, except in accordance with the regular policy of the school to assign, grade, promote, or demote white children similarly situated." Educational measurement comes into the picture on this decision, but only because the rules appeared to have been applied to blacks and whites in unequal manner. A cultural bias in the tests has not been suggested in this, or any of the other decisions, as yet.

In *Green v. School Board of City of Roanoke, Virginia* (U.S. Court of Appeals, Fourth Circuit, 1962), the court reviewed individually the action of the school board in granting nine transfer applications and denying thirty. Twelve of the thirty denials were effected because the results of these pupils' aptitude and achievement tests placed them below, or in a few cases only slightly above, the median of the classes in the white schools they wished to attend. In regard to these twelve pupils, the court upheld the denial as to one who had performed very poorly in the aptitude test, ordered the admission of one pupil who was academically well above the median of the pupils in the school to which he was applying, and ordered the state board to reexamine the applications of the remaining ten pupils. Again, the court reiterated that it had on several occasions recognized that residence and aptitude or scholastic achievement criteria might be used by school officials in determining pupil assignment as long as racial or other discriminatory factors were not applied.

One of the newest developments in the litigation concerns *de facto* segregation found principally in the North and West. *De facto* segregation can be defined as racial concentrations in the public schools caused by other than "the sanction of law" declared unconstitutional by the United States Supreme Court in the *Brown* decision. Rather, these racial concentrations (also called racial imbalances) are caused by sociological and economic factors which result in housing patterns wherein nearly all Negroes live in definite areas, and Negro students attend the neighborhood school designated by school officials according to attendance zones.

Few cases in the North arose out of the *Brown* decision before 1960. The major impact on the North began to be felt as a result of dissatisfaction with the condition of racially imbalanced schools arising from the operation of the neighborhood school plan.

The case of *Taylor v. Board of Education of City School District of New Rochelle* (U.S. Court of Appeals, Second Circuit, 1961), arising in New York State, is an example of litigation involving a district in the North. The plaintiffs alleged that the district had gerrymandered the boundaries so that the schools were essentially segregated. The enrollment in one school was approximately 90 percent black, while neighboring schools maintained a substantially white enrollment. The enrollment plan included provisions for students to request transfers to other schools, but such students were required to be recommended by the principal and classroom teacher as being able to perform at an academically satisfactory level in the grade to which he was assigned. The court ruled that the board of education could not impose any standard of academic achievement or emotional adjustment as a requirement for transfers, and that each transferring child should be assigned to the same grade in the school to which he was transferring as he would have been assigned had he remained at the segregated school.

> **Cause no. 5:** *Another type of challenge is that placement criteria which consist only of educational measurement in academic areas are insufficient. The purpose of the school is much wider than the learning of the "three R's."*

What happens when the program is not completely individualized, and in fact includes a considerable amount of homogeneous grouping; and the students from the lower socioeconomic levels are grouped together in the lower tracks, separate from the students from higher socioeconomic levels. This very fact of separation, regardless of the fairness or unfairness of the test, might be considered discriminatory—*to both groups*. The purpose of the school is wider than the three R's—it is a preparation for citizenship and for living together. This challenge may be more subtle, but it may also be finally getting at the very heart of the matter.

After all, one of the purposes of the school is to aid in the socialization of the students. Socialization might be defined as the manner in which the individual defines reality. Acceptable social behavior occurs when the student defines reality in a manner which fits into society's expectations. As the student is socialized, he learns society's definition for acceptable and unacceptable behavior, and in the process learns what to expect from others.

Socialization is an important objective of formal schooling. The school could be a powerful positive agent in the process. One is led to wonder at the artificiality of the school socialization when the disadvantaged student's classmates are all remarkably like him, and the advantaged student's classmates are all similarly advantaged.

This point of view is exemplified by the case of *Blocker* v. *Board of Education of Manhasset, New York* (U.S. District Court, Second Circuit, 1964), in which the court questions the use of educational measurements, even if they are applied equally to blacks and whites. The court declares that the learning involved in the academic subjects is just a part of the total purpose of the schools. The court said:

The denial of the right not to be segregated cannot be assuaged or supported by evidence indicating that underachievement in the three R's may be due in whole or in part to low socioeconomic level, home influence or measured intelligence quotient. The role of public education in our democracy is not limited to these academic subjects. It encompasses a broader preparation for participation in the mainstream of our society. Public education is the very foundation of good citizenship.

This opinion is a somewhat new direction for the court, for it has suggested that educational measurement in academic areas cannot be the sole criteria for deciding on transfer requests.

From the foregoing discussion, it can be seen that citizens who believed their schools had not complied with the desegregation provision of *Brown* were told by the courts to first exhaust all existing channels for remedy. The courts also refused to take charge of the schools, on the assumption that this was the responsibility of school officials. When the courts did begin listening to challenges of certain school procedures used to assign students to different schools, they refused to read bias into the rules. That is, if the rules *could be* applied legitimately to all students, the court could not assume that the rules *would not be so applied*. The citizens had to wait until alleged instances of unfair treatment under the rules occurred, and then to return to the bench with these challenges. In such cases, the court did acknowledge that certain rules, fair on the face, had been applied in a discriminatory manner.

In all of these instances, the use of educational measurements has not been challenged, if they are used indiscriminately for all students. But the fourth challenge listed, in which the court began looking closely at the application of the rules, coupled with the fifth challenge, in which the court acknowledged that education was more than the three R's, indicated a trend toward closer scrutiny of administrative procedures to accomplish desegregation. This trend leads to the following challenge:

> **Cause no. 6:** *Are the educational measurements used as selection and placement criteria "less equal" to the student from the lower socioeconomic levels? Is there cultural bias involved in the tests themselves?*

The section of chapter 5 dealing with cultural bias in ability grouping procedures should be reconsidered at this point.

It is the authors' belief that two types of bias are possible here, and that it is important to differentiate between them. Here is an example which should illustrate the first:

To be capable of functioning at a satisfactory level in our society, students must be reasonably facile at certain basic mathematical operations. All functioning citizens must deal with money, and thus should be capable of carrying out simple arithmetic operations with money, as well as understanding things like interest, percentages, and loans. They should know something about the way things are measured and counted, and know the fundamentals of decimals and fractions. A basic mastery level in mathematics must include a number of other concepts.

Now if a *good* test is written to measure the level to which students have mastered these basic and fundamental concepts; and the results show that students from the higher socioeconomic levels have mastered the concepts far better than have students from the lower socioeconomic levels, that is one type of bias. This is a bias in the culture, not in the test. It is the culture which should be castigated. The test is "fair"; it is reporting the world as it exists. And this type of information is important to the school officials as they make decisions about the school's program. In a program of individualized instruction, the student starts his own private studies at his current performance level. If that means that the lower socioeconomic status students must be starting lower than those from the upper levels, so be it—to do any differently would be unfair to these low-scoring students. *Let us strongly emphasize* that we are talking about a *hypothetical situation* in which a test accurately indicates the level of mastery of each student in areas of fundamental importance.

The second type of bias is in the test itself—that is, the test is unfair to certain subgroups in the tested population. For example, consider using a vocabulary test which consists of word recognition tasks. The student is presented with a stimulus word (for example: *file*). His task is to choose from four other words (fool, cabinet, picture, test) the word most like the stimulus word. In this case, he should choose *cabinet*. Now if we assembled a random sample of children from advantaged areas and a second sample from disadvantaged areas and gave them a free association task ("I am going to say a word. You say the first word it reminds you of"), it is quite likely that the two groups would have different association lists. Even if many of the associations are the same on the two lists, the most common ones on the one would probably not be the same as the most common associations on the second. However, *most tests have been constructed from word association lists collected primarily from advantaged children*. What if the most common associate of the advantaged children *is* the concept "a place to store things" which stimulates words like "drawer," "cabinet," and "folder." But for the disadvantaged children, it may be that the most common associate is the concept "a device to smooth things with" and it stimulates "sandpaper," "rough" and "not smooth." While the example is completely hypothetical, it can be seen that the question is more difficult for the one group than for the other—simply because the culture in which the disadvantaged group lives has given them different word associations than the ones upon which the test was normed.

There is a second way that a reading test can have this kind of more subtle bias. A reading comprehension test generally consists of a paragraph to read, followed by a question or two dealing with the paragraph. If the story told in the paragraph is an experience known to the student, the questions will be much easier to answer (to be sure, the student may not even have to read the paragraph to answer the questions). If it is a completely foreign experience, the questions are much more difficult. What if the topics are these: construction of a kite, a trip on a jet airplane, use of a bird feeder, a playful kitten named Taffy, and regular six-month appointments with the dentist. Is it fundamentally important that children should know about these experiences? Probably not. Are advantaged children more likely to have had each of these experiences than disadvantaged children? Probably so. If this is true, the advantaged children might be able to answer the questions *without* reading the paragraph. They should at least be able to visualize the situation quickly. The disadvantaged child will have to conceptualize a new and foreign situation ("A bird feeder? Is that a man who stands on the corner throwing little pieces of bread to birds?") before they can respond to the questions.

There may be more hidden types of bias in the test results. For example, in selecting a test for use in a district it is important to have a test which is reliable. Reported reliabilities for commonly used achievement test batteries generally exceed 0.80, and school officials use test results "knowing" that the results are reliable. But the reliabilities reported by the publishers are for heterogeneous cross-sections of the student population in this country. These reliability figures may be too high if the district's population tends to be a minority group. It is well known that the reliability of a group's test scores *decreases* as the group becomes more homogeneous (that is, as the range of ability in the group decreases). The point is, if the group at hand is not typical of the norming group, and in fact is quite homogeneous—all black, or all from low socioeconomic levels—the reliability of their scores might be much lower than the figures reported in the publisher's manual.

If the disadvantaged students in a district tend to congregate at the lower tracks or ability groups while the advantaged students are likewise segregated into the upper levels, it is not surprising that certain citizens would question the procedures which placed them in that peculiar manner. Such questioning has been brought to the courts. A review of certain aspects of the *Hobson* v. *Hansen case* (U.S. District Court, D.C. Circuit, 1967), in which citizens did successfully challenge the placement criteria, follows.

HOBSON V. HANSEN: THE TRACK SYSTEM

The suit was filed by Julius Hobson, a Negro economist, against the Washington, D.C., school superintendent, Carl Hansen.[1] Besides ruling that the tracking system, in which students were grouped at four levels on the basis of ability, should immediately end, Judge J. Skelly Wright extended the prohibition against *de jure* segregation (that is, legally sanctioned by law), which had been set down in the *Brown* case, to also include *de facto* segregation (not legally sanctioned,

---

[1] The opinion, handed down in 1967, was appealed but upheld.

but existing anyway). He ordered the district to immediately integrate the teaching staffs at all schools.

The plaintiff's arguments against the tracking system which led to the judge's ruling to eliminate this system deserve close attention. Although the case was centered on the Washington, D.C., schools, the arguments are general enough to have applicability in a wide variety of other districts.

The track system in the Washington, D.C., school system was begun in 1956. In the *Hobson v. Hansen* case, the plaintiffs charged that this system was implemented as a technique for maintaining segregation in the face of a court order to end this practice. The school authorities denied the claim, and countered:

. . . the track system is and always has been a legitimate pedagogical method of providing maximum educational opportunity for children of widely ranging ability levels; and that any racial effect is but an innocent and unavoidable coincidence of ability grouping [p. 442].

The court acknowledged that, on its face, the system initiated by the district in 1956 was not in violation of the law, and that the superintendent of schools was probably motivated by a sincere conviction that this was the best way to handle the diverse student body in the Washington schools. The court indicated its intention to also study the operation of the system, to determine if, operationally, it was depriving certain students of equal opportunity. In this light the court said:

. . . although the track system cannot be dismissed as nothing more than a subterfuge by which defendants are attempting to avoid the mandate of *Bolling v. Sharpe,* neither can it be said that the evidence shows racial considerations to be absolutely irrelevant to its adoption and absolutely irrelevant in its continued administration. To this extent the track system is tainted [p. 443].

The court, however, did not intend to base its decision on any notion of intentional racial segregation. The plaintiffs convinced the court that the system denied equal educational opportunity to the poor and to the majority of black students, contrary to the guarantees of the Fifth Amendment.

The track system's advocates contend that this technique will allow for greatest individual self-development through the use of curricula differentiated by ability level. The objectives include equality of education and the attainment of quality education. The chief author of the system, Superintendent Hansen, writing for the President's Commission on Goals in 1960, lists the purposes as: "To guard the rights of the individual. To ensure his development. To enlarge his opportunity" (p. 444).

The plaintiffs contended that the tracking system was perpetuating socioeconomic and racial segregation. The socioeconomic bias can be substantiated with data from the Washington schools. The following table is taken from section IV-D of *Hobson* v. *Hansen*.

Table 11
Percentage of Students in Special Academic and General Tracks

Income Level	Number of Schools	1964	1965
High	3	7.8–34.6%	8.1–40.1%
Middle	4	44.8–62.7%	43.9–63.0%
Low	4	67.5–85.5%	64.8–87.9%

The *Special Academic* and *General* tracks mentioned above are levels 4 and 3 in a four-level system. Note that in each case, and for both years, as the socioeconomic level *decreases,* the percentage of students in the lowest two levels *increases*. The correlation shown by these data is inverse and perfect. The data shown was based on high schools in this district. Other data, for junior high schools and elementary schools, led to the same conclusions.

Racial bias can also be illustrated by other data from this case:

Table 12
Ratio of Negroes to Whites in Special Academic Track

	School Year	Total School Enrollment		Percentage in Special Academic Track	
		% Negro	% White	% Negro	% White
Elementary	1964	89.5	10.5	95.0	5.0
	1965	91.0	9.0	95.0	5.0
Junior high	1964	87.6	12.4	94.7	5.3
	1965	89.5	10.5	96.4	3.6

Again, the special academic track is the lowest track. In each case listed in the table, the proportion of black students in the lowest track exceeds their proportion in the school. Conversely, the proportion of whites in the lowest track is less than the proportion of whites in the school. If not by intent, then at least in operation the system was racially biased. In the words of the court:

> Clearly, then, race cannot be considered irrelevant in the operation of the track system. Even if the effects of tracking are not racially motivated, the Negro student nonetheless is affected [p. 457].

Whatever the underlying purpose of the tracking system in the Washington, D.C., schools, it was operating in a manner which tended to separate and insulate classes and races from each other. And in a very real sense, this result was a function of the techniques (measures) used by the school authorities to place the students in the tracks. The court addresses this problem as follows:

> The reason for the track system's separative effect (and concomitant cushioning effect as well) inheres largely in the placement methods used in the District, pupils being programmed on the strength of their performances in class and on standardized aptitude tests, both of which criteria are heavily—and, as it turns out, unfairly—weighted against the disadvantaged student [p. 458].

The operation of an ability grouping system depends upon the initial measurement of a student's maximum ability, followed by the availability of compensatory programs for students who are not currently working at their maximum performance level. If these compensatory programs operate effectively, the students would presumably be brought up through the levels until he reaches his own maximum performance level. This principle was espoused by the founders of the D.C. ability grouping program, when they declared:

> When the four-track system was put into operation in 1956, the intent was not to make pigeon-holes into which pupils would be permanently sorted like mail of different classes [p. 458–459].

The administration of this district attempted to facilitate flexibility through transfers from one track to another, and through cross-tracking, which implies that the student can take courses outside their own track placement. In *Hobson* v. *Hansen* the court had considerable difficulty in determining the amount of upgrading and cross-tracking which actually occurred. The authors have similarly had very limited success in obtaining such information from districts which practice ability grouping extensively. The information presented in *Hobson*, however, indicated that approximately 3 percent to 8 percent of the students were upgraded out of the lowest (special academic) track. The lower figure is for elementary schools. The administration, in setting up the program, had stated that:

> . . . the basic curriculum has two purposes. One is to offer slow learners a curriculum from which they may graduate with honor. The other is to help retarded students overcome their academic deficiencies so that they will be eligible for transfer to the general or even the college preparatory tracks [p. 459–460].

The figures seem to imply that about 92–97 percent of the students originally assigned to the special academic track belong to the slow learners group, while 3–8 percent are the "retarded students" who have overcome their academic deficiencies. If the example given in chapter 5, dealing with chance misplacement of students due to the several types of errors possible in the placement device, is any indication, the 3–8 percent figure is simply too low. Why is the figure low? Is it the fault of the instructional materials, which do not stimulate the students to raise their performance level? Are remedial programs inadequate or poorly designed? Do teachers underestimate the potential of their students? Or are the students who are not upgraded already at the level of their maximum performance? The answer is not totally clear, but the evidence strongly suggests that the fault lies more in ill-conceived administrative practices than in the innate disabilities of the students. The administration had stated that "Pupil placement in a curriculum must never be static or unchangeable. Otherwise, the four-track system will degenerate into a four-rut system." The court responded that "(t)he tragedy has occurred" (p. 463–464).

An ability grouping system in which about 5 percent of the students are moved is not totally inflexible. But the odds for movement once a student is assigned are pretty long, and the students and teachers are surely aware of this picture.

When school administrators introduce compulsory ability grouping procedures into the schools, they must realize that such a decision incurs the obligation to live up to the promises made as part of the procedures. They must not allow "ability grouping" to be a ruse whereby some students are simply shunted off from the mainstream of the educational program. The program must have effective mechanisms whereby all students will be brought up to their maximum potential.

In chapter 5 the fundamental assumptions underlying ability grouping were presented. In *Hobson* v. *Hansen,* Judge Wright ruled that the Washington, D.C., schools (at that time) were not fulfilling any of them. The failure of the third assumption (inflexibility in the system) was discussed above. The second assumption deals with the availability of adequate compensatory and remedial programs so that underachieving students could move to their maximum performance levels. In commenting on the compensatory education programs in the school, the court comments:

> There is substantial evidence, however, that neither the remedial nor the compensatory education programs presently in existence are adequate; rather that disadvantaged students consigned to the lower track tend simply to get the lesser education, not the push to a higher level of achievement [p. 469, 470].

The court commended the school for their attempts toward these kinds of programs, but added:

> But as yet they have not gone far enough. They cannot obscure the sad fact that the vast majority of disadvantaged school children in the school system, if not altogether untouched by remedial and compensatory programs, are at best touched only in passing [p. 473].

The first assumption dealt with the ability of the school to measure maximum performance levels for students from widely disparate backgrounds. The information presented in chapter 5 about testing errors includes most of the evidence presented by the plaintiffs in this case. After a lengthy review of this kind of information, the court comments:

> None of this is to suggest either that a student should be sheltered from the truth about his academic deficiencies or that in-

struction cannot take account of varying levels of ability. It is to say that a system that presumes to tell a student what his ability is and what he can successfully learn incurs an obligation to take account of the psychological damage that can come from such an encounter between the student and the school; and to be certain that it is in a position to decide whether the student's deficiencies are true, or only apparent. The District of Columbia school system has not shown that it is in such a position [p. 492].

SUMMARY

The historical overview presented heretofore indicates the ever-broadening scope of school administrative practices which are under scrutiny by the courts. Whereas educational measurements had been a peripheral topic before *Hobson,* this landmark case brought them dramatically into the arena.

Educational measurement has made substantial contributions to education in the past and will continue to do so in the future. We endorse the court's opinion that students should not be sheltered from knowledge of their academic deficiencies. School decision-makers with a population which includes a considerable racial or socioeconomic mix must take the initiative to seek out and change administrative procedures which put students with disparities in educational opportunity at a disadvantage. When such administrative procedures exist, the public can and should seek redress in the courts. The courts appear to be looking at such challenges with considerable sympathy.

When the *Brown* decision was rendered, it was viewed as a significant step forward for the plight of the segregated American black. In many ways *Brown* has proved to be a catalyst—however gradual—to the integration of public schooling in the South. While *Brown* may be considered of positive value to the Southern black, there is a serious question whether *Brown* has been at all effective in addressing itself to the racial problems of a large number of American blacks located in the North and West.

The ineffectiveness of the *Brown* decision lies in the restrictiveness of its application. The Supreme Court in 1954 was presented with, and asked to rule upon, a particular form of racial segregation—segregation which was created or maintained by affirmative state action. In its decision, the court addressed itself restrictively, and seemingly exclusively, to this form of segregation. The language used by the court in its decision leaves no doubt that *de jure* segregation (that characterized by some form of state action) violates the equal protection clause of the Fourteenth Amendment. The court in *Brown,* however, did not go further in its ruling than the facts before it might permit. The court did not address itself to the possibility that there might exist segregated schooling, of an equally deleterious and inherently unequal nature, that is caused not by state action but rather by various social factors that promote and maintain a rigid form of racial imbalance.

While *de jure* segregation was a condition endemic to the South, the North and West were free of such a form of racial separation. Instead, in the North and West, economic, social, and political factors can and did interrelate to enforce effective and long-term racial separatism—separatism which was arguably permissible because of the absence of state action. The practical effect of *Brown* was to create a constitutional prohibition against the Southern form of segregation but leave undecided the constitutional propriety of *de facto* segregation.

In the years following *Brown,* various suits raising the issue of the constitutionality of *de facto* segregation have been brought before Northern federal courts. With the notable exception of several cases (refer to *Hobson* v. *Hansen,* 1967; *Blocker* v. *Board of Education of Manhasset, New York,* 1964; and *Barksdale* v. *School Commission,* 1963) federal courts have almost uniformly asserted the inapplicability of *Brown* to the issue of *de facto* segregation. Five federal courts of appeals have held that the Fourteenth Amendment, as interpreted by *Brown,* imposes no duty on the part of state or local governmental officials to eliminate *de facto* segregation (*Bell* v. *School City,* 1963; *Downs* v. *Board of Education,* 1964; *Offermann* v. *Nitkowski,* 1967; and *Deal* v. *Board of Education,* 1965). Federal district courts have reached similar conclusions when the issue has been raised before them (*Webb* v. *Board of Education,* 1963; *Olson* v. *Board of Education,* 1966; and *Henry* v. *Godsell,* 1958).

Because of the restrictive ruling handed down in *Brown,* lower courts have rarely attempted to expand the applicability of *Brown* to situations involving *de facto* segregation:

The Supreme Court itself has been, so far, unwilling to entertain the issue of the equal protection clause and its relationship to *de facto* segregation.

REFERENCES

Barksdale v. School Commission, 1963, 237 F. Supp. 543.

Bell v. School City, 1963, 324 F. 2d 209.

Blocker v. Board of Education of Manhasset, New York, 1964.

Brown v. Board of Education, 1954, U.S. Reports, V. 347, 483–496.

Calhoun v. Latimer, 1963, 321 F. 2d 302.

Carson v. Warlick, 1956, 238 F. Supp. 724.

Deal v. Board of Education, 1965, 369 F. 2d 55.

Dove v. Parham, 1960, 282 F. 2d 256.

Downs v. Board of Education, 1964, 336 F. 2d 988.

Green v. School Board of Roanoke, Virginia, 1962, 304 F. 2d 118.

Groves v. Board of Education of St. Mary's County, Md., 1958, 164 F. Supp. 621.

Henry v. Godsell, 1958, 165 F. Supp. 87.

Hobson v. Hansen, 1967, 269 F. Supp. 491.

Jones v. School Board of City of Alexandria, Virginia, 1960, 278 F. 2d 72.

Monroe v. Board of Commissioners of the City of Jackson, Tennessee, 1964, 229 F. Supp. 580.

Offermann v. Nitkowski, 1967, 378 F. 2d 22.

Olson v. Board of Education, 1966, 250 F. Supp. 1000.

Pettit v. Board of Education of Harford County, 1960, 184 F. Supp. 452.

Shuttlesworth v. Birmingham Board of Education of Jefferson County, Alabama, 1958, 162 F. Supp. 372.

Taylor v. Board of Education of City School District of New Rochelle, 1961, 294 F. 2d 36.

Thompson v. County School Board of Arlington County, 1956, 166 F. Supp. 529.

Webb v. Board of Education, 1963, 223 F. Supp. 466.

INDEX

Ability grouping. *See* Grouping; *also* Homogeneous grouping
Accountability, teacher, 201–205
Accounting for the variance, 40–41, 45
Achievement
 self-defined, 62, 63
 corridors of, 62–63 (*see also* Corridor approach)
Achievement grouping, 101–102, 105–106
Achievement tests, 17, 24–25, 30–34
 tryout period for, 31
 time schedule for, 31–34
 for decision-making about individual students, 54
 costs of, 79
 primary uses of, 79–80
 measuring growth by, 80, 85–87
 and use of norms for comparison, 80–82
 and raw score conversion, 82–85
 for fixed time interpretations, 87–89
 reliability of, 197
"Action before crisis" philosophy, 58–59
Actuarial method of recruitment, 177–178, 180
Adjustment inventories, 196
Administrators
 homogeneous grouping and, 119–122
 and teachers, 157
 use of attitude survey by, 160–168
 interest of, in staff, 161
Affective objectives, 6
Age-grouping, 99, 104
Alexander, William M., 185, 189
Analysis
 in cognitive domain, 6, 7, 8
 organization as unit of, 148–149
Anderson, H. E., Jr., 103, 124
Anderson, R. H., 103, 124, 145
Anti-school feeling, 212
Application (in cognitive domain), 6
Armentrout, W. D., 208
Association
 predictive, 39–49
 measures of, 46–49
 statistical, 47
Attitude survey, 160–168
 Coughlan's School Survey, 162–165
 deficiencies in, 165–166
 effective use of, 166–167
Attitudes
 community, toward school program, 14
 measurement of, 14, 19, 35, 59, 75–76, 196, 213–233
 and curriculum relevance, 25–26
 and participation in school activities, 26, 35–39
 continuous assessment of, 53, 59, 76, 187, 232–233
 time required to change, 57–58
 and grouping practices, 102–103
 changed by in-service program, 140–143
 and behavior, 140–143, 212–213
 pattern of, 164
 trends in (faculty), 187
 community, to school bond issue, 211–230

Baehr, Milany E., 149 n., 168
Bales, Carol, 145
Barksdale v. School Commission, 255, 256
Barr, A. S., 193, 207
Bauthues, Donald, 174, 177, 178 n., 189
Beggs, Donald L., 83 n., 97, 202, 204, 207, 208, 225, 233
Behavior
 unlikelihood of major change in, 4, 5
 classification of objectives of, 5–8
 and program objectives, 8–12, 18–19
 and in-service program, 18–19, 127, 133–135, 136–137, 140–143, 144
 specifying outcomes, 24–28
 measurement of, 30–39
 student, in community, 35, 205
 and attitudes, 140–143, 212–213
 finding correlates of, in measurement, 143
 student, changed by teacher in-service program, 144
 norms of, for teachers, 163
Bell Adjustment Inventory, 196
Bell v. School City, 255, 256
Belongingness, 148
Bent, R. K., 189
Biddle, Bruce J., 175, 190
Bidwell, Charles E., 157, 168
Blocker, Clyde E., 159 n., 170
Blocker v. Board of Education of Manhasset, New York, 245, 255, 256
Blommers, Paul, 43, 45, 49, 76, 223, 227, 233
Bloom, Benjamin S., 5, 6, 7, 20
Blum, Milton L., 151 n., 168
Boardman, C. W., 189
Bond issue, school, community attitudes and, 211–230
Borg, Walter R., 101, 103, 124, 207
Borgsmiller, Patricia A., 199, 207
Bowers, N. D., 193, 209
Braun, R. H., 103, 124
Brayfield, Arthur H., 159, 169
Brown v. Board of Education, 236, 254–255, 256
Burns, Robert K., 149 n., 160, 169

Calhoun v. Latimer, 239, 256
Campbell, R., 148 n., 169
Career patterns, men and women, 181–182
Carson v. Warlick, 237, 239, 256
Caste system, 112–113
Chandler, B. J., 159 n., 169
Change
 behavioral, difficult to bring about, 4, 5 (*see also* Behavior)
 and program objectives, 8–12
 length of time for, and test spacing, 57–58

257

to keep up with needs of society, 114
teacher as principal agent of, 119
planning for, 127
and in-service program, 127, 139–144
and job obsolescence, 129
in attitudes and values affecting behavior, 140–143, 213
in personal relationships, 143–144
as measure of teacher effectiveness, 201–205
Charters, W. W., Jr., 181 n., 187, 189
Chase, F. S., 154, 157, 169
Check list for studying morale, 154
Chi-square tables, 38
Citizenship, education for, 244, 245
Clark, Maurice P., 145
Class load, 183–184, 185
Climate
learning, and evaluation, 3–8
emotional, in in-service program, 130–131
permissive, in interview, 152
See also Environment
Clinical method of recruitment, 177, 178, 180
Coefficient of correlation, 49
Coefficient reliability, alternate forms, 107 n.
Coffman, W. E., 157, 169
Cognitive capacity, affective factors in, 116
Cognitive objectives, 5–6
See also Knowledge
Community
intellectual tone of, 5
attitude of, toward school program, 14
reporting test results to, 91–95
as a factor in teacher recruitment and retention, 175, 176
pressure groups in, 184, 235
teacher effectiveness and pupil behavior in, 205
attitudes of, to school bond issue, 211–230
relationship of school with, 230–232, 236
Comparison
of learning curves, 74
use of norms for, 80–82
and test results, 92
Compensatory education, 253
Competition
with self, 60
between students, 60–61, 67–70
Comprehension (cognitive domain), 6, 7–8
improved, 24–25
Computer management with corridor approach, 65–72
Conant, J. B., 124
Conference discussion, 167
Consumer Price Index, 231
Continuous assessment, 13–14, 17
cost of, 14–15
basic concepts of, 53–59
of teacher attitudes, 59, 187
individualized, 59–73
other uses for, 73–76
of community attitudes, 76, 232–233
in-service and, 139
of staff morale, 168
Control group, outcome evaluation experiment, 28–30
Conversion of raw scores, 82–85, 91
Cooperation, district, 162

Corey, Stephen M., 212 n.
Correlation coefficient, 49
Corridor approach, 17, 61–63
deciding number of corridors, 63–64
computer-managed, 65–72
curriculum flexibility and, 72–73
student placement and, 73
Coughlan, Robert J., 76, 147 n., 149 n., 169
School Survey, 162–165
Court cases, desegregation, and educational measurement, 236–256
Crockett, Walter H., 159, 169
Cronbach, Lee J., 107, 124
Cross-tracking, 251–253
Cultural bias
grouping and, 104, 111–117, 123
in ability testing, 246–248
Cumulative profiles, 90
Curriculum
increased relevance of, 25–26
corridor system and, 72–73
specialized, 102
for flexible grouping, 120–122
development of, and morale, 157

Dagne, Frank A., 145
Davidson, H. H., 202, 207
Davis, Frederick B., 97
Deal v. Board of Education, 255, 256
Decentralization, 161–162
Decision-making
and achievement tests, 54
and sampling, 58, 213–214
and continuous assessment, 58–59, 232–233
and ability grouping, 104–105
school, and teacher morale, 156–157
recruitment, models for, 178–181
and assessing teacher effectiveness, 206–207
statistical procedure and, 227–230
Deitrich, F. R., 103, 124
Deming, W. E., 223, 233
Descriptive ratings, 196
Desegregation
litigation over, and educational measurement, 20, 236–256
causes for delays in, 236–248
and the track system (*Hobson v. Hansen*), 248–254
Detail profiles, 164
Diagnosis
individual, 59
by attitude survey, 160–161
Dickson, William J., 147 n., 170
Difference score, 180
Directive interview, 152
Disadvantaged children
scholastic aptitude tests and, 114–117
undereducation of, 115
See also Cultural bias
"Discrimination" technique to measure morale, 154 n.
Discussion techniques, 167
Douglass, Harl R., 183, 186, 189
Dove v. Parham, 240, 256
Downs v. Board of Education, 255, 256
Drews, E. M., 103, 124

Eash, M. J., 101, 102, 124
Edwards Personal Preference Schedule, 196
Ekstrom, R. B., 101, 124
Ellena, William J., 190

Ellers, A., 103, 124
Environment
  work, and morale, 153–154
  classroom, established by teacher, 193, 201
  school, and teacher characteristics, 194
  school, and teacher effectiveness, 201–202
  See also Climate
Epley, T. M., 103, 124
Errors
  measurement, 106–111, 123, 197
  of inference, in School Survey, 165–166
  probability of, 218
  Type I, Type II, 228
Evaluation
  learning climate a function of, 5–8
  in objectives taxonomy, 6
  responses to, 7
  learning geared to techniques of, 7–8
  tied to specification of behavioral change, 10–11
  continuous, 13–15, 17 (see also Continuous assessment)
  of teacher effectiveness, 14, 19–20, 193–207
  time schedule in, 15–16
  outcome (experiment), 16–17, 23–49
  of in-service program, 18–19, 127–128, 137–144
  of whether group or individual measurement is required, 53–54
  individual, 59
  as part of learning process, 60–61
  or student achievement, in-service program on (example), 129–137
  subjectivity in, 198–199
  of teachers, by students, 199–200
  See also Tests
Evans, Kathleen M., 207
Expectations
  self-defined, 62, 63
  teacher, and pupil performance, 118–119, 202–205
  and job satisfaction, 157
  teacher, of rewards, 159–160
  public, of schools, 203
Exploratory Committee on Assessing the Progress of Education, 28

Face validity, 239, 240, 242
Feedback
  to student, 96
  survey, 161–162
Financial problems, school, and community attitudes, 211–230
Fixed time interpretations
  standard scores and, 87–88
  misuse of grade equivalents with, 88–89
Flanders, Ned A., 202, 207, 208
Forced-choice format, personality measures, 196–197
Forgetting, 33
Free association test, 247
Free response procedure, morale measurement, 154 n., 155
Frequency counts, 35–39
  measures of association and, 46–49

Getzels, J. W., 148 n., 151 n., 169
Gifted pupils, grouping and, 105
Glass, Gene V., 49, 50
Goals. See Objectives
Gold, M., 202, 208

Goldberg, M. L., 101 n., 102, 103, 124
Golden, William P., Jr., 145
Good, Carter V., 216, 224, 233
Goodlad, J. I., 102, 124
Grade equivalents, 82–83, 86–87, 90, 95–96, 204
  misuse of, with fixed time interpretations, 88–89
Green v. School Board of City of Roanoke, Virginia, 243, 256
Gross, C. F., 201, 208
Gross National Product, 231
Group
  reference, for use with achievement test scores, 83–84, 88, 92
  work, 147–148
  pressure, 184, 235
Group performance and attitude, continuous assessment of, 73–76
Group preferences, 53
Grouping
  ability, 18, 99–101, 122–123 (see also Homogeneous grouping)
  corridor, 64
  within-class, 99
  based on special handicaps, 99, 100
  for teachability, 99, 100
  by age, 99, 104
  based on learning styles or learning problems, 100
  achievement, 101–102, 105–106
  heterogeneous, 105, 107
  See also Tracking
Groves v. Board of Education of St. Mary's County, Md., 238, 256
Guba, E. G., 151 n., 169
Guion, Robert M., 151, 169

Haas, C. Glen, 128 n., 145
Hakstian, A. Ralph, 49, 50
Handicapped children, grouping of, 99, 100
Hansen, Carl, 248, 250
  Hobson v. Hansen, 106, 115, 248–254, 255, 256
Harris, C. W., 124
Havumaki, S., 202, 208
Hays, William B., 34, 48, 50
Heilman, J. D., 208
Henry, Nelson B., 145
Henry v. Godsell, 255, 256
Herrick, Virgil E., 145
Herzberg, Frederick, 150 n., 159, 169
Hickey, Michael, 177, 189
Hieronymus, A. N., 83 n., 97, 208, 225, 233
Hill, Kennedy T., 202, 208
Hobson, Julius, 248
Hobson v. Hansen, 106, 115, 248–254, 255, 256
Homogeneous grouping, 18, 99–101, 122–123
  student achievement and, 101–102
  review of research in, 101–104
  teacher attitude and, 102
  student attitude and, 102–103
  basis for, 103–104
  errors in, due to cultural bias, 104, 111–117, 123, 246–248
  dimensions of, 104–106
  assumptions of, 105–106
  errors in, due to measurement errors, 106–111, 123
  errors in, due to using IQ as determinant, 107–111, 117

errors in, due to infrequent testing, 111, 123
results of misclassification, 118–122, 236–256
review panel for changing, 119–120, 123
administrative considerations, 119–122
curricular considerations, 120–122
court cases involving, 236–256
See also Grouping
Hoppock, R., 154 n., 169
Horst, Paul, 196, 208
Howell, W. J., 103, 124
Hughes, J. M., 190
Hutson, P. W., 190
Hyman, Herbert H., 223, 233

Ideal profile approach, 179–180
Individual differences, 63, 116, 131
Individualized continuous assessment, 59–73
Individualized corridor approach. *See* Corridor approach
Individualized instruction, 59–60
Input measures, 12, 13
In-service program
evaluation of, 18–19, 127–128, 137–144
and changed behavior, 127, 140–144
defined, 128
reasons for, 128–129
example of, 129–137
design phase of, 132–136
stating outcomes behaviorally, 133–135, 136–137
and prior information, 138–139
and continuous assessment, 139
Insko, Chester A., 151 n., 169
Intelligence quotient (IQ)
grouping based on, 103, 107–111
errors due to use of, 107–111, 117
Intelligence tests, 115 n.
Interaction
group, in in-service program, 143–144
teacher-administrator, 157
student-teacher, 158
of teacher characteristics and school environment, 194
of factors bearing on teacher effectiveness, 196
Interest inventories, 196
Interview
to measure morale, 151–152
of teaching candidates, 177

Jacobson, Lenore, 118, 125, 202, 208
Jardine, Alex, 145
Jensen, Arthur R., 115 n.
Job adjustment, morale and, 149–151, 153–154
Job descriptions
teacher characteristics and, 174–177
in teacher recruitment, 180
Job obsolescence, 129
Job satisfaction
and job expectations, 157
and job performance, 159–160
Johnson, M., Jr., 101, 125
Jones, R. E., 193, 207
Jones v. School Board of City of Alexandria, Virginia, 241, 256
Justman, J., 124

Kierstead, R., 103, 124
Kincaid, D. J., 103, 124
Kinnick, B. Jo, 145

Kleinman, Lou, 175, 189
Knowledge
in cognitive domain, 6
recall of, 7
demonstrated on achievement test, 24–25
and participation in adult world, 25, 35, 205
changed through in-service program, 139–140
prior to accepting teaching position, 183–185
Knox, W. B., 189
Koos, Frank H., 183, 189
Koos, Leonard V., 190
Koplyay, J. B., 159 n., 169
Kranzler, Gerald D., 202, 208
Kuder Preference Record, 196

Lang, G., 202, 207
Lawler, E. E., 149 n., 159, 160, 170
Learning climate. *See* Climate
Learning curves, comparison of, 74
Learning program
as experimental conditions, 4–5
objectives of, 8–12
community attitude to, 14
areas of, needing continuous assessment, 58–59
evaluation a continuing part of, 60–61
Learning skills, classified, 5–7
Least-squares condition, 42 n.
Lennon, R. T., 107, 125
Leton, D. A., 103, 124
Lindquist, E. F., 34, 43, 45, 48, 49, 50, 76, 208, 223, 227, 233
Lipham, J., 148 n., 169
Lippitt, R., 202, 208
Listening, active, 152
Longitudinal investigation, 35–36
School Survey, 165
Low achievers, reporting test results of, 95
Ludwig, David J., 202, 208

McClusky, Howard, 154 n., 170
Maehr, Martin J., 202, 208
Maslow, A. H., 149, 170
Mathis, Claude, 159 n., 169, 170
Matthes, William A., 202, 208
Mausner, B., 169
Maves, Harold J., 145
Mayer, G. Roy, 202, 208
Mayo, Elton, 147 n., 170
Measurement
costs and benefits of, 12–15
attitude, 14, 19, 35, 59, 75–76, 196, 213–232
of staff morale, 19, 76, 151–153, 168
of behavioral outcomes, 30–39
association, 46–49
of random variations, 62
of growth, by achievement test, 80, 85–87
of teacher effectiveness, 174, 193–207
of reasons for leaving positions, 184–185
of community attitudes, 230–232
and litigation over school practices, 236–256
and cultural bias, 246–248
See also Evaluation
Measurement errors, 62, 106–111, 123, 197

Mental ability scores. See Intelligence quotient (IQ)
Mental hygiene, 186
Middle-class culture, 113–114
Miller, Antoinette, 158, 170
Millman, J., 101, 125
Mills, H. H., 186, 189
Mitzel, Harold E., 174, 175, 190, 201, 208
Monroe, W. S., 125
Monroe v. Board of Commissioners of the City of Jackson, Tennessee, 239, 256
Morale
 staff, measurement of, 19, 76, 151–153, 168
 in work group, 147–148
 concept of, 147–151
 and identification with goals of organization, 148
 and organization as unit of analysis, 148–149
 and job adjustment, 149–151
 defined, 151
 work environment and, 153–154
 research on, in schools, 153–160
 teacher characteristics and, 154–156
 decision-making, expectations, and, 156–157
 curriculum development and, 157
 student-teacher relationships and, 158
 salary and, 158–159, 183
 performance and, 159–160
 attitude survey and, 160–168
 continuous assessment of, 168
Morse, N. C., 151 n., 170
Motivation
 student, and scholastic aptitude tests, 116
 achievement, 117
 for professional fulfillment, 150
"Motivation-hygiene" theory, 150 n.
Motor skills, 6
Multiple regression equation, 179 n.

National Assessment, 28
Needs categories, 149 n.
Nelson, Robert H., 182, 190
Nondirective interview, 152
Norms
 use of, for comparison, 80–82
 national, 81
 standard score, 82, 84–85
 local, 92
 behavioral, of teachers, 163
 School Survey findings in terms of, 165
Nylin, Donald W., 145

Objectives
 educational, generalities not warranted, 5
 behavioral, classification of, 5–7
 and changes in behavior, 8–12
 clear specification of, 14
 of in-service program, 132–136
 of organization, acceptance of, 148
 attainment of, and teaching effectiveness, 206
 teaching, definition of, 206
 school, wider than learning of "three R's," 244–245
Observation, evaluating teachers by, 198–201
Offermann v. Nitkowski, 255, 256
Olson v. Board of Education, 255, 256

Oppenheim, A. N., 215, 233
Opportunism, 195
Organization
 acceptance of goals of, 148
 as unit of analysis, 148–149
 formal and informal structures in, 149
 cooperation within, 162
Otis, A. S., 107, 125
Otis-Lennon Mental Ability Test, 107
Otto, H. J., 102, 125
Outcome evaluation (experiment), 16–17, 23–49
 specifying behavioral outcomes, 24–28
 control group, 28–30
 measuring outcomes, 30–39
 statistical significance and predictive association, 39–49
Output measures, 12, 13, 14, 20
Overestimating, cost of, 46

Pacing, 120
Palmer, Dale, 175, 190
Parents, reporting test results to, 95–96
Parker, J. Cecil, 145
Passow, A. H., 124
Percentiles, 82, 83–84, 88, 90, 96
Performance
 test, reporting complete range of, 91–92
 trends in, 92–94
 pupil, and teacher expectations, 118–119, 202–205
 teacher, and morale, 159–160
 student, as measure of teacher effectiveness, 201–205
Permissiveness, 152
Personality measures, 195–198
Pettit v. Board of Education of Harford County, 242, 256
Phi coefficient, 47
Planning
 and input and output measures, 12–15
 short- and long-range, 13, 189
 and predictive association, 41–46
 for change, 127
 of in-service program, 131, 132
 and survival curves, 189
Porter, L. W., 149 n., 159, 160, 170
Post-test, 16
Precision interval, 45
Predictive association
 statistical significance and, 39–49
 strength of, 41–46
 measures of, 47–49
Predictor variable, 44–45
Preference tests, 196
Pre-service teacher, 128
Pressure groups, 184, 235
Pre-test, 15
 for questionnaire, 217
Probability, 37, 39–49
Product-moment correlation, 45 n.
"Professional fulfillment" motivators, 150
Profile
 cumulative, 90
 detail and summary, 164
 ideal, 179–180
Program evaluator, 129–130, 133, 136
Projections, 41
Psychomotor objectives, 6
Public opinion polls, 53
Pupil progress reporting, 59–60

Questionnaire
 morale, 152–153

attitude survey, 161, 162–163, 165–166, 214–217
  distortions in, 165–166
  bond issue survey, 214–217
  developing of, 215–217
  tryout of, 217
  adequate return for, 223–227
  and statistical procedure, 227–230
Random variations, measurement of, 62
Ranking, 80, 88
Rating scales, 196, 199
Raw scores, 86
  conversion of, 82–85, 86
Reavis, W. C., 190
Recall items, 134
Recruitment of teachers
  research on, 173–178
  situational factors in, 175–176
  district-specific factors in, 176–177, 178, 179
  clinical and actuarial methods of, 177–178, 180
  factors affecting, 178–181
  gathering data to improve, 186–189
Redefer, Frederick L., 154 n., 170
Reduction in variance, 47
Reference group, use of, with test scores, 84, 88, 92
Relevance, curriculum, and student attitude, 25–26
Reliability
  of teacher interview, 177
  of achievement tests, 197, 248
  of personality measures, 197–198
  of rating scales, 199
Reliability coefficient, alternate forms, 107 n.
Remedial programs, 253
Renck, Richard, 149 n., 168
Research
  on homogeneous grouping, 101–104
  on morale in schools, 153–160
  on teacher recruitment and retention, 173–178
  on teacher effectiveness, 193–194
  on community attitude, 211–232
  factors affecting quality of, 223–224
Retention of teachers, 181–186
  gathering data to improve, 186–189
Review panel for homogeneous grouping, 119–120, 123
Reward system, 129, 159–160
Richardson, Richard C., 159 n., 170
Roethlisberger, F. J., 147 n., 170
Rosencranz, Howard A., 175, 190
Rosenthal, Robert, 118, 125, 202, 208
"Rubber scales," 84, 88
Rugg, H., 208
Ryans, David G., 174, 175, 190

Salary, morale and, 158–159, 183
Sampling
  size of sample and test accuracy, 54–56, 58
  continuous program of, 58
  and attitude measurement, 75–76
  national sample, 81
  of community attitude, 213–214, 231
  and questionnaire technique, 214–217
  size of sample and accuracy of prediction, 217–227, 231
Sandiford, P., 198, 208
Sarason, I. G., 196, 208

Sarason, Seymour B., 202, 208
Saylor, J. G., 185, 189
Scates, Douglas E., 214, 233
Scholastic aptitude tests, disadvantaged children and, 114–117
School
  population of, and grouping, 104
  and teacher recruitment and retention, 175, 176
  environment of, and teacher characteristics, 194
  environment of, and teacher effectiveness, 201–202
  bond issue for, and community attitudes, 211–230
  relations of, with community, 230–232, 236
  litigation over practices of, 236–256
  objectives of, 244–245
School Survey (Coughlan), 162–165
Schultz, R. E., 155, 170
Scores
  standard, 82, 84–85, 87–89, 90
  raw, conversion of, 82–85, 86
  School Survey questionnaire, 163
  difference, in ideal-profile method, 180
Scott, William E., Jr., 178, 190
Segregation
  de facto, 243, 248–249, 255–256
  de jure, 248
  See also Desegregation
Self-concept, teacher, 195
Self-contained classroom, 99
Self-fulfilling prophecy, 118–119, 202
Selltiz, Claire, 215, 233
Sentence completion test, 155
Shannon, J. R., 225, 233
Sharma, C. L., 156, 170
Shilland, P. D., 154 n., 170
Shuttlesworth v. Birmingham Board of Education of Jefferson County, Alabama, 238, 239, 256
Sievers, C., 103, 125
Simple Randomized Design, 34
Situations list, 154
Snedecor, George W., 225, 233
Snyderman, B. B., 169
Social acceptability of test response, 142
Socialization
  staff, and in-service program, 129, 135–136
  as function of school, 244
Socioeconomic bias in school, 250
Spaulding, R. L., 202, 209
Specialist (consultant), role of, 26, 40
Staines, J. W., 202, 209
Standard deviation, 44
  reduced, 45 n.
Standard error of measurement, 62, 107, 108, 110, 111
Standard scores, 82, 84–85, 87–89, 90
Standards and norms, 80. See also Norms
Stanines, 85, 96
Statistical significance and predictive association, 39–49
Statistical techniques, 33–34, 37–39
  formal testing of hypothesis, 227–230
Stendler, Celia, 209
Strayer, Floyd J., 154 n., 170
Streaming, 99–101. See also Tracking
Strong Vocational Interest Blank, 196
Structured interview, 152
Students
  and the relevant curriculum, 25–26

"upward mobile," 70–72
measuring attitudes of, 75–76
reporting test results to, 96
achievement of, and grouping, 101–102
attitudes of, and grouping, 102–103
gifted and slow, 105
underachieving, 106
and teacher morale, 158
as evaluators of teachers, 199–200
teacher effectiveness measured by performance of, 201–205
performance of, and teacher expectations, 202–205
Subjectivity of teacher evaluation, 198–199
Subjects
efficient use of, 56–57
grouping and, 104–105
Suehr, John H., 155, 170
Summary profiles, 164
Survey questionnaire, 152–153, 161, 162–163, 165–166, 214–217, 223–230
Survival curves, 187–189
Synthesis (cognitive domain), 6

Taylor v. Board of Education of City School District of New Rochelle, 243, 244, 256
Teachability, grouping for, 99, 100
Teacher effectiveness
criteria for, 193–194
personality measures and, 195–198
evaluated by expert observation, 198–201
rating scales and, 199
student rating of, 199–200
measured by student performance, 201–205
measured by student behavior in community, 205
decision-making model and, 206–207
Teacher morale, 148
measurement of, 151–153
research on, 153–160
and teacher characteristics, 154–156
and curriculum development, 157
and job expectations, 157, 160
and relationships with students, 158
and salaries, 158–159, 183
and job satisfaction, 159–160
and the attitude survey, 160–168
continuous assessment of, 168
Teacher Reaction Inventory, 157
Teachers
recruitment and retention of, 19, 173–180, 181–189
measuring effectiveness of, 19–20, 174, 193–207
reporting test results to, 90–91
attitude of, toward grouping, 102
expectations of, and pupil performance, 118–119, 202–205
in-service education for, 127–144
pre-service, 128
excellent, rewards for, 129
individual differences among, 131
and administrators, 157
and students, 158
who leave teaching, 173, 176, 182–186
characteristics of, and job descriptions, 174–177
decision-making on hiring, 178–181

career patterns of men and women, 181–182
trends in attitudes of, 187
survival curves for, 187–189
as establishers of classroom environment, 193, 201
characteristics of, and school environment, 194
measuring personality of, 195–198
evaluation of, by observation, 198–201
accountability of, for pupil performance, 201–205
and decision-making model, 206–207
See also Teacher effectiveness *and* Teacher morale
Teachers' aides, 123
Teaching load, 183–184, 185
Telfer, Richard G., 145
Temperament tests, 196
Tests
reporting results of, 89–96
infrequent, and grouping errors, 111
to determine grouping, 114
aptitude, and disadvantaged children, 114–117
emotional and psychological responses to, 116
recall items, 134
personality, 195–198
test-retest format, 197
reliability of, 197–198, 248
ability, cultural bias in, 246–248
Thelen, H. A., 99, 125
Thompson, Michael L., 182, 190
Thompson v. County School Board of Arlington County, 239–240, 241–242, 256
Thorndike, Robert L., 145, 202, 209
Thorpe, Louis P., 209
"Three-variable" approach, 148 n.
Time schedule
in evaluation, 15–16
for achievement test, 31–34
for continuous assessment, 57–58
Toops, Herbert A., 178 n., 190
Tracking, 99–101
and *de facto* segregation, 248–254
inflexibility in, 251–253

Underachievers, grouping and, 106
Underestimating, cost of, 46
Unstructured interview, 152
"Upward mobile" students, 70–72

Validity
of evaluation project, 16
of personality measures, 197–198
face, 239, 240, 242
Values, changing of, 140–143
Vroom, Victor, 153, 159, 170

Webb, W. B., 193, 209
Webb v. Board of Education, 255, 256
West, J., 103, 125
Wick, J. W., 61, 103, 125
Wilcox, J., 103, 125
Work group, work environment, and morale, 147–148, 153–154
Wright, J. Skelly, 115, 248, 253

Yager, R. E., 103, 125
Yeomans, Alice V., 214, 233